Also by Jody Wilson-Raybould

From Where I Stand:
Rebuilding Indigenous Nations
for a Stronger Canada (2019)

"Indian" in the Cabinet:
Speaking Truth to Power (2021)

True Reconciliation:
How to Be a Force for Change (2022)

Reconciling History

A Story of Canada

Jody Wilson-Raybould
& Roshan Danesh

McClelland & Stewart

Hardcover edition published 2024

Library and Archives Canada Cataloguing in Publication
data is available upon request.
ISBN: 978-0-7710-1723-0
ebook ISBN: 978-0-7710-1762-9

Jacket design by Terri Nimmo
Jacket art: "Family" carving by Jackson Robertson, illustrated by Dylan Browne
Typeset in Adobe Caslon by Erin Cooper
Printed in the United States of America

McClelland & Stewart,
a division of Penguin Random House Canada Limited,
a Penguin Random House Company
www.penguinrandomhouse.ca

1 2 3 4 5 28 27 26 25 24

Penguin
Random House
McCLELLAND & STEWART

For the Musgamagw Dzawada̱'enux̱w peoples,
whose strength, forethought, vision, and leadership
is reflected in the Kingcome Pole, and continues to
guide so many of us today and into the future.

Contents

"Where common memory is lacking, where people do not share in the same past, there can be no real community. Where community is to be formed, common memory must be created."

—Georges Erasmus

Odoodem (TOTEM POLE)

I come from We Wai Kai, a small First Nations community on an island off the west coast of Canada. You may know it as Cape Mudge on Quadra Island. Quadra is one of the largest of the Gulf Islands, and a place of insurmountable beauty. While writing this I am sitting down by the water—Discovery Passage—out front of my small house on Indian Reserve No. 10, as it has been classified under Canada's Indian Act. As is typical in the summer months, one can expect to see orca and humpback whales pass by and eagles fly overhead, as well as cruise ships on the Alaska route.

While Cape Mudge is my home, it is not actually a full answer to the question of where I am from. Cape Mudge is a place, but I am from a people and a nation as well as a place. My people, the Musgamagw Tsawataineuk and Laich-Kwil-Tach, are part of the Kwakwaka'wakw Nation, also known as the Kwak'wala-speaking peoples.

Like peoples around the world, my people are organized around families, clans, and tribes. The term *Musgamagw* essentially means "four groups living together." We are four tribes who together are one people. Each tribe has roles and responsibilities that must be fulfilled to help everyone survive and thrive. We also are part of broader kinship groups and confederacies—the Kwakwaka'wakw—as part of supporting, caring for, and ensuring the safety and well-being of one another. In our telling of our origin stories and history, this coming together of groups was in response to threats and challenges—a Great Flood.

The way I just told you part of the story of my people is not the most typical way we would tell that story. Art is. At once time-bound and timeless, our art conveys our worldview, identity, history, and teachings. Whether in the form of masks, cedar baskets, carvings, paintings, dance, or song, our art educates us about who we are, how we got here, and what roles and responsibilities we have to each other.

For me, it has always been our carvings, such as our totem poles, that have stood out for their telling of the story of who we are, across time and across space. Our word for totem is *ki'kw*. The Algonquin word *odoodem* is where the word "totem" in English is derived from. *Odoodem* means "clan," or "kinship group." Typically, clans for First Nations peoples are based on animals. The animals appear, and clans form, in our origin stories. Those stories speak to the roles, responsibilities, relationships, and knowledge that each clan has and must carry through time in order for human and social well-being to exist

When a totem pole is carved, it is a telling of the history of a peoples, a family, and their lineage, and of their rights, responsibilities, and relationships. Look at the Musgamagw Dzawada̲'enux̱w pole in the picture. It stands at Gwa'yi, or Kingcome, the home of my grandmother Pugladee, Ethel Pearson. The pole was carved by a group of artists, including Willie Seaweed and Herbert Johnson.

What do you see when you look at it?

Here is what I see.

I see our history. The crests—the Thunderbird (at the top), Wolf, Raven, and Head Winter Dancer, a portrayal of First Ancestor (at the bottom)—represent one of the four tribes (*gukwa̲lut*) of the Musgamagw Dzawada̲'enux̱w. In showing each of them, the pole conveys how we are connected as one, have love and charity for one another, and have responsibilities to each other and for the land and resources.

I see our law. In our system of governance, when understandings and agreements are reached, they need to be validated publicly. Witnessing is critical, and it binds the community, and every

Musgamagw Dzawada̱'enux̱w Totem Pole, Gwa'yi (Kingcome)

member, to the agreements that have been reached. This is reflected and confirmed in the Potlatch, our central institution of governance. The collective decision to erect a pole would take place only through an agreement reached through our governance process, and publicly witnessed and validated.

I see forms of wealth. In our teachings, our unity and connection are a form of wealth, and representing our relations with each other conveys that. In other words, I see family, so I see wealth. Many totems also represent wealth—both material and immaterial—through the placing of a copper on a pole (in many First Nations cultures, coppers are a symbol of wealth, carrying their own name, history, and value).

Now this may surprise you, but when I look at this totem pole, I also see the reality of Canada's history of colonization of Indigenous Peoples, and the struggle of my people for justice. This is not visible in the carving itself but in viewing this pole in its context.

The pole was erected in 1936 following the death of King George V of England. Even though this death occurred at one of the darkest times for First Nations in British Columbia and for Indigenous Peoples across Canada—the Indian Act was controlling our lives, the residential "school" system was breaking up our families, our governance systems were ignored and, in some instances, outlawed, and we were legally barred from raising issues of land rights—the pole was erected as a tribute to the late King. The decision to do this reflects the relational worldview of our, and other, Indigenous Peoples. It is in upholding and strengthening proper, healthy, and just relationships that true happiness, prosperity, and meaning in life is found. Even when one's partner is not upholding that relationship—or perhaps even especially when one's partner is not upholding that relationship—there is a responsibility to uphold it oneself.

Raising the pole was also an act of resistance, defiance, and strength. Because while the pole was being erected in memory of King George V, it also symbolizes the enduring resilience and unity

Musgamagw Dzawada̱'enux̱w Chiefs and community at pole raising, 1936

of my people in the face of the Crown's effort to divide and conquer us. At the time the pole was raised, speeches were made by leadership in Kwak'wala about what was happening to them, such as the banning of the Potlatch, and what needed to be done. Chief Dick Webber, who was among those who spoke, delivered a warning: "I can see it coming, we will forget who we are . . . and we will say bad things to each other . . . the day will come when you forget our unity, honour, love, respect . . . to one another . . . I know that day will come—I know it is coming really soon . . ."[1]

As Chief Glen Johnson conveyed, the pole would help to educate the children and youth, and the generations to come, about our identity. It would show them that in the face of the Indian Act band system, which divided our people into smaller units and forced us onto reserves—like the reserve I am sitting on as I write this—the

Musgamagw Dzawada̱'enux̱w Totem Pole, 1967

pole reinforced our unity and identity, governed under our laws.[2] The pole was and is a reminder to not forget who you are, to not forget that we are ultimately one with each other.

As my grandmother said of the Kingcome Valley: "We never stopped our traditions in this beautiful valley." This pole is proof of that.

In the totem pole is a valuable lesson about how we talk about history and tell stories of how we arrived at this moment in time. Poles need to be viewed from multiple angles. They protrude, jut, and cut. If you look at one just from straight ahead you will miss something. If you look at it from one side or the other, you will see something new or different. You will gain further insights by viewing it in various ways. You need to stand under it; and glimpsing it from a distance will give you yet another valuable perspective. If you want to understand the pole you need to view it in isolation as well as be immersed in the context of all you can learn, see, and know about it.

The totem pole guides us through this book. It urges us to tell the history of Canada in a way that makes us look from different angles, to see its dimensions, its curves, and its cuts. To see that history has an arc, just as the totem pole rises, but that the details along the way also hold important meanings. To recognize, just as our carvers do, that the story of the past is always there to be retold, recast, and reconsidered, and to be conveyed to generations to come. To understand that in the act of retelling, meaning is found and strength is built.

When it comes to telling the history of Canada and, in particular, the history of the relationship between Indigenous and non-Indigenous people, we need to accept that we are not telling a story of peoples who have viewed themselves as in clan or kinship relations. Yes, we all have relations as human beings and groups, but much of the history of Canada with respect to Indigenous Peoples has been rooted in failing to see how we are connected and interdependent, to see how we must recognize and respect one another. The way in which our history has traditionally been told demonstrates this. This telling of history has not been a common and shared enterprise. In many ways, it has been an exclusive and siloed one. Peoples and groups have told their stories, and within, between, and amongst those peoples and groups, some have dominated and controlled how the stories are told, often emphasizing certain voices and experiences over those of others.

In the words of Dene leader Georges Erasmus, Canada lacks a "common memory."

History-telling today is breaking away from this exclusivity—and not just in Canada. In other places around the world, voices that have traditionally been marginalized, whose stories and experience have been ignored or left in the shadows, are telling and retelling history from their perspective. At this moment, we understand more than we have before about the historical experiences of women, young people, oppressed groups, the economically vulnerable, and others. This is important. It is like looking at the totem from a different perspective or angle; it lets us see something in a new way, which then educates us about how to approach the challenges of today and tomorrow.

This retelling is important in another way as well. It brings us closer to being able to tell a shared story, continuing the effort to understand the complex and evolving relations between groups of humanity and to help build patterns of greater justice and cohesion. At a time in humanity's history when our challenges encompass and impact all of us—climate change, conflict and war, pandemics, economic well-being—we need to deepen our ways of thinking about what we share. This includes finding ways to understand honest and truthful shared stories of our past that honour, reflect, and include the distinct voices and experiences of all peoples. Like the totem pole, these stories will let us see, hear, feel, touch, and understand our origins and connections.

This is why I've chosen to tell the story of Canada here the way I do. It is an "oral history"—a telling of history in the voices and words of those who lived it, and in supporting documents. In doing so—through the voices of Indigenous and non-Indigenous people throughout the history of Canada, and before—I am trying to do what the totem pole beckons us to do, which is to look and see from many different perspectives.

In telling this oral history, we must acknowledge the countless voices that could not be included because of the reality that they have been ignored or not heard in our past, and what they said has not been recorded or remembered. The way the story is told also reflects fundamental aspects of our history—about who holds power, about what beliefs were held, about what voices matter, about traditions and cultural practices, including how knowledge was transmitted, and about the course of events. At times, Indigenous voices are predominant. At other times, the voices of those of European descent are predominant. While the story reflects shifts and change, it also reveals things that stay the same.

Of course, there are countless voices, especially as we look further into the past, that we cannot hear, or hear only in the faintest of whispers. But in that silence, if we recognize it, we can also recognize vital realities and truths.

This book is guided by the structure of the Kingcome pole and the crests of the tribes carved into it.

We start at the bottom, with one of our representations of our First Ancestor—Head Winter Dancer, or Cedar Man. Indeed, all of the crests on the pole, whether of a human form, such as the Cedar Man, or of an animal, can be understood as different representations of the First Ancestor. This is a reflection of how intrinsic and integrated our teachings are, and how our worldview speaks of the relationship between humans and the natural world. In this part of the book, we will hear voices tell the story of these lands before the arrival of Europeans. This crest is of the Kwikwasut'inuxw First Nation, or Gilford.

As we move up the pole, we see the Raven—in my culture, and many other Indigenous cultures, a "trickster" and transformer. We will hear voices tell the story of early relations between Indigenous and non-Indigenous people and how, like in dealings with the trickster, it was uncertain what was happening and what might happen. And how, over time, possibility and even hope transformed into patterns of oppression and colonization. This crest is of Dzawada̱'enux̱w, or Kingcome.

Further up, we find the Wolf, in my culture (and others) representing loyalty and strong ties. We will hear voices tell the story of Indigenous resilience and advocacy, and the emergence of relations and venues that supported that advocacy. This crest is of Haxwa'mis, or Wakeman.

At the top, we find the Thunderbird, in my culture representing power, protection, and strength. We will hear voices tell the story of trying to build transformed relations between Indigenous and non-Indigenous people, and how such a transformation is central to the strength and future of Canada. This crest is of Gwawa'enuxw, or Hopetown.

When I look at the pole, I see an image of my own people and my peoples' story, and I try to understand what that means for my people today and into the future. I hope that when you read this oral history, it will have a similar effect. That when you hear the voices of Indigenous and non-Indigenous people telling the story of their relations you will be able to situate yourself within it and be able to assess, anew, what that may mean for you—and for all of us—today and tomorrow.

This history includes voices from our past and present, woven together to tell our collective story of how and why we are.

And we who are here today are called to witness this retelling of our past, and to play our part in shaping the future.

PART I

First Ancestor

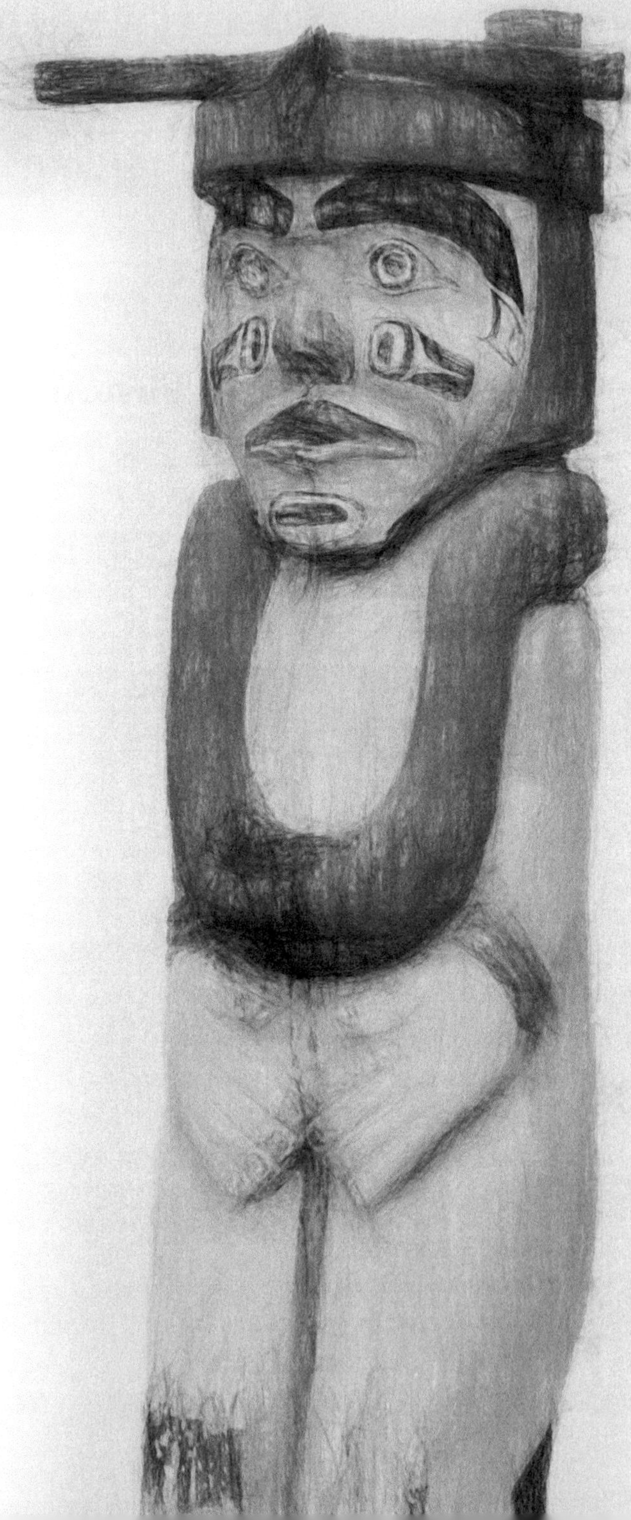

I find the face of the First Ancestor at the base of the Kingcome pole a little haunting. When I stare at him, the eyes are always elusive—looking past me at things I cannot fully see. I imagine this is because the eyes see something clearly that we, today, struggle to glimpse because it was so long ago—the beginning of time, of our story, and of history itself. The First Ancestor sees beyond our typically limited views, and in doing so challenges us to try to see what he sees: how we came to be.

For my people, the First Ancestor is seeing how our people survived and grew after the Great Flood. He sees how we formed our vital relationship with the sea and the creatures within it. In the Kwakwaka'wakw legend of the dawn of time, one of our central teachings, *maya'xa̲la*, is also conveyed. *Maya'xa̲la* is the teaching of respect—to treat all others, and all things in creation, the way you wish to be treated. To do unto others as you would have them do unto you. Yes, there is a similarity between *maya'xa̲la* and the Golden Rule that is a central teaching in many traditions.

I also understand the haunting eyes of the First Ancestor to be reflecting something important about beginnings: how they always involve an absolute and all-consuming immersion in the experience of a new reality. Consider the birth of a child, where in a single moment one has entered a new world. We call it a birth because there is no history at birth, only future. Everything is yet to unfold. The only story we have in that moment is of how we began. And as time passes and our stories grow, we keep retelling our beginning to help us make sense of who we are, what is happening to us, and why.

In traditions across the globe, in the various religions, legends, and mythologies that are passed down from generation to generation, there is always an origin story. Some of these are familiar, like the story of Adam and Eve, for example. Or the stories of Shatarupa and Manu in Hinduism, Pandora in Ancient Greece, and many others. Science, of course, has its own stories. Growing up I heard of "Lucy," the fossil skeleton of a human ancestor who at the time of discovery in 1974 was believed to be the oldest such fossil yet found.

Whether from legend and myth or the study of human evolution, learning about the First Ancestor has the same fundamental purpose for everyone—to help us make sense of our existence today. These stories help give us an identity and connection to others, including giving us something to share with past, present, and future generations. They are also like a compass, pointing us to the direction we must look if we want to understand how we arrived at this moment in time.

There is no single First Ancestor story amongst Indigenous Peoples. There is, and always has been, tremendous diversity amongst the peoples who live on the lands that now make up Canada. First Nations and Inuit, who have been here since the beginning, have many different and distinct stories about how they came to be. The Métis, who formed in more recent times with both First Nation and European roots, have connections to the origin stories of different traditions, as well as stories of how they came to be a people that are distinct to them.

First Nations and Inuit stories, as you will see, do share some features—in particular, a rooting in the natural world. The beginning of human beings is inseparable from the force and power, and life-giving qualities, of the world around us. But there are also distinctions in these stories that often reflect the diversity of the natural world and the climates, geographies, and living beings in different places.

Listening to these stories is important if we want to understand the history of Canada, the legacy of colonization, and our challenges today. These stories are critical foundations that have shaped and reflect Indigenous worldviews and cultures, as well as governance, legal, and social systems—the systems that have been present on the lands for the longest of times. We need to understand the roots of these systems so that we can more fully understand how they have shaped what has come to be Canada. These systems continue to operate and impact how we live today.

Put simply, if we want to reconcile, as we so often say we do, we need to know from where we came. And for that, we need to start at the beginning.

<<<< >>>>

For the thousands of years before the arrival of Europeans, First Nations and Inuit owned, occupied, and governed the lands now known as North America. In some First Nations traditions, the story of creation is that of "Turtle Island," a name now commonly used by some First Nations to refer to these lands. An example of this is from of the Ojibwe.

FROM THE OJIBWE, THE STORY OF TURTLE ISLAND

The story of Turtle Island begins with a great flood. The Great Spirit had decided to flood the world and create a new land where the Ojibwe people could live and prosper. The Great Spirit called upon the muskrat to find land, and the muskrat dove into the flood waters and eventually found a great turtle swimming beneath the waves. The turtle was carrying a great load of mud on its back, and the muskrat asked the turtle if he could use the mud to create land. The turtle agreed, and the muskrat began to shape the mud into land, creating Turtle Island.[1]

First Nations creation stories are distinct and diverse. They often recount relations between humans, animals, and the forces of the natural world. Almost always, First Nations creation stories involve significant climate events, as well as interactions with animals.

FROM THE IROQUOIS, WHOSE TERRITORY IS WITHIN WHAT IS NOW KNOWN AS ONTARIO AND QUEBEC

Long before the world was created there was an island, floating in the sky, upon which the Sky People lived. They lived quietly and happily. No one ever died or was born or experienced sadness. However one day one of the Sky Women realized she was going to give birth to twins. She told her husband, who flew into a rage. In the center of the island there was a tree which gave light to the entire island since the sun hadn't been created yet. He tore up this tree, creating a huge hole in the middle of the island. Curiously, the woman peered into the hole. Far below she could see the waters that covered the earth. . . . She fell through the hole, tumbling towards the water below.

Water animals already existed on the earth, so far below the floating island two birds saw the Sky Woman fall. Just before she reached the waters they caught her on their backs and brought her to the other animals. Determined to help the woman they dove into the water to get mud from the bottom of the seas. One after another the animals tried and failed. Finally, Little Toad tried and when he reappeared his mouth was full of mud. The animals took it and spread it on the back of Big Turtle. The mud began to grow and grow and grow until it became the size of North America.

Then the woman stepped onto the land. She sprinkled dust into the air and created stars. Then she created the moon and sun.[2]

Sky Woman Geezhigo-Quae by Donald Chrétien

FROM THE MI'KMAQ, WHOSE TERRITORY IS WITHIN WHAT IS NOW KNOWN AS ATLANTIC CANADA

Life began with the number 7. First, there was the Giver of Life, who made everything. Then there was the sun, we call Nisgam, our Grandfather. And it's the sun that gives us our shadows, and it's important that we have shadows. And they are our spirits, it gives us our lifeblood. And then, the third entity was the Earth, Ootsitgamoo. And upon the Earth, all life is given to us from our Mother Earth we call Oetsigitpogooin. Not too long after everything was created, the Life-Giver caused a bolt of lightning to strike and hit the earth. It formed the shape of a person. The head was in the direction of the rising sun. And the arms were outstretched and the feet were in the direction of the setting sun.

It was not until the second bolt of lightning that hit the earth, that the first one who spoke, we call Gellulaskiv in our language, Glooscap. He was given his toes, his fingers, his hands and he was given 7 sacred parts to his head. He had to listen to his world. When we are born, the first thing we hear is our mother's heartbeat. Also Glooscap was given his eyes, so he could look and see his world around him. He also was given two holes in his nose, from there, he sensed his place in this world. He also was given his mouth, to drink the water that is in abundance for everybody. Also to be able to share the food that we eat, that comes from Mother Earth. We take the medicines that we gather from the animals and the birds and the plants and the trees. And last that came from Glooscap's mouth was words.

And our Elders teach us that if we can listen first and look and sense and share our food, our medicines, our water, and the air and then to be able to speak. Then in this way, we have been able to honour and give respect to all life and everything around us.[3]

Reflecting the oral tradition of First Nations, creation stories have been passed on orally from generation to generation. They are also communicated and conveyed in other ways, such as through art. For example, carvings are sometimes used to tell First Nations creation stories.

FROM THE HAIDA, FROM HAIDA GWAII OFF THE WEST COAST OF WHAT IS NOW KNOWN AS BRITISH COLUMBIA

In the beginning there was Raven and Butterfly.

They played amongst the stars. They played tag and hide and seek. They played until they got tired of the games. They looked for something else to play with.

They found the Earth.

Raven Butterfly and the First Haida by Ron Russ

They went to Rose Spit which is on the northernmost tip of Haida Gwaii. They walked in the sand.

Soon they noticed something squirt water into the sky. They went to investigate and found a clam. They started to play with the clam. Soon they saw a movement in the clam. They saw human forms in the clam. The humans closed the clam to hide from Raven and Butterfly. No matter how hard they tried to open the clam it wouldn't open.

Raven talked quietly to the humans. Soon the humans opened the clam to see what was talking to them. They got braver and came out of the clam.

Soon [B]utterfly got tired of the humans and flew away.

The humans started to climb all over Raven. Soon Raven got tired of the humans climbing on him. Raven flew away.

There were still some humans on Raven. They started to tickle Raven. Soon Raven shook and some fell off.

Where the Humans landed they started to make villages.

That is how Haida Gwaii was given to the Haida people.[4]

The legend of Sedna is often identified as the central creation story of Inuit. Similar to First Nations stories, it speaks to the overwhelming power of nature. But Inuit Nunangat (the land, water, and ice of the homeland of Inuit) also has a distinct climate and geography that influences many aspects of Inuit teachings and culture.

FROM INUIT, THE LEGEND OF SEDNA

Sedna was a beautiful Inuit girl who was pressured into marriage by her father. Unknown to Sedna, her new husband was actually a raven who fed her fish and kept her in a nest on an island far away from her family. Her father, who missed Sedna terribly, went in his kayak to rescue her but the raven, with his special powers, called up a storm. The father panicked and pushed Sedna into the cold water.

As she clung to the kayak, her frozen fingers and hands were broken off and fell into the sea where they became seals, whales and other sea mammals. Sedna could no longer struggle and sank into the water where she became a goddess of the sea. Her frustration and anger continue to be expressed through the creation of storms and high seas. Inuit hunters have treated Sedna with respect for centuries to ensure she will allow Inuit to harvest her bounty. Today some hunters still sprinkle a few drops of fresh water into the mouths of sea mammals they harvest to thank Sedna for her generosity.[5]

Ancient Inuit legends also speak to the ways of life of their people, and modes of survival and the ability to thrive. The legend of Kiviuq is one such legend. It reflects on the relationship between the vast lands, water, ice, and often harsh climate and the ways in which Inuit lived in that environment.

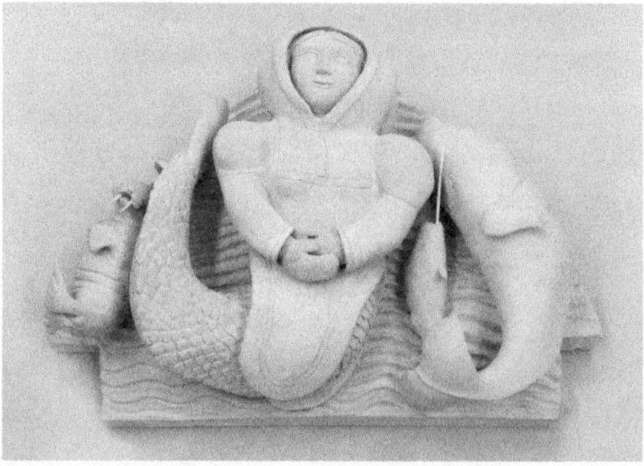

Sedna with Friends by Bart Hanna Kappianaq

FROM INUIT, THE LEGEND OF KIVIUQ

Kiviuq was paddling his kayak along the shore when he came upon an igloo. He saw an old bumblebee lady inside. There were also skeletons of men stacked up against the wall. When she tried to look up, her old sagging eyelids got in the way. So she took out her ooloo and cut off her eyelids. When Kiviuq saw that, he fainted and fell down into the igloo. The bumblebee woman took off Kiviuq's kamaks and hung them on the drying rack. One of the dead heads spoke to Kiviuq, "If you don't get back your kamaks and leave right now, you'll end up like me." But Kiviuq had a spirit helper. The bird picked up Kiviuq's kamak. Just as Kiviuq snuck by the old woman, he felt her ooloo slash through his parka. Kiviuq ran down to his kayak and paddled out to sea as fast as he could. The old woman waded into the water, slashing the air with her ooloo. Then she pleaded with Kiviuq to come back to be her husband and stay with her. But Kiviuq kept on paddling. In a rage, the bumblebee woman threw her ooloo after him into the water and the wash from the ooloo froze. And that's the sea ice today.[6]

<<<< >>>>

Kwakwa̱ka̱'wakw Potlatch, 1914

Ever since I was a child, I have heard about the history of my people. This is, of course, an innately human thing. Children are raised to know where they have come from. This is part of how we form our identities and preserve and pass on knowledge and teachings. We all come from peoples with pasts, presents, and a future. We all have knowledge passed on to us about our people, and with it a responsibility to share that knowledge with the generations to come. Transmitting this history helps us be connected across generations, and rooted to the communities, cultures, and ways of life that are vital to shaping who we are and how we live our lives.

Inevitably, these histories we tell of peoples—these stories—also include moments of rupture and shift. Moments where something was changed or transformed in massive ways, for good or ill. For my people, and for First Nations and Inuit across Canada, one of these central moments was when Europeans first came to our lands.

Prior to that moment, long-standing ways of life, systems of governance, cultures, and traditions had formed and been in place, rooted in our distinct and diverse worldviews, teachings, and belief systems. The arrival of Europeans did not immediately disrupt or impact these in significant ways. That would come later, as the destructive violence of colonization fully asserted itself.

The arrival of Europeans, colonization, the formation of Canada, and everything that has occurred since has also never stopped the telling of the story of our people. So, as I was growing up Kwakwaka'wakw in Cape Mudge, as well as in Vancouver, Port Hardy, Comox, and a few other places, life always included hearing these stories, and stories of how we had lived since the First Ancestor. How we governed ourselves through the Potlatch in the Big House. How we organized our families and society in accordance with the principle of balance, including balance between humans and the natural world, between genders, between groups of peoples, within a family or community, or in how we lived and organized our own lives. How we have always believed that spirits animate all things in Creation, and that we are in a necessary and integrative relationship with all things in existence that demands we live in harmony and proper relations with each other. How wealth is measured by how much one gives away to others and not how much one possesses for oneself, and as such a central function of the Potlatch is for a family to give to others. How we are primarily a fishing people, with an economy built on sea and land.

This knowledge of the history of my people, and our teachings and values, is what has grounded me through all of life's trials and tribulations. It is this knowledge that has shaped my identity and the choices I have made and continue to make in life. It is this knowledge that, more than anything, has made me who I am today. As I said in one very public moment of my life:

> I was taught to always hold true to your core values and principles and to act with integrity. These are the teachings of my parents, my grandparents, and my community.
>
> I come from a long line of matriarchs and I'm a truth teller, in accordance with the laws and traditions of our Big House.
>
> This is who I am, and this is who I always will be.[7]

What is still little understood, however, is that just as the knowledge about my people has shaped how I live my life, the Canada that we live in today has also been shaped in far-reaching and profound ways by the worldviews, cultures, and ways of life of First Nations and Inuit that were present before Europeans arrived, and of the Métis Nation who formed later on. As well, when we talk today about First Nations, Inuit, and Métis rights, and the struggle for their recognition and implementation, we are talking about rights that have an inextricable connection to aspects of the culture, societies, economies, relationships with land, governance, and laws that existed prior to the arrival of Europeans. This will come into focus as we move through later parts of this book.

To understand and make sense of the history of Canada, we need to understand what existed here before Canada. And, even earlier, before Europeans arrived on our shores. In addition to looking back through time, we need to also understand how Indigenous ways of life continue to influence and shape Canada today and will do so into the future.

To do this, we need to start by looking at what the First Ancestor saw after the beginning—as we moved from the First to the many, and as communities and societies grew.

In reading this part of the book, it is also important to reflect on the fact that the ways in which we tell and pass on the histories of our peoples involve choices. One of those choices is about how, in telling our stories, we talk about our relationship with other peoples, and with humanity. Are our stories of our friends or enemies? Do we describe ourselves as distinct yet connected and part of a whole, or separate and in competition or conflict? Does the way we tell our stories provide a foundation for positive relations between peoples?

Reflecting the worldviews and cultures of First Nations, Inuit, and Métis, Indigenous Peoples often tell our histories in ways that emphasize the building of positive relations and connections within our families and communities, and between peoples. Doing this is not to avoid or deny the reality of hardships, conflict, and injustice. Rather, it is to help to continue to advance the essential work of building more just and harmonious relations from generation to generation.

So, while the voices in this part of the book are primarily Indigenous, one can already hear how they reflect the idea that achieving balance and harmony is paramount. This will become clearer in later parts of the book, where even in the face of colonization and racism, the belief and desire to achieve proper and just relations remains ever-present.

<<<< >>>>

As First Nations and Inuit had predominately oral traditions, we do not have written records authored by them about their way of life from prior to contact with Europeans. But First Nations and Inuit have continued to pass on orally—and in writing after Europeans arrived—their knowledge of life prior to contact. There was tremendous diversity amongst these peoples and societies. This is seen in the number of different Indigenous languages, and where they are spoken. While accounts of pre-contact life all emphasize the importance of land, they vary in their descriptions of the political, cultural, economic, and social systems that existed. For some, life was primarily nomadic; for others, it included various forms of village and settled life.

TECUMSEH, A SHAWNEE CHIEF, 1811

Before the palefaces came among us, we enjoyed the happiness of unbounded freedom and were acquainted with neither riches, wants, nor oppression.[8]

BLACK ELK, AN OGLALA SIOUX HOLY MAN

The Sun comes forth and goes down again in a circle, the Moon does the same, and both are round. Even the seasons form a great circle in their changing, and always come back again to where they were. The life of a man is a circle, from childhood to childhood, and so it is in everything where power moves.

. . .

In the old days when we were a strong and happy people, all our power came to us from the sacred hoop of the nation and so long as the hoop was unbroken the people flourished.

. . .

And I saw that the sacred hoop of my people was one of many hoops that made one circle, wide as daylight and as starlight, and in the centre grew one mighty flowering tree to shelter all the children of one mother and one father . . . The flowering tree was the living centre of the hoop, and the circle of the four quarters nourished it. The East gave peace and light, the South gave warmth, the West gave rain, and the North with its cold and mighty wind gave strength and endurance.[9]

LENA NOTTAWAY, AN ALGONQUIN MATRIARCH

Long time ago we didn't have any cabins. We lived in wigwams made of bark. In the winter it was no problem to sleep in the bush. We had rabbit fur clothing, you could not freeze or get cold with it. It wasn't necessary to have a fire. We used spruce boughs for bedding, and we wouldn't get wet. I didn't even have a tent, even after I got married.

Everybody lived all over the place. We had half-way houses, built like teepees so anybody could sleep in them on their way from one place to another.

. . .

If you wanted something you would trade moccasins, or tools, or whatever you had.

. . .

Long time ago, we had no place to sell furs, we only trapped when we needed fur for ourselves. We would hunt so we had enough food to last for a week or two. . . . In the summer no one stayed in one place for long. We scattered in small groups, gathered our own foods, fish, ducks, blueberries. We had to keep moving all the time. . . . Long time ago, we had no money for guns, so we used bow and arrow, and slingshots. There used to be so many ducks and geese we could get close to them. If we wanted potatoes or onions, we found them growing wild in the bush, we could find them winter or summer.

. . .

Long time ago, before the white man came, it was better. Nobody ever got sick. But after the white man came, and put the logs in the water, by and by everything was spoiled. Even the taste of the water, even the medicine in the bush. Then many people began to get sick. It wasn't us, it was them, they spoiled everything. Long time ago, before the white man came, we never had any shortage of food. Only after the white man came was there shortage.[10]

CHIEFS OF THE SHUSWAP, OKANAGAN, AND COUTEAU TRIBES OF BRITISH COLUMBIA, WRITING TO PRIME MINISTER SIR WILFRID LAURIER, 1910

When they first came among us there were only Indians here. They found the people of each tribe supreme in their own territory, and having tribal boundaries known and recognized by all. The country of each tribe was just the same as a very large farm or ranch (belonging to all the people of the tribe) from which they gathered their food and clothing, etc., fish which they got in plenty for food, grass and vegetation on which their horses grazed and the game lived, and much of which furnished materials for manufactures, etc., stone which furnished pipes, utensils, and tools, etc., trees which furnished firewood, materials for houses and utensils, plants, roots, seeds, nuts and berries which grew abundantly and were gathered in their season just the same as the crops on a ranch, and used for food; minerals, shells, etc., which were used for ornament and for plants, etc., water which was free to all. Thus, fire, water, food, clothing and all the necessaries of life were obtained in abundance from the lands of each tribe, and all the people had equal rights of access to everything they required.[11]

First Nations and Inuit had complex systems of governance, law, social organization, and family that were reflections of their distinct world-views, spiritualities, and cultures. While these systems are not static, and have continued to change over time, they also reflect teachings, values, and principles that are constant. Relations between First Nations were also varied and complex. They could include conflict, and even war, but more often were harmonious. Diplomatic protocols, structures, and processes governed these relations between and amongst First Nations, such as the well-known Great Law of Peace.

HAUDENOSAUNEE (IROQUOIS), EXCERPTS FROM THE GREAT LAW OF PEACE, DESCRIBING DEMOCRATIC POLITICAL RELATIONS BETWEEN THE SENECA, CAYUGA, ONEIDA, ONONDAGA, AND MOHAWK, 1451

2. Roots have spread out from the Tree of the Great Peace, one to the north, one to the east, one to the south and one to the west. The name of these roots is the Great White Roots and their nature is Peace and Strength.

   If any man or any nation outside the Five Nations shall obey the laws of the Great Peace and make their disposition [swear their allegiance] to the Lords of the Confederacy, they may trace the Roots to the Tree and if their minds are clean and they are obedient and promise to obey the wishes of the Confederate Council, they shall be welcomed to take shelter beneath the Tree of the Long Leaves.

. . .

24. The chiefs of the League of Five Nations shall be mentors of the people for all time. The thickness of their skins shall be seven spans, which is to say that they shall be proof against anger, offensive action and criticism. Their hearts shall be full of peace and good will and their minds filled with a yearning for the welfare of the people of the league. With endless patience, they shall carry out their duty. Their firmness shall be tempered with a tenderness for their people.

. . .

92. If a nation, part of a nation, or more than one nation within the Five Nations should in any way endeavor to destroy the

Great Peace by neglect or violating its laws and resolve to dissolve the Confederacy, such a nation or such nations shall be deemed guilty of treason and called enemies of the Confederacy and the Great Peace.

. . .

93. Whenever a specially important matter or a great emergency is presented before the Confederate Council and the nature of the matter affects the entire body of Five Nations, threatening their utter ruin, then the Lords of the Confederacy must submit the matter to the decision of their people and the decision of the people shall affect the decision of the Confederate Council. This decision shall be a confirmation of the voice of the people.[12]

Some Europeans set out to study the way of life, culture, and traditions of First Nations and Inuit, and in the process of those studies recorded what they heard from First Nations and Inuit about life prior to contact. The birth of the field of study known as anthropology has many of its foundations in Europeans studying Indigenous Peoples in different parts of the world, including what is now Canada. These descriptions by early anthropologists reflect the attitudes and beliefs of Europeans at the time—some of which we now recognize as racist—while also providing descriptions of Indigenous culture and society, including as described to them by the peoples they were studying. One of the more well-known of these Europeans was Franz Boas, sometimes called the "father" of anthropology, who spent time with Inuit, Kwakwaka'wakw, and the Nuu-chah-nulth, among others. Another was Diamond Jenness, who was one of Canada's leading anthropologists in the early 1900s, and who spent many years studying Indigenous Peoples across the county, including significant amounts of time in the North amongst Inuit.

FRANZ BOAS

After all the many little adventures, and after a long and intimate intercourse with the Eskimos, it was with feelings of sorrow and regret that I parted from my Arctic friends. I had seen that they enjoyed life, and a hard life, as we do; that nature is also beautiful to them; that feelings of friendship also root in the Eskimo heart; that, although, the character of their life is so rude as compared to civilized life, the Eskimo is a man as we are; that his feelings, his virtues, and his shortcomings are based in human nature, like ours.[13]

As these bays open into Davis Strait the formation of the ice is retarded and its extent diminished, and consequently some peculiarities in the arrangement of the life of the Eskimo are observed here. The only occupation of the Nugumiut and the inhabitants of Ukadlik is sealing with the harpoon on the floe of the inner parts of the bay. Near Ukadlik the tide holes east and west of Allen Island abound with seals. In winter, when the seals take to the open ice, the village of this group of families is established near Roger's Island, where the floe of the bay forms the hunting ground.[14]

The structure of the 'namima [clan] is best understood if we disregard the living individuals and rather consider the 'namima as consisting of a certain number of positions to each of which belongs to a name, a "seat" or "standing place," that means rank, and privileges. There number is limited, and they form a ranked nobility. I am told that among the thirteen tribes of the region extending from Fort Rupert to Nimpkish River and Knight Inlet, there are 658 seats. These names and seats are the skeleton of the 'namima, and individuals in the course of their lives, may occupy various positions and with these take the names belonging to them.[15]

It is good that you should have a box in which your laws and stories are kept. My friend, George Hunt, will show you a box in which some of your stories will be kept. It is a book I have written on what I saw and heard when I was with you two years ago. It is a good book, for in it are your laws and your stories. Now they will not be forgotten."[16]

DIAMOND JENNESS

By isolating myself among the Eskimos . . . I had followed their wanderings day by day from autumn round to autumn.

I had observed their reactions to every season, the disbanding of the tribes and their reassembling, the migrations from sea to land and from land to sea, the diversion from sealing to hunting, hunting to fishing, fishing to hunting, and then to sealing again. All these changes caused by their economic environment I had seen and studied; now, with a greater knowledge of the language, I could concentrate on other phases of their life and history.[17]

Based on knowledge of the life of First Nations and Inuit that has been passed on from generation to generation, there are many summary descriptions of how their societies were structured and organized prior to the arrival of Europeans. While these summaries provide only a glimpse of what life was like, they can help us understand aspects of what was disrupted, impacted, and changed by the arrival of Europeans.

ROYAL COMMISSION ON ABORIGINAL PEOPLES, AND PAUKTUUTIT INUIT WOMEN OF CANADA, DESCRIBING LIFE PRIOR TO THE ARRIVAL OF EUROPEANS

In the southeastern region of North America, the Cherokee were organized into a confederacy of some 30 cities—the greatest of which was nearly as large as imperial London when English explorers first set eyes on it. Further south, in Central and South America, Indigenous peoples had carved grand empires out of the mountains and jungles long before Cortez arrived.

In northern North America, Aboriginal cultures were shaped by environment and the evolution of technology:

- The plentiful resources of sea and forest enabled west coast peoples to build societies of wealth and sophistication.

- On the prairies and northern tundra, Aboriginal peoples lived in close harmony with vast, migrating herds of buffalo and caribou.

- In the forests of central Canada, Aboriginal peoples harvested wild rice from the marshes and grew corn, squash and beans beside the river banks, supplementing their crops by fishing, hunting and gathering.

- On the east coast and in the far north, the bounty of the sea and land—and their own ingenuity—enabled Aboriginal peoples to survive in harsh conditions.[18]

Prior to contact with Europeans, Inuit were entirely self-sufficient. They lived in small, autonomous, nomadic groups, dependent upon hunting, fishing and gathering for survival and for all their physical

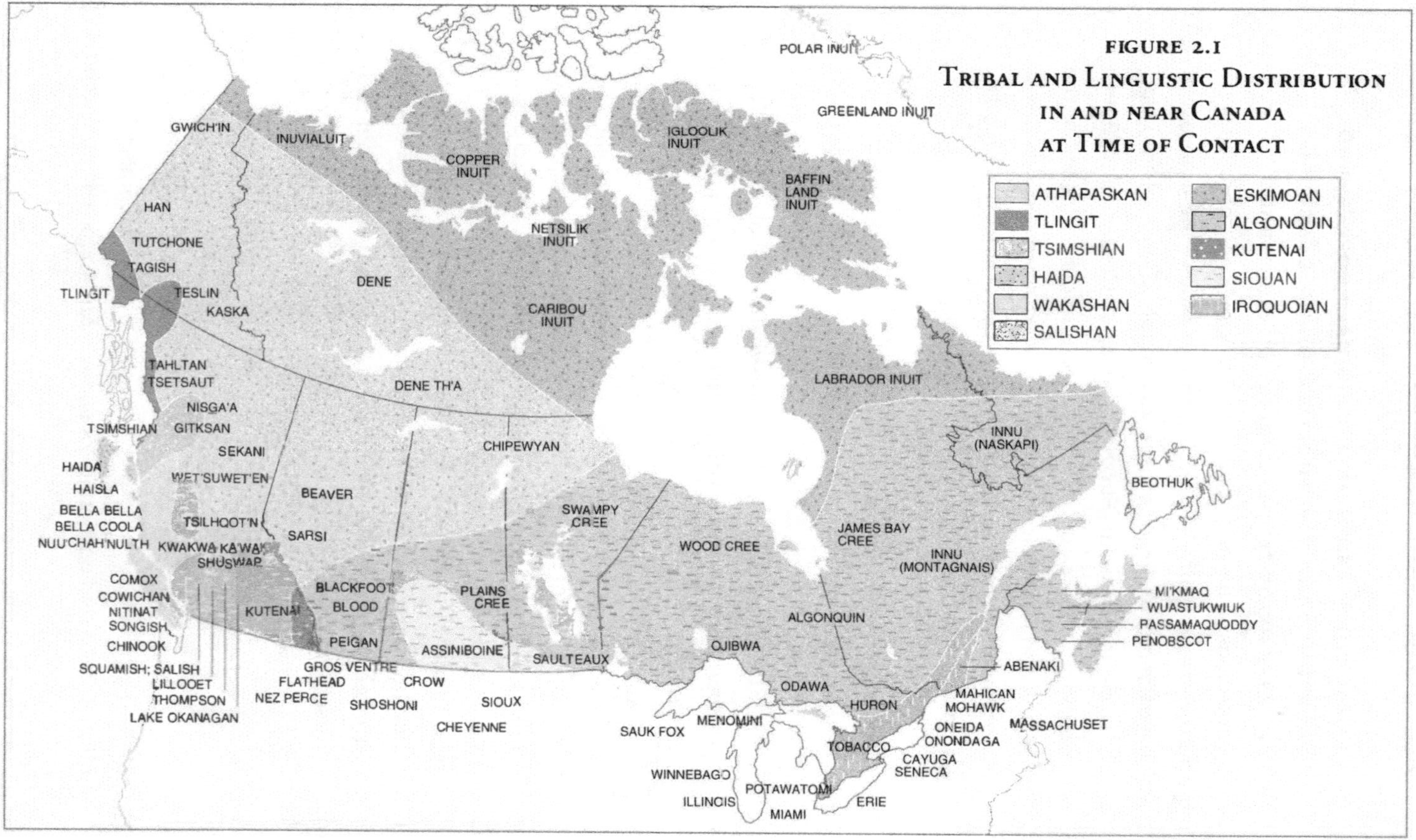

Tribal and linguistic distribution in and near Canada at time of contact (RCAP, 1996)

> needs. Customary law was followed, characterized by its informal nature, flexibility, and its reliance upon social pressures to ensure that people acted appropriately. Inuit had developed a rich material culture, based primarily upon hunting and fishing technology. Spirituality centered upon beliefs in animal and human-like spirits, including the spirits of deceased relatives.[19]

<<<< >>>>

Typically, our telling of history begins with a moment in time. We may choose this beginning moment for any number of reasons—a big event, an important person, a transition, or a change. For Canada, we know the moments in time we typically use, such as the arrival of Europeans, or Confederation.

The message of the First Ancestor, the foundation of the totem pole, is that we should be less concerned with *when* we began, and more concerned with *how* and *why*. It is in the how and the why of our existence, our reality, that meaning lies. What led to our emergence? What were the forces that shaped our birth? How did those forces lead to our first ways of being as individuals and together?

It is the first answers to these questions that we have begun to witness here, through these glimpses into the way of life of the peoples who first inhabited these lands. As we move up the pole and examine the Raven, we will see new forces come into play—and we will come to understand how they shaped and reshaped the ways of being of those who were here, and those who came from far away.

PART 2 Raven

In 1910, the leaders of the Secwépemc (Shuswap), Nlaka'pamux (Okanagan), and Syilx Peoples (Couteau) in the interior of British Columbia wrote a petition to Prime Minister Wilfrid Laurier. The petition recounted their experience since the arrival of Europeans and was also a plea for help—for intervention to stop the growing harms and threats that were occurring. The decision to send the petition was not unique. Indigenous Peoples both before and after Confederation were ringing the alarm bell in a variety of ways about the forms of oppression they were experiencing.

When I read the petition—just as when I read other petitions, like that of the Mi'kmaq to Queen Victoria in 1841—I experience the full range of emotions. In particular, I feel pride in the strength shown by these peoples trying to stand up to the harms being perpetrated against them. I am also inspired by the resilience they demonstrate in continuing to try to find a peaceful way of living together despite all that has been taken from them.

I also experience anger—especially at the fact that much of what is voiced in this petition from more than a hundred years ago continues to be spoken in the voices of Indigenous people today as they call for change. These words from 1910 could have been uttered in any of the countless Chiefs meetings I attended throughout my life. For example:

> We never accepted these reservations as settlement for anything nor did we sign any papers or make any treaties about the same. They

> thought we would be satisfied with this, but we never have been satisfied and never will be until we get our rights.[1]

But more than anything, when I read the petition, I see the Raven. I see the movement from the depth and distance of the eyes of the First Ancestor on the Kingcome pole to the fierceness and complexity in the eyes of the Raven.

The Raven possesses strength and power. The Raven symbolizes creation, transformation, knowledge, and prestige as well as the complexity of nature and the subtlety of truth. Sometimes the Raven is referred to as a "keeper of secrets," because he helps us by exposing truths—revealing secrets that if kept hidden could potentially harm us. While the Raven effects change, his mode of making change is also as a mischief maker. There is both light and dark in the Raven. The Raven can shape-shift. And sometimes we are tricked, thinking that what is happening benefits us, when really it will result in harm.

Some peoples, such as the Tlingit, also speak of the Raven as a Creator—but one who, in the act of creation, also brings mayhem and trouble. Often, this element of darkness, of tricking, of mayhem is reflective of the idea of selfishness—a sense that, ultimately, the Raven creates out of his own interest, and to feed his own needs.

In the petition, the interior Chiefs state that "We had never known white chiefs to break their word so we trusted." This reflects the experience of many Indigenous Peoples in their early interactions with Europeans—that there existed patterns of mutual interdependence, sharing, and trust in early relations. These patterns were expressed in multiple ways with both French and English settlers, including in military alliances; the formation of the agreements and treaties, such as the Peace and Friendship Treaties in the 1800s; and the establishment of trade relations. They were also expressed in the fabric of lives, with peoples increasingly living in contact with each other, often next to each other, and, in some instances, even with

Chief "Louis" Clexlixqen of Tk'emlúps (Kamloops), Chief Basil "Dick" David of Stuxtéws (Bonaparte), and Chief "John" Chelahitsa of sp'áxmen (Douglas Lake), Ottawa, 1908

each other as intermarriage occurred. The distinct Métis Nation, culture, and society was formed in this way.

But the story the Chiefs tell does not end there. They go on to share how the Europeans were saying one thing and doing another. Trying to pull a trick.

The Europeans said they would only use "these pieces of land for a few years, and then would hand them back to us in an improved condition; meanwhile they would give us some of the products they raised for the loan of our land. Thus, they commenced to enter our 'houses,' or live on our 'ranches.'" Trusting in this, the nations welcomed them in accordance with what their teachings always said:

> With us when a person enters our house he becomes our guest, and we must treat him hospitably as long as he shows no hostile intentions. At the same time we expect him to return to us equal treatment for what he receives. Some of our Chiefs said, "These people wish to be partners with us in our country. We must, therefore, be the same as brothers to them, and live as one family. We will share equally in everything—half and half—in land, water and timber, etc. What is ours will be theirs, and what is theirs will be ours. We will help each other to be great and good."[2]

By the time the Chiefs petition was written, however, the possibility for good had ended. The dark side of the Raven became evident. Self-interest and greed were paramount. The taking never stopped—whether of land, of wealth, of freedom, of autonomy:

> What have we received for our good faith, friendliness and patience? Gradually as the whites of this country became more and more powerful, and we less and less powerful, they little by little changed their policy towards us, and commenced to put restrictions on us. Their government or chiefs have taken every advantage of our friendliness, weakness and ignorance to impose on us in every way. They treat us as

> subjects without any agreement to that effect, and force their laws on us without our consent and irrespective of whether they are good for us or not. They say they have authority over us.[3]

This movement from interdependence to imposition, from co-operation to colonization, from potential good to demonstrable evil, from sharing to possessing is the mayhem that comes about when the dark side of the Raven is dominant.

This arc in the experience of early relations with Europeans shared by the Secwépemc, Nlaka'pamux, and Syilx Chiefs is shared by all First Nations and Inuit. While the specific expressions of the shifts toward increasing harm and violence are diverse, the reality of the trajectory of change was universal. It is important that we keep a focus on both the specific and the universal. In the specific, we gain a glimpse into the human dimensions of what occurred—how the lives of particular individuals, families, and communities were impacted and shaped; what they felt and thought. In the universal, we gain insight into the narratives that explain how we got to where we are today, and what those narratives may mean for where we go tomorrow. We need to understand both—the lived experiences and the narrative they are a part of—if we wish to understand history.

So, as we move up the Kingcome pole—as we tell our story—we need to ensure that we are not tricked. The pole may move up in a straight line, but it is also expressing that things change, often in confusing and bewildering ways, and that we need to be able to see things for what they truly are. To not be tricked by one story when there are other stories that must also be heard.

We cannot be scared by the fierceness of the Raven's eyes. We need to look into them—and be willing to see whatever they see and confront the truth.

What they show is that, gradually, a goal of the Europeans in this period of our story was to stop the building of the totem pole at the Raven. That the mayhem, mischief, and trouble would be so complete there would be no one left who could carve the Wolf and the Thunderbird.

<<<< >>>>

Europeans came to the lands that are now known as North America as part of efforts taking place around the world to build economic wealth, spread Christianity, and address struggles for power between rulers. It was these dynamics that set off centuries of conquest and colonization of different parts of the world. The "Doctrine of Discovery," which has its roots in directives from the papacy, provided a justification for this movement across the globe. At the core of the doctrine was the belief that any lands where there were no Christians living were considered uninhabited and therefore could be "discovered." Any non-Christians who happened to be on those lands were viewed as not inhabiting them as human beings. As such, the lands and resources could be taken as if they were empty—terra nullius—and any people on them were treated as slaves, and to be converted to Christianity.

POPE NICHOLAS V, 1452

[I]nvade, search out, capture, vanquish, and subdue all Saracens, Pagans whatsoever. Reduce their persons to perpetual slavery. Convert them to his and their use in profit.[4]

ROMANUS PONTIFEX, AUTHORIZING KING AFONSO OF PORTUGAL TO CONQUER AFRICA AND BEYOND, AND TO ENGAGE IN THE SLAVE TRADE, 1455

[T]o invade, search out, capture, vanquish, and subdue all Saracens and pagans whatsoever, and other enemies of Christ wheresoever placed, and the kingdoms, dukedoms, principalities, dominions, possessions, and all movable and immovable goods whatsoever held and possessed by them and to reduce their persons to perpetual slavery, and to apply and appropriate to himself and his successors the kingdoms, dukedoms, counties, principalities, dominions, possessions, and goods, and to convert them to his and their use and profit.[5]

PASSAGE FROM THE SERMON OF A PURITAN PREACHER IN NEW ENGLAND REGARDING EMPTY LAND, 1609

Some affirm, and it is likely to be true, that these savages have no particular property in any part or parcel of that country, but only a general residency there, as wild beasts in the forest; for they range and wander up and down the country without any law or government, being led only by their own lusts and sensuality. There is no *meum* and *teum* [mine and thine] amongst them. So that if the whole land should be taken from them, there is not a man that can complain of any particular wrong done unto him.[6]

In 1497, King Henry VII of England gave direction to explorer John Cabot reflecting the Doctrine of Discovery. This resulted in the first English claim to "discover" lands that would eventually make up Canada. The first French claim to "discover" these lands was by explorer Jacques Cartier in the 1530s. The goals of conversion to Christianity and civilization of peoples that Europeans believed to be savages were present right from the beginning.

KING HENRY VII, DIRECTION TO THE EXPLORER JOHN CABOT AND HIS SONS FOR THE DISCOVERY OF NEW AND UNKNOWN LANDS, 1496

We have also granted to them and to any of them, and to the heirs and deputies of them and of any one of them, and have given licence to set up our aforesaid banners and ensigns in any town, city, castle, island or mainland whatsoever, newly found by them.

And . . . may conquer, occupy and possess whatsoever such towns, castles, cities and islands by them thus discovered that they may be able to conquer, occupy and possess, as our vassals and governors lieutenants and deputies therein, acquiring for us the dominion, title and jurisdiction of the same towns, castles, cities, islands and mainlands so discovered . . .[7]

JACQUES CARTIER, REFLECTING ON HIS ENCOUNTER WITH MI'KMAW, 1534

We recognize that this folk could easily be converted to our faith.[8]

KING CHARLES II, INSTRUCTIONS TO THE COLONIAL OFFICE, 1670

And you are to consider how the Indians and slaves may be best instructed in and invited into the Christian religion, it being both for the honour of the Crown and of the Protestant religion itself, that all persons within any of our territories, though ever so remote, should be taught the knowledge of God, and be made acquainted with the mysteries of salvation.[9]

When Europeans first arrived in what is now Canada, there was a recognition by both Europeans and First Nations of the significant differences they observed about each other. Some of their respective ways of living caused confusion and questioning. What was being observed was how fundamentally different worldviews, belief systems, and cultures manifested themselves in different social, economic, and political systems and patterns. While the Doctrine of Discovery had a focus on the taking up of lands and conversion to Christianity, some early contact and interaction between First Nations and Europeans was marked by co-operation, peace, and friendship. This included the formation of economic and trade relations, as well as other patterns of mutual support. In these early days, when the number of Europeans was quite small, there was also often reliance by Europeans on First Nations peoples for aspects of their survival.

ANDREW GRAHAM, CHIEF TRADER AT YORK FACTORY, COMMENTING ON CREE PEOPLE, EARLY 1600S

They have no manner of government or subordination amongst them. The father or head of a family owns no superior, obeys no command. He gives his advice and opinion of things, but has no authority to enforce obedience. The youth of his family obey his directions; but it is rather filial affection and reverence than in consequence of a duty exacted by a superior. When several tents or families meet to go to war, or to the Factories to trade, they choose a leader; but it is only a voluntary obedience. Everyone is at liberty to leave him when he pleases; and the notion of a commander is quite obliterated when the journey or voyage is over. Merit alone gives the title to distinction; and the possession of qualities that are held in esteem, is the only method of obtaining affection and respect out of his own house.[10]

FR. PAUL LA JEUNE, WRITING ABOUT THE MONTAGNAIS, SOMETIME BETWEEN 1633 AND 1634

The savages say that it [the beaver] is the animal well-beloved by the French, English, and Basques—in a word, by the Europeans. I heard my host [a Montagnais Chief] say one day jokingly, . . . "The beaver does everything perfectly well, it makes kettles, hatchets, swords, knives, bread; and in short, it makes everything." He was making sport of us Europeans, who have such a fondness for the skin of this animal and who fight to see who will give the most to these Barbarians to get it; they carry this to such an extent my host said to me one day, showing me a beautiful knife, "the English have no sense; they gave us twenty knives like this for one Beaver skin."[11]

CHIEFS OF THE SHUSWAP, OKANAGAN, AND COUTEAU TRIBES OF BRITISH COLUMBIA, WRITING TO PRIME MINISTER SIR WILFRID LAURIER, 1910

The "real whites" we found were good people. We could depend on their word, and we trusted and respected them. They did not interfere with us nor attempt to break up our tribal organizations, laws, customs. They did not try to force their conceptions of things on us to our harm. Nor did they stop us from catching fish, hunting, etc. They never tried to steal or appropriate our country, nor take our food and life from us. They acknowledged our ownership of the comity, and treated our chiefs as men. They were the first to find us in this country. We never asked them to come here, but nevertheless we treated them kindly and hospitably and helped them all we could. They had made themselves (as it were) our guests.[12]

KAHGEGAGAHBOWH (GEORGE COPWAY), ON THE OJIBWE NATION

Among the Indians there have been no written laws. Customs handed down from generation to generation have been the only laws to guide them. Everyone might act different from what was considered right did he choose to do so, but such acts would bring upon him the censure of the nation, which he dreaded more than any corporeal punishment. . . .

This fear of the nation's censure acted as a mighty band, binding all in one social, honorable compact. They would not as brutes be whipped into duty. They would as men be persuaded to the right.[13]

While there were early patterns of co-operation, the taking up of lands was always a focus for England and France and was driven by competition and conflict in the political and economic relations between

Europeans. In the decades and centuries after contact, this taking up of land would occur through various means, including wars, treaties, and the establishment of settlements.

There were instances where lands were simply granted by European powers to their own people, sometimes on a massive scale. A well-known example is the Hudson's Bay Company. Founded in 1670, the company was a central force in the English settlement of what would become known as Canada. It was given a monopoly by King Charles II over "Rupert's Land," a region that encompasses the Hudson Bay drainage basin. This effectively gave the Hudson's Bay Company control of the fur trade, allowing them to play a government-like role over a vast area for almost two centuries. The Hudson's Bay Company sold Rupert's Land to Canada in 1869, while continuing to operate elsewhere. The sale absolved the company of any responsibility to Indigenous Peoples.

ROYAL CHARTER OF THE HUDSON'S BAY COMPANY, 1670

WE HAVE given, granted and confirmed, and by these Presents, for Us, Our Heirs and Successors, DO give, grant, and confirm, unto the said Governor and Company, and their Successors, the sole Trade and Commerce of all those Seas, Streights, Bays, Rivers, Lakes, Creeks, and Sounds, in whatsoever Latitude they shall be, that lie within the Entrance of the Streights commonly called Hudson's Streights, together with all the Lands and Territories upon the Countries, Coasts and Confines of the Seas, Bays, Lakes, Kivers [*sic*], Creeks, and Sounds aforesaid, that are not already actually possessed by or granted to any of our Subjects or possessed by the Subjects of any other Christian Prince or State, with the Fishing of all Sorts of Fish, Whales, Sturgeons, and all other Royal Fishes, in the Seas, Bays, Inlets, and Rivers within the Premisses, and the Fish therein taken, together with the Royalty of the Sea upon the Coasts within the Limits aforesaid, and all Mines Royal, as well discovered as not discovered, of Gold,

Silver, Gems, and precious Stones, to be found or discovered within the Territories, Limits, and Places aforesaid, and that the said Land be from henceforth reckoned and reputed as one of our Plantations or Colonies in America, called *Rupert's Land*.

AND FURTHER, WE DO by these Presents, for Us, Our Heirs and Successors, make, create and constitute, the said Governor and Company for the Time being, and their Successors, the true and absolute Lords and Proprietors, of the same Territory, Limits and Places aforesaid, and of all other the Premisses . . .[14]

FIRST ORDER OF BUSINESS FOR THE DOMINION OF CANADA, UPON TRANSFER OF RUPERT'S LAND, 1870

[The federal government agreed that] Any claims of Indians to compensation for lands required for purposes of settlement shall be disposed of by the Canadian government in communication with the Imperial Government; and the Company shall be relieved of all responsibility in respect of them.[15]

Growing conflict between the French and the English, beginning in the latter part of the seventeenth century and continuing through the Seven Years' War (1756–63), was a factor in many of the changes in their relations with First Nations, as European powers looked for allies to bolster their positions and advance their colonial aspirations. As such, military alliances between First Nations and Europeans also emerged in various places. For example, the Iroquois were one of several First Nations that fought alongside and against European powers.

IROQUOIS CHIEF COMMENTS, REPORTED BY JESUITS, 1670

They ask, who does Onontio [the French Governor] take us for? He is angry that we are going to war: he wants us to lay down our hatchets and leave his allies in peace. Who are his allies? How does he expect us to recognize them, when he claims to take under his protection all the peoples discovered by those who go to spread the word of God across all these lands, and when every day, according to what we hear from our people who escape the cruel fires, they make new discoveries and enter into nations that have never been anything but enemies to us?[16]

OBSERVATIONS ABOUT THE IROQUOIS MADE BY ANTOINE-DENIS RAUDOT, INTENDANT OF NEW FRANCE, EARLY EIGHTEENTH CENTURY

They devoted all their energies to inducing the other nations to surrender and give themselves to them. They sent them presents and the most skilful people of their nation to lecture them and tell them that if they did not give themselves up, they would be unable to avoid destruction, and those who fell into their hands would suffer the cruellest torments; but if on the contrary they wished to surrender and disperse to their cabins, they would become the masters of other men.

. . .

In previous years, the Iroquois came in fairly large contingents at certain times during the summer and then left the river free, but this year they have changed their purpose and divided into small detachments of 20, 30, 50 or 100 at most, along all the passages and places on the river, and when one group leaves another takes its place. They are small, well-armed contingents that are constantly moving so as to occupy the entire river and prepare ambushes everywhere, emerging unexpectedly and attacking Montagnais, Algonquin, Huron and French indiscriminately.[17]

As their numbers grew and their claims to land expanded, the English also started formalizing roles and offices to conduct "Indian Affairs" and eventually, in the 1750s, established an "Indian Department" and appointed a "Superintendent for Indian Affairs." The mandate included "political relations with Indian people, protection of traders, boundary negotiations and the enlistment of Indian people during times of war."[18] *These were the early steps in the establishment of formal government offices regarding Indigenous Peoples, and which, over time, would have a role and focus on exerting control over Indigenous Peoples.*

SUPREME COURT JUSTICE WILLIAM JOHNSON, IN *CHEROKEE NATION V. GEORGIA*, ON NATIONHOOD, 1831

I cannot but think that there are strong reasons for doubting the applicability of the epithet "state" to a people so low in the grade of organized society as our Indian tribes most generally.[19]

DUNCAN CAMPBELL NAPIER, SECRETARY OF THE INDIAN DEPARTMENT, ON THE DUTIES OF INDIAN DEPARTMENT OFFICERS, 1837

It is essential that they should conciliate the good-will of the several tribes, and possess their confidence; hear and determine their endless complaints and difficulties, and when necessary report upon them to the secretary in charge of the Department for the consideration of the Governor in Chief; protect and support the chiefs in preserving subordination in their Tribes; and distribute in detail the Presents, provisions, etc., which the Indians, through the bounty of their Great Father the King, have enjoyed ever since the conquest in 1759. Much discretion and judgement are required for the faithful and satisfactory discharge of those duties. In war the Officers of the Department commanded the Indians, when embodied for service in the field, as auxiliaries to Her Majesty's regular troops.[20]

The recognition that First Nations sovereignty, occupation, and ownership of lands had to be dealt with was also reflected in instructions to

English colonizers—over time—that the Doctrine of Discovery did not and could not be applied. The Royal Proclamation of 1763 from King George III made clear that for First Nations lands to be acquired, they must be ceded or purchased—they could not just be taken. The Royal Proclamation was expressive of the shift to treaty-making that had begun. Treaties were a tool that Europeans were familiar with. For Europeans, treaties were, in accordance with their own political traditions and legal orders, the ways in which relations between powers and rulers were documented and confirmed. One focus in European treaty-making was in delineating land boundaries. Another focus was to confirm the terms of political arrangements and alliances, as part of the structuring of power relations.

KING GEORGE III, EXCERPTS FROM THE ROYAL PROCLAMATION, 1763

[I]t is just and reasonable and essential to our Interest, and the Security of our Colonies, that the several Nations or Tribes of Indians with whom We are connected, and who live under our Protection, should not be molested or disturbed in the Possession of such parts of our Dominions and Territories as not having been ceded to or purchased by Us, are reserved to them, or any of them, as their Hunting Grounds . . . any Lands whatever, which, not having been ceded to or purchased by Us as aforesaid, are reserved to the said Indians, or any of them.

. . .

[A]nd We do hereby strictly forbid, on Pain of our Displeasure, all our loving Subjects from making any Purchases or Settlements whatever, or taking Possession of any of the Lands above reserved, without our especial leave and Licence for that Purpose first obtained.

And We do further strictly enjoin and require all Persons whatever who have either wilfully or inadvertently seated themselves

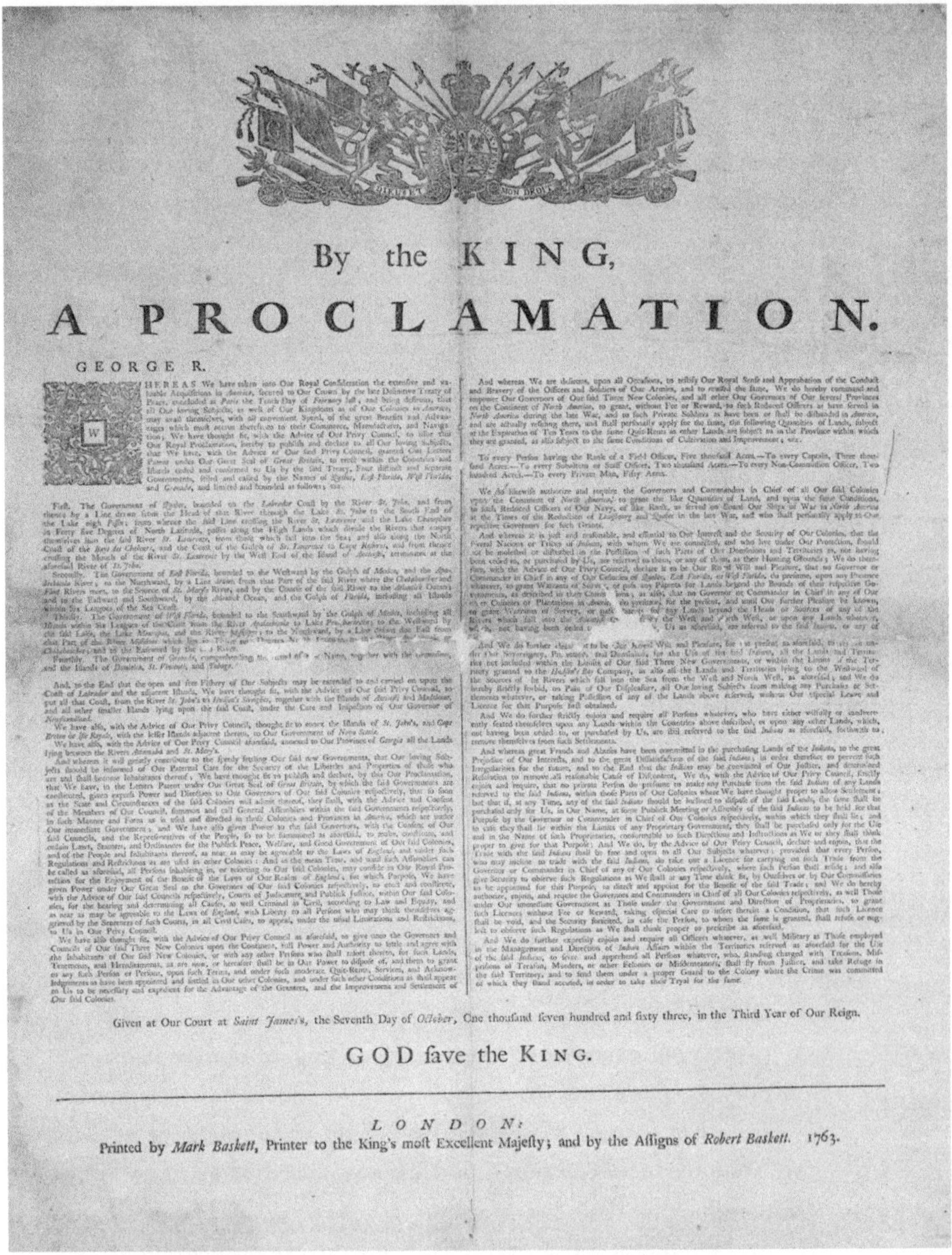

DIEU ET MON DROIT
By the KING,
A PROCLAMATION.
GEORGE R.
Given at Our Court at Saint James's, the Seventh Day of October, One thousand seven hundred and sixty three, in the Third Year of Our Reign.
GOD save the KING.
LONDON:
Printed by Mark Baskett, Printer to the King's most Excellent Majesty; and by the Assigns of Robert Baskett. 1763.

Royal Proclamation, 1763

upon any Lands within the Countries above described or upon any other Lands which, not having been ceded to or purchased by Us, are still reserved to the said Indians as aforesaid, forthwith to remove themselves from such Settlements.

And whereas great Frauds and Abuses have been committed in purchasing Lands of the Indians, to the great Prejudice of Our Interests. And to the great Dissatisfaction of the said Indians: in order therefore to prevent such Irregularities for the future, and to the End that the Indians may be convinced of Our Justice and determined Resolution to remove all reasonable Cause of Discontent, We do, with the Advice of our Privy Council strictly enjoin and require, that no private Person do presume to make any Purchase from the said Indians of any Lands reserved to the said Indians, within those Parts of Our Colonies where We have thought proper to allow Settlement; but that if, at any Time, any of the said Indians should be inclined to dispose of the said Lands, the same shall be purchased only for Us, in Our Name, at some publick Meeting or Assembly of the said Indians to be held for that Purpose . . . .[21]

ROYAL INSTRUCTIONS TO THE GOVERNOR OF NOVA SCOTIA, 1719

And whereas we have judged it highly necessary for our service that you should cultivate and maintain a strict friendship and good correspondence with the Indians inhabiting within our said province of Nova Scotia, that they may be induced by degrees not only to be good neighbors to our subjects but likewise themselves to become good subjects to us; we do therefore direct you upon your arrival in Nova Scotia to send for the several heads of the said Indian nations or clans and promise them friendship and protection in [H]is Majesty's part; you will likewise bestow upon them in our name as your discretion shall direct such presents as you shall carry from hence for their use.[22]

ROYAL INSTRUCTIONS TO GOVERNOR JAMES MURRAY OF QUEBEC, 1763

And whereas Our Province of Quebec is in part inhabited and possessed by several Nations and Tribes of Indians, with whom it is both necessary and expedient to cultivate and maintain a strict Friendship and good Correspondence, so that they may be induced by Degrees, not only to be good Neighbours to Our Subjects, but likewise themselves to become good Subjects to Us; You are therefore, as soon as you conveniently can, to appoint a proper Person or Persons to assemble, and treat with the said Indians, promising and assuring them of Protection and Friendship on Our part, and delivering them such Presents, as shall be sent to you for that purpose.[23]

First Nations also had protocols and traditions of confirming relations with other peoples that were structured in accordance with their own legal orders. But the form and nature of these protocols were very different than European traditions of treaties: they were grounded in values and standards of responsibilities to each other and to the land, the importance of ceremony and the sacred nature of the relations and bonds that we form, and the importance of demonstrating mutual respect. Reflecting this, First Nations assented to treaties with Europeans in different ways. One of these was through presenting wampum to officials. Wampum, made of white and purple seashells from the Atlantic Ocean, is woven into belts. Particular patterns symbolize events, alliances, and peoples. Wampum was used to form relationships, propose marriage, atone for murder, or even ransom captives. The Two Row Wampum Belt of the Iroquois symbolizes an agreement of mutual respect and peace between the Iroquois and European newcomers. The principles embodied in the belt are a set of rules governing the behaviour of the two groups. The wampum belt tells us that neither group will force their laws, traditions, customs, or language on each other, but will coexist peacefully.

Two Row Wampum

ONONDAGA NATION, DESCRIBING TWO ROW WAMPUM, C. 1613

It is agreed that we will travel together, side by each, on the river of life . . . linked by peace, friendship, forever. We will not try to steer each other's vessels.[24]

GRAND CHIEF MIKE MITCHELL OF THE AKWESASNE, DESCRIBING THE TWO ROW WAMPUM AT THE CONCLUSION OF THE TREATY OF ALBANY, 1664 (THE FIRST FORMAL ALLIANCE BETWEEN THE BRITISH CROWN AND INDIGENOUS PEOPLES IN NORTH AMERICA)

[S]ymboliz[ing] two paths or two vessels travelling down the same river together. One, a birch bark canoe, will be for the Indian people, their laws, their custom and their ways. The other, a ship, will be for the white people and their laws, their customs and their ways. We shall each travel the river together, side by side, but in our own boat. Neither of us will try to steer the other's vessel.[25]

ELLEN GABRIEL, MOHAWK ACTIVIST AND ARTIST, DESCRIBING THE IMPORTANCE OF THE TWO ROW WAMPUM TREATY

Kw'swenh:tha or the Two Row Wampum Treaty is a significant agreement in history of the relationship between European monarchs and Indigenous peoples. Ka'swenh:tha is more than visionary. As a principled treaty it is grounded in an Indigenous intellect providing an insight and a vigilant awareness of the inevitability of the evolution of society. Ka'swenh:tha is an instrument of reconciliation for contemporary times if openness, honesty, respect, and genuine concern for present and future generations is a foundational priority.[26]

One example of an early treaty was the Treaty of Niagara between more than twenty First Nations in parts of what would become Ontario and Quebec. The Treaty of Niagara was affirmed through the gifting of wampum by the Crown official to the assembled Chiefs. It was to establish peace and alliance, which was of particular concern to the British, as conflict was increasing with the French.

MINAVAVANA, AN OJIBWA CHIEF FROM WEST OF MANITOULIN AT MICHILIMACKINAC, REGARDING TREATY-MAKING, 1761

Englishman, although you have conquered the French you have not yet conquered us! We are not your slaves. These lakes, these woods and mountains, were left to us by our ancestors. They are our inheritance; and we will part with them to none. Your nation supposes that we, like the white people, cannot live without bread, and pork and beef! But, you ought to know, that He, the Great Spirit and Master of Life, has provided food for us, in these spacious lakes, and on these woody mountains.

Englishman, our Father, the king of France, employed our young men to make war upon your nation. In this warfare, many of them have been killed; and it is our custom to retaliate, until such time as the spirits of the slain are satisfied. But, the spirits of the slain are to be satisfied in either of two ways; the first is the spilling of the blood of the nation by which they fell; the other, by covering the bodies of the dead, and thus allaying the resentment of their relations. This is done by making presents.

Englishman, your king has never sent us any presents, nor entered into any treaty with us, wherefore he and we are still at war; and, until he does these things, we must consider that we have no other father or friend among the white man, than the king of France . . .

You have ventured your life among us, in the expectation that we should not molest you. You do not come armed, with an intention to make war, you come in peace, to trade with us, to supply us with necessities, of which we are in much want. We shall regard you therefore as a brother; and you may sleep tranquilly, without fear of the Chipeways. As a token of our friendship we present you with this pipe, to smoke.[27]

SIR WILLIAM JOHNSON, SUPERINTENDENT OF INDIAN AFFAIRS, UPON EXCHANGE OF PRESENTS AND AFTER PRESENTING THE COVENANT CHAIN AND WAMPUM BELTS TO ASSEMBLED CHIEFS, C. 1764

Brothers of the Western Nations, Sachems, Chiefs and Warriors;

You have now been here for several days, during which time we have frequently met to renew and Strengthen our Engagements and you have made so many Promises of your Friendship and Attachment to the English that there now remains for us only to exchange the great Belt of the Covenant Chain that we may not forget out mutual Engagements.

I now therefore present you the great Belt by which I bind all your Western Nations together with the English, and I desire that you will take fast hold of the same, and never let it slip, to which end

> I desire that after you have shewn this Belt to all Nations you will fix one end of it with the Chipeweighs at St. Marys [Michilimackinac] whilst the other end remains at my house, and moreover I desire that you will never listen to any news which comes to any other Quarter. If you do it, it may shake the Belt.[28]

What are now commonly referred to as the Peace and Friendship Treaties were entered into in the east between England and the Mi'kmaq, Maliseet, and Passamaquoddy between 1726 and 1779. These treaties were intertwined with establishing and supporting trade and commercial relations—including in furs and fish—as well as managing conflict and war. Geopolitics between the English and French, as well as between the newly created United States and Britain, were factors in some of the treaties.

1752 PEACE AND FRIENDSHIP TREATY BETWEEN HIS MAJESTY THE KING AND JEAN-BAPTISTE COPE (DESCRIBED AS THE CHIEF SACHEM OF THE MI'KMAQ INHABITING THE EASTERN PART OF NOVA SCOTIA)

2. That all Transactions during the late War shall on both sides be buried in Oblivion with the Hatchet, and that the said Indians shall have all favour, Friendship & Protection shewn them from this His Majesty's Government.
3. That the said Tribe shall use their utmost endeavours to bring in the other Indians to Renew and Ratify this Peace, and shall discover and make known any attempts or designs of any other Indians or any Enemy whatever against His Majesty's Subjects within this Province so soon as they shall know thereof and shall also hinder and Obstruct the same to the utmost of their Power, and on the other hand if any of the Indians refusing to ratify this Peace, shall make War upon the Tribe who have now confirmed the same; they shall

upon Application have such aid and Assistance from the Government for their Defence, as the case may require.

4. It is agreed that the said Tribe of Indians shall not be hindered from, but have free liberty of Hunting & Fishing as usual: and that if they shall think a Truckhouse needful at the River Chibenaccadie or any other place of their resort, they shall have the same built and proper Merchandize lodged therein, to be Exchanged for what the Indians shall have to dispose of, and that in the mean time the said Indians shall have free liberty to bring for Sale to Halifax or any other Settlement within this Province, Skins, feathers, fowl, fish or any other thing they shall have to sell, where they shall have liberty to dispose thereof to the best Advantage.[29]

A MI'KMAW CHIEF FROM CAPE BRETON, SPEAKING AT THE BURYING THE HATCHET CEREMONY, 1761

As long as the Sun and Moon shall endure, as long as the Earth on which I dwell shall exist, in the same state, you this day see it, as long will I be your friend and ally, submitting myself to the Laws of your Government, faithful and obedient to the Crown.[30]

Relations between Europeans and Indigenous Peoples resulted in the emergence of a people with their own community, culture, and homeland. In the Red River Settlement, the Métis Nation was born, with other Métis settlements stretching outward. The Métis would emerge as a vital political, cultural, and social force in the historic and contemporary reality of Canada, and as a distinct Indigenous People recognized in Canada's Constitution.

A MÉTIS VOYAGEUR, DESCRIBING THE MÉTIS IDENTITY, 1850S

Where do I live? I cannot say. I am a Voyageur—I am a Chicot mister. I live everywhere. My grandfather was a Voyageur; he died on the voyage. My father was a Voyageur; he died on the Voyage. I will also die while on voyage and another Chicot will take my place. Such is the course of our life.[31]

AUDREY POITRAS, DESCRIBING THE PRIDE, RESILIENCE, AND ROOTS OF THE MÉTIS

Our flag represents the faith that the Métis culture shall live on forever. We are Indigenous to this country because we were born of the land long before Canada was a country.[32]

The Red River Métis formed their own systems of governance and law, reflecting their distinct worldview, culture, and traditions. Their language—Michif—and modes of social organization set them apart from their roots in European and First Nations populations. From the outset of their emergence, the Métis also struggled with opposition to their reality as a distinct people.

WILLIAM MCGILLIVRAY, CHIEF PARTNER OF THE NORTH WEST COMPANY, REFLECTING ON MÉTIS PEOPLE AND THE BATTLE OF SEVEN OAKS, 1818

The assemblage of half-breeds requires a little further comment; we need not dwell here upon the organization of that class of men. You are yourself, Sir personally aware, that although many of them, from the ties of consanguinity and interest, are more or less connected with the North-West company's people, and either as clerks or servants, or as free hunters, are dependent on them; yet they one and all look upon themselves as members of an independent tribe of natives, entitled to a property in the soil, to a flag of their own, and to protection from the British Government.

It is absurd to consider them legally in any other light than as Indians; the British law admits no filiation of illegitimate

Métis flag

children but that of the mother; and as these persons cannot in law claim any advantage by paternal right, it follows, that they ought not to be subjected to any disadvantages which might be supposed to arise from the fortuitous circumstances of their parentage.[33]

MÉTIS BUFFALO HUNT LAW, 1840

A codified portion of these laws contained the following provisions:

a. No buffalo to be run on the Sabbath-Day.

b. No party to fork off, lag behind, or go before, without permission.

c. No person or party to run buffalo before the general order.

d. Every captain with his men, in turn, to patrol the camp, and keep guard.

e. For the first trespass against these laws, the offender to have his saddle and bridle cut up.

f. For the second offence, the coat to be taken off the offender's back, and be cut up.

g. For the third offence, the offender to be flogged.

h. Any person convicted of theft, even to the value of a sinew, to be brought to the middle of the camp, and the crier to call out his or her name three times, adding the word "Thief," at each time.[34]

LOUIS RIEL, 1885

When the Government of Canada presented itself at our doors it found us at peace. It found that the Metis people of the North-West could not only live well without it . . . but that it had a government of its own, free, peaceful, well-functioning, contributing to the work of civilization. . . . It was a government with an organized constitution, whose jurisdiction was all the more legitimate and worthy of respect, because it exercised over a country that belonged to it.[35]

DR. THELMA CHALIFOUX, DESCRIBING HER RESPONSIBILITY AND ROLE AS A SENATOR, 1999

[P]artly education and partly bringing the issues forward, especially for the Métis because we are truly the forgotten people.[36]

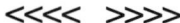

<<<< >>>>

We cannot pinpoint a moment in time in our past when the potential and possibility of constructive and positive relations between Indigenous Peoples and the Crown was lost; of when hopes of living side by side in harmony was replaced with violent and oppressive colonial forces. I imagine that at times it felt like this change occurred stealthily: a bit more land taken up, an increasing number of outsiders showing up, and growing claims that new laws or rules applied. I imagine that at other times the change felt rapid, stark, and brutal, including the experiencing of the ravages of disease, of children being taken away, of violence and death. One could say then, that for Indigenous Peoples colonization felt simultaneously like it occurred gradually and all at once.

Of course, the emergence of oppressive and destructive forces did not occur at the same time, in the same way, for all Indigenous

Peoples. The pace and scale of settlement varied in different parts of the country—most notably in the West and North. In some places, treaties and alliances that had been entered into, even when being violated, did alter how various intrusions took place. Patterns of relations, including intermarriage, in local communities and regions also led to differences. And we also know that as these oppressive forces mounted, distinct impacts on women and men were also experienced, including the imposition of European attitudes regarding gender roles and responsibilities that saw, in some places, matrilineal systems disrupted, and women increasingly dispossessed of their leadership roles and marginalized from public life.

Yet, while we cannot set the clock for when the destructive forces of colonization fully took root, there is a moment in time—one that impacts all Indigenous Peoples in a similar, destructive way—that we can and must identify. It is a date we all know. Confederation. The "founding" of Canada.

July 1, 1867. Despite whatever happened before that date—however hopeful it may have been at times, and however complex and destructive it was becoming—the founding of Canada was a demarcation line.

When the settlers, the French and English, sat down to form this country and claim a form of sovereign independence over these lands under their own laws, First Nation, Inuit, and Métis peoples were not part of it. We were not invited, asked, or welcome to be there. Rather, we were a subject matter, a topic. It was determined that—like the "postal service," "the borrowing of Money on the Public Credit," "Navigation and Shipping," the "Criminal Law," and a host of other topics—"Indians, and Lands reserved for the Indians" was an exclusive responsibility of the federal government (as distinct from the provinces) in the British North America Act.

With the absence of First Nations, Inuit, and Métis at Confederation, it became a *fait accompli* that in many ways the most destructive phase of colonialism was yet to come. Canada

Fathers of Confederation by Rex Woods

was born in denial of the prior presence of Indigenous Peoples on these lands. To legitimize and justify its existence, Canada would have to act as if our non-existence was a reality. And that is what happened.

Whether we're talking about the Indian Act, the continued taking of lands and entrenchment of the reserve system, the forced relocation of whole families and communities, the denial of basic individual rights and freedoms, or the residential "school" system, one thing is glaringly clear: an effort was being made to create a Canada where Indigenous peoples did not exist and, indeed, had never existed.

It is a hard truth that the growing oppression of Indigenous Peoples and, ultimately, the exclusion of Indigenous Peoples from the founding of Canada, was akin to an original sin. Atoning for that original sin, making amends and reparations, is the work to which Canadians from coast-to-coast-to-coast are increasingly committed. To do that work properly requires understanding why the sin happened, and what its impacts have been.

<<<< >>>>

Despite some early progress in the relations between Europeans and Indigenous Peoples, destructive and oppressive forces also continued to grow in the decades prior to Confederation. This included disease, violence, and the taking of lands and resources in other parts of what would become Canada. As the debate, dialogue, and effort by Europeans to further settle and form the country emerged, Indigenous Peoples were increasingly marginalized. Smallpox was particularly destructive. For example, it is estimated the Haida people went from a population of approximately twenty thousand prior to 1770 to less than six hundred by the end of the nineteenth century, primarily as a result of the disease. In some instances, the smallpox was intentionally spread among Indigenous Peoples by Europeans. At various times, other diseases such as tuberculosis would also have devastating impacts.

LORD GEOFFREY AMHERST, A BRITISH MILITARY LEADER IN THE AMERICAS, 1763

You will Do well to try to Innoculate [*sic*] the Indians by means of Blankets, as well as to try Every other method that can serve to Extirpate this Execrable Race. I should be very glad your Scheme for hunting them Down by Dogs could take effect. . .[37]

NORTH COAST HAIDA CHIEF KOWE, DESCRIBING THE DEVASTATION OF DISEASE, 1795

[T]he small Pox swept off two-thirds of the people.[38]

A HUDSON'S BAY COMPANY REPORT DOCUMENTING DISEASE, 1829

Immense numbers of them were swept off by a dreadful visitation of the smallpox, that from the appearance of some individuals that bear marks of the disease, may have happened fifty or sixty years ago [1769–79]. The same disease committed a second ravage, but less destruction than the first about ten years afterwards.[39]

Out west, the newest of the colonies, the Colony of Vancouver Island, was established in 1849. The original instructions to James Douglas, the chief factor of the Hudson's Bay Company and first governor of the new colony, was that treaties needed to be completed with the local First Nations to access lands and resources. This resulted in fourteen treaties being completed with First Nations on Vancouver Island. But this early recognition of First Nations' connection to their lands on the west coast—and as such the necessity to complete treaties—would soon change. Treaty-making stopped, and land was increasingly taken up by settlers on Vancouver Island and the mainland of what would eventually become British Columbia. As a result, over almost the entirety of British Columbia, the territories of First Nations were claimed by the Crown with no treaty or any other arrangement in place.

Land Settlement Notice, 1906

TSTASS-AYA AND TSQUEN-ES-TEN, SNUNEYMUXW ELDERS, DESCRIBING SOME OF THE ORAL HISTORY REGARDING EARLY INTERACTION AND TRADE ON THE COLONY OF VANCOUVER ISLAND

[T]he Hudson Bay men said to the Indians, "this coal that is here . . . is no good to you and we would like it but we want to be friends, so if you let us come and take as much of this black rock as we would need, we will be good to you." Each chief then received a bale of Hudson Bay Blankets, and a lot of shirts, and some tobacco like rope.[40]

SECRETARY OF THE HUDSON'S BAY COMPANY ARCHIBALD BARCLAY, INSTRUCTIONS TO JAMES DOUGLAS TO COMPLETE TREATIES, 1849

With respect to the rights of the natives, you will have to confer with the chiefs of the tribes on that subject, and in your negotiations with them you are to consider the natives as the rightful possessors of such lands only as they are occupied by cultivation, or had houses built on, at the time the island came under the undivided sovereignty of Great Britain in 1846. All other land is to be regarded as waste, applicable for the purposes of colonization. The right of fishing and hunting will be continued to the natives, and when their lands are registered, and they conform to the same conditions with which other settlers are required to comply, they will enjoy the same rights and privileges.[41]

JOSEPH TRUTCH, CHIEF COMMISSIONER OF LAND AND WORKS, DESCRIBING THE SHIFT AWAY FROM TREATY-MAKING TO DENIAL OF FIRST NATIONS CONNECTION TO LANDS, 1870

[F]or the past 10 years at least during which I have resided in this Colony—the Government appears to me to have striven to the extent of its power to protect and befriend the Native race, and its declared policy has been that the Aborigines should, in all material respects, be on the same footing in the eye of the law as people of European descent, and that they should be encouraged to live amongst the white settlers in the country, and so, by their example, be induced to adopt habits of civilization. In the more settled districts the Indians do now reside mostly in the settlements working for the white settlers—eating similar food and wearing similar clothing and having to a great extent relinquished their former wild primitive mode of life.

. . .

But the title of the Indians in the fee of the public lands, or any portion thereof, has never been acknowledged by Government – but, on the contrary, is distinctly denied. In no case has any special arrangement been made with any of the tribes of the Mainland for the extinction of their claims of possession – but these claims have been held to have been fully satisfied by securing to each tribe, as the progress of the settlement of the country seemed to require, the use of sufficient tracts of land for their wants for agricultural and pastoral purposes.

. . .

I will only remark further, on the general subject of the condition of the Indians in the Colony, that it is unhesitatingly acknowledged to be the peculiar responsibility of Government to use every endeavour to promote the civilization – education – and ultimate Christianization of the native races within our territory, and that any practical scheme for advancing this object which it would be within the scope of the pecuniary ability of the Colony to carry into effect would be adopted with alacrity . . .[42]

THE TIMES (UK), FROM AN OCCASIONAL CORRESPONDENT ON "INDIANS IN BRITISH COLUMBIA," 1877

First and foremost, there is a question of the unextinguished Indian Title in the soil. The Canadian policy is to recognize this title, but the Crown has not recognized it—at least on the mainland portion of the Province, and some, indeed, say that the Crown from the first has distinctly denied it in the Colony of British Columbia. It would cost a great sum of money to extinguish the Indian title here, and if it be not extinguished this Province, which contains about one-third of all the Indians in Canada, will be in this respect an exceptional area. Who is to find the money for the purpose? The practical difficulties in settling this question are so great that it has not been raised at present, there being some hope that the Commissioners may adjust matters so as to prevent the necessity of its being raised. But what guarantee can there be that the Indians themselves will not raise it at some future, perhaps not distant, time?[43]

On the Prairies, what was called the Red River Resistance was forming in the late 1860s as a result of the arrival of new anglophone settlers, whose very existence increased tensions with the Métis and First Nation populations. The health and welfare of the Métis, especially, was becoming increasingly precarious, as their land was being appropriated and previous promises by the Europeans broken. Resistance emerged as a recurring aspect of Métis life and culture. It was an essential part of protecting their identity and reality as une nouvelle nation—a "new" nation of people both part of but distinct from Indigenous and European traditions.

LOUIS RIEL, DESCRIBING THE RESISTANCE OF THE MÉTIS PEOPLE

We may be a small community and a Half-breed community at that—but we are men, free and spirited men, and we will not allow even the Dominion of Canada to trample on our rights.[44]

Louis Riel, 1869

We have allowed ourselves to fall into the hands of a Government which only thinks of us to pillage us. Had he only understood what God did for us before Confederation, we should have been sorry to see it coming. And the half-breeds of the North-West would have made conditions of a nature to preserve for our children that liberty, that possession of the soil, without which there is no happiness for anyone; but fifteen years of suffering, impoverishment and underhand, malignant persecution have opened our eyes; and the sight of the abyss of demoralization into which the Dominion is daily plunging us deeper and deeper every day, has suddenly, by God's mercy, as it were, stricken us with horror.[45]

We must cherish our inheritance. We must preserve our nationality for the youth of the future. The story should be written down to pass on.[46]

As England continued to become more dominant over the French in North America, through the second half of the eighteenth century, the focus further shifted from alliances with Indigenous Peoples for military purposes to a desire to control, subjugate, and "civilize" them. The seeds of the weapons of oppression that would be fully unleashed after Confederation—such as the Indian Act—were being planted.

DUNCAN CAMPBELL SCOTT, A CAREER CIVIL SERVANT WHO IMPLEMENTED "INDIAN" POLICY IN THE EARLY TWENTIETH CENTURY, DESCRIBING ASPECTS OF THAT POLICY FROM BEFORE CONFEDERATION

The civilization of the Indian became the ideal; the menace of the tomahawk and the firebrand having disappeared, the apparent duty was to raise him from the debased condition into which he had fallen owing to the loose and pampering policy of former days. Protection from vices which were not his own, and instruction in peaceful occupations, foreign to his natural bent, were to be substituted for necessary generosity.[47]

ARCHIBALD ACHESON, GOVERNOR GENERAL OF BRITISH NORTH AMERICA, DESCRIBING POLICY TOWARD INDIGENOUS PEOPLES, 1837

[I]nducing the Indians to change their present ways for more civilized Habits of Life, namely their Settlement . . . compact Settlements should be formed . . . giving them Agricultural Implements, but no other Description of Presents.[48]

In Britain, the 1837 House of Commons Select Committee on Aborigines began considering new policies based on a worldwide view of Britain's imperial role. The committee was informed by field reports from missionaries stating that Indigenous Peoples were in urgent need of Christianity and the other trappings of civilization. Reflecting ideas of racial superiority and the need to civilize Indigenous Peoples, the attitudes and beliefs that would be the basis of the residential school system also were becoming deeply rooted and expressed in policy. This included the Gradual Civilization Act of 1857, which sought to assimilate Indigenous Peoples and laid a policy focus on assimilation that would continue in Canada until the second half of the twentieth century.

SIR JAMES KEMPT, GOVERNOR GENERAL OF BRITISH NORTH AMERICA, 1828–30, ON "INDIAN" POLICY

1st. To collect the Indians in considerable numbers, and settle them in villages with a due portion of land for their cultivation and support.

2nd. To make such provision for their religious improvement, education, and instruction in husbandry as circumstances may from time to time require.

3rd. To afford them such assistance in building their houses; ration; and in procuring such seed and agricultural implements as may be necessary, commuting when practicable a portion of their presents for the later.[49]

REPORT OF THE HOUSE OF COMMONS SELECT COMMITTEE ON ABORIGINES, 1837

In the foregoing survey we have seen the desolating effects of unprincipled Europeans with Nations in a ruder state. There remains a more gratifying subject—the effect of fair dealing and of Christian instruction upon heathens. True civilization and Christianity are inseparable: the former has never been found, but as a fruit of the latter. As soon as they were converted, they perceived the evils attendant upon their former ignorant wandering state; they began to work, which they never did before; they perceived the advantage of cultivating the soil;

they totally gave up drinking; they became industrious, sober and useful.[50]

LORD SYDENHAM, THE COLONY'S GOVERNOR GENERAL, WRITING WHEN THE BAGOT COMMISSION WAS ESTABLISHED, 1841

Thus circumstanced, the Indian loses all the good qualities of his wild state and acquires nothing but the vices of civilization. He does not become a good settler, he does not become an agriculturalist or mechanic. He does become a drunkard and debauchee, and his females and family follow the same course. He occupies valuable land, unprofitably to himself and injuriously to the country. He gives infinite trouble to the government, and adds nothing either to the wealth, the industry, or the defence of the province.[51]

BAGOT COMMISSION OF INQUIRY, MAIN PRINCIPLES THAT WOULD COME TO INFORM ASPECTS OF INDIAN POLICY

Indians should be gathered in settlements, instructed in agriculture, and placed in the hands of teachers "of strictly moral and religious character" who would gradually elevate them to the standards of Europeans. . . .

Indian parents had too much influence on their children, so a system of "labour or industrial schools" should be created, where the children could live all the time. . . .

Since Indian life was thought to be so degenerate, an escape hatch should be offered to those who could earn it. Any Indian "qualified by education, knowledge of the arts and customs of civilized life and habits of industry and prudence" should be given a limited title to up to 200 acres of communal Indian lands, and at the same time a once-and-for-all payment in furniture, stock or tools. In return for this, he would forfeit all future claims to the communal property of the tribe. . . .

All land not handed over to Individuals in this way should be surrendered to the government, to be sold for the benefit of the tribe. Obviously, the commission had in mind that within a few years, Indian reserves would no longer exist. . . .

The annual gifts paid to Indians in compensation for land surrenders, and for loyalty during the colonial wars, should be discontinued. . . .[52]

Harms and challenges also began to increase for Inuit. While there had been earlier contact between Inuit and Europeans, it had been relatively limited in nature and seasonal, primarily related to the European whaling industry. But in the 1850s, year-round shore stations were established. Among the harmful impacts of contact with the Europeans was a rising rate of disease that was soon decimating the Inuit population.

CHARLES FRANCIS HALL, AN ARCTIC EXPLORER WHO TOOK MUCH INUIT TESTIMONY, C. 1861–62

The days of the Inuit are numbered. There are very few of them left now. Fifty years may find them all passed away, without leaving one to tell that such a people ever lived.[53]

A MISSIONARY STATIONED IN CUMBERLAND SOUND, EARLY 1900S

I have more than once . . . pointed out to these wretched people the whalers, the sure and certain goal to which they are traveling. The extermination of the whole of the Eskimo population in Cumberland Sound and elsewhere is only a matter of time, if some check is not put to these awful practices.[54]

As mentioned, First Nations, Inuit, and Métis were not present at Confederation, physically or in spirit. There had been little debate or discussion about Indigenous Peoples—and none with Indigenous Peoples—in the process of making the decision to form the country of Canada. In fact, there was only one provision of the British North America Act regarding Indigenous Peoples, and it was about the exclusive jurisdiction of the federal government over "Indians." At the same time, the lands of the newborn country were primarily placed under the ownership and jurisdiction of the provinces. The purpose of placing "Indians" under the jurisdiction of the federal government was explicitly understood as a matter of maintaining control over the Indigenous population. For some, this meant the full assimilation, or even eradication, of Indigenous Peoples.

BRITISH NORTH AMERICA ACT, 1867

91 [I]t is hereby declared that . . . the exclusive legislative authority of the Parliament of Canada extends to all matters coming within the classes of subjects next herein-after enumerated . . .

(24) Indians, and Lands reserved for the Indians.[55]

LORD DENNING, IN *R. V. SECRETARY OF STATE*, ON THE 1867 BRITISH NORTH AMERICA ACT, 1973

Save for that reference in s. 91(24), the 1867 Act was silent on Indian Affairs. Nothing was said about the title to property in the "lands reserved for the Indians," nor to the revenues therefrom, nor to the rights and obligations of the Crown or the Indians thenceforward in regard thereto. But I have no doubt that all concerned regarded the royal proclamation of 1763 as still of binding force. It was an unwritten provision which went without saying. It was binding on the legislatures of the Dominion and the provinces just as if there had been included in the statute sentence: "The aboriginal peoples of Canada shall continue to have all their rights and freedoms as recognized by the royal proclamation of 1763."[56]

In the early years after Confederation, the formation of laws, policies, and practices of oppression deepened. A policy goal became to fully assimilate Indigenous Peoples and deny any official relationship of Indigenous Peoples to their lands.

JOSEPH TRUTCH, CHIEF COMMISSIONER OF LAND AND WORKS, REGARDING THE CONNECTION OF INDIGENOUS PEOPLES TO THEIR LANDS, 1867

The Indians really have no right to the lands they claim, nor are they of any actual value or utility to them; and I cannot see why they should either retain these lands to the prejudice of the general interests of the Colony, or be allowed to make a market of them either to the Government or to Individuals.[57]

WILLIAM SPRAGUE, DEPUTY SUPERINTENDENT GENERAL OF INDIAN AFFAIRS, DESCRIBING THE PURPOSE OF CANADA'S EARLY LEGISLATION REPLACING TRADITIONAL INDIGENOUS POLITICAL INSTITUTIONS WITH ELECTED BAND COUNCILS, LATE 1800S

The Acts [Act to provide for the organization of the Department of the Secretary of State of Canada and for the Administration of the Affairs of the Indians and An Act for the gradual enfranchisement of Indians] framed in the years 1868 and 1869, relating to Indian affairs, were designed to lead the Indian people by degrees to mingle with the white race in the ordinary avocations of life. It was intended to afford facilities for electing, for a limited period, members of bands to manage, as a Council, local matters; that intelligent and educated men, recognized as chiefs, should carry out the wishes of the male members of mature years in each band, who should be fairly represented in the conduct of their internal affairs.

Thus establishing a responsible, for an irresponsible system, this provision, by law, was designed to pave the way to the establishment of simple municipal institutions.[58]

DUNCAN CAMPBELL SCOTT, DESCRIBING A PROPOSED BILL ON CANADA'S POLICY TOWARD INDIGENOUS PEOPLES, 1920

I want to get rid of the Indian problem. I do not think as a matter of fact, that the country ought to continuously protect a class of people who are able to stand alone. That is my whole point. I do not want to pass into the citizens class people who are paupers. That is not the intension of the Bill. But after one hundred years, after being in close contact with civilization it is unnerving to the individual or to a band to continue the state of tutelage, when he or they are able to take this position as British Citizen or Canadian Citizenship to support themselves and stand alone. That has been the whole purpose of education and advancement since earlier times.

Our object is to continue until there is not a single Indian in Canada that has not been absorbed into the body politic and there is no Indian question and no Indian Department, that is the whole object of this Bill.[59]

From the outset, Indigenous people recognized what was happening, resisted these changes, and worked to maintain their governing systems and ways of life.

CHIEF POUNDMAKER (CREE), 1887

Our old way of life is gone. But that does not mean we should become imitation white men. Our beliefs are good. No man has yet shown me anything better.[60]

Chief Poundmaker, 1885

PETITION OF THE CLAN MOTHERS OF ST. REGIS TO THE GOVERNOR GENERAL OF CANADA, DEMANDING THE REINSTITUTION OF INDIGENOUS GOVERNANCE, 1898

We have considered the elective system as not being intended for us Indians and we would therefore return to our old method of selecting our life chiefs according to our Constitution of Iroquois government.[61]

CHIEF DAN GEORGE OF THE TSLEIL-WAUTUTH NATION, FROM "A LAMENT FOR CONFEDERATION," REFLECTING ON CANADA'S POLICIES TOWARD INDIGENOUS PEOPLES, 1967

When I fought to protect my land and my home, I was called a savage. When I neither understood nor welcomed his way of life, I was called lazy. When I tried to rule my people, I was stripped of my authority.[62]

The Christian churches played a central role in implementing policies of assimilation and oppression, including operating most of the residential school system. This role of the churches in civilizing and assimilating Indigenous Peoples, which had been present in various forms since the arrival of Europeans, continued as part of official government policy after the formation of Canada.

REV. SAMUEL ROSE, PRINCIPAL OF MOUNT ELGIN RESIDENTIAL SCHOOL, 1852

[The education of these] youths has been regarded by me as the work of no ordinary character; an education solemnly important in his connection to the future, with the unborn periods of the time. . . . These youths are to form the class whose histories is to be a most important epoch in the history of the nations to which they belong. . . . This class is to spring a generation, who will either perpetuate the manners and customs of their ancestors, or being *intellectually*, *morally* and *religiously* elevated, take their stand among the improved, intelligent nations of the earth, their part in the great drama of the world's doing; or off [*sic*] want of necessary qualifications, to take their place and perform their part, be despised and pushed off the stage of action and ceased to be![63]

REPORT OF THE ALBERTA METHODIST COMMISSION, DESCRIBING ATTITUDES TOWARD INDIGENOUS PEOPLES, 1911

The Indian is the weak child in the family of our nation and for this reason presents the most earnest appeal for Christian sympathy and cooperation. . . . [W]e are convinced that the only hope of successfully discharging this obligation to our Indian brethren is through the medium of the children, therefore education must be given the foremost place.[64]

MEMORANDUM OF THE CONVENTION OF CATHOLIC PRINCIPALS, DESCRIBING ATTITUDES TOWARD INDIGENOUS PEOPLES, 1924

All true civilization must be based on moral law, which Christian religion alone can give. Pagan superstition could not suffice . . . to make the Indians practice the virtues of our civilization and avoid its attendant vices. Several people have desired us to countenance the dances of the Indians and to observe their festivals; but their habits, being the result of free and easy mode of life, cannot conform to the intense struggle for life which our social conditions require.[65]

Building on legislation that was passed prior to Confederation, the Indian Act (1876) was the foundation for a deepening oppression of Indigenous Peoples. The original Indian Act had 122 sections, which formalized and entrenched oppressive measures aimed at assimilating and civilizing "Indians." These included: the segregation of First Nations people onto reserves; the banning of ceremonies, including the Potlatch and Sun Dance; limitations on basic human rights, including freedom of mobility; the imposition of a system of administrative control from Ottawa, which sought to replace traditional structures of governance; and the laying of a foundation for removing children from their parents and establishing the residential school system. Almost every aspect of daily life on reserves was brought under the control and regulation of federal officials. While through political and legal advocacy there have been amendments to the Indian Act, the act itself remains in force and its framework in place to this day.

PRIME MINISTER SIR JOHN A. MACDONALD ON INDIGENOUS PEOPLES

[Indians] are simply living on the benevolence and charity of the Canadian Parliament, and . . . beggars should not be choosers.[66]

[W]e have been pampering and coaxing the Indians; that we must take a new course, we must vindicate the position of the white man, we must teach the Indians what law is; we must not pauperise them, as they say we have been doing.[67]

I have reason to believe that the agents as a whole . . . are doing all they can, by refusing food until the Indians are on the verge of starvation, to reduce the expense . . .[68]

INDIAN ACT, 1876, CHAPTER 18

An Act to amend and consolidate the laws respecting Indians . . .

2. The Minister of the Interior shall be Superintendent-General of Indian Affairs, and shall be governed in the supervision of the said affairs, and in the control and management of the reserves, lands, moneys and property of the Indians in Canada by the provisions of this Act.[69]

PRIME MINISTER SIR JOHN A. MACDONALD, DESCRIBING THE PURPOSE OF THE INDIAN ACT, 1887

[N]othing in their way of life that was worth preserving . . . [and] . . . the great aim of our legislation [the Indian Act] has been to do away with the tribal system and assimilate the Indian people in all respects with the other inhabitants of the Dominions as speedily as they are fit to change.[70]

ROYAL COMMISSION ON ABORIGINAL PEOPLES, DESCRIBING THE INDIAN ACT, 1996

In the midst of the treaty-making process going on in western Canada, the first *Indian Act* as such was passed in 1876 as a consolidation of previous Indian legislation. Indian policy was now firmly fixed on a national foundation based unashamedly

CHAP. 18.

An Act to amend and consolidate the laws respecting Indians.

[*Assented to 12th April, 1876.*]

WHEREAS it is expedient to amend and consolidate the laws respecting Indians: Therefore Her Majesty, by and with the advice and consent of the Senate and House of Commons of Canada, enacts as follows:— Preamble.

1. This Act shall be known and may be cited as "*The Indian Act*, 1876;" and shall apply to all the Provinces, and to the North West Territories, including the Territory of Keewatin. Short title and extent of Act.

2. The Minister of the Interior shall be Superintendent-General of Indian Affairs, and shall be governed in the supervision of the said affairs, and in the control and management of the reserves, lands, moneys and property of Indians in Canada by the provisions of this Act. Superintendent General.

TERMS.

3. The following terms contained in this Act shall be held to have the meaning hereinafter assigned to them, unless such meaning be repugnant to the subject or inconsistent with the context:— Meanings assigned to terms in this Act.

1. The term "band" means any tribe, band or body of Indians who own or are interested in a reserve or in Indian lands in common, of which the legal title is vested in the Crown, or who share alike in the distribution of any annuities or interest moneys for which the Government of Canada is responsible; the term "the band" means the band to which the context relates; and the term "band," when action is being taken by the band as such, means the band in council. Band.

2. The term "irregular band" means any tribe, band or body of persons of Indian blood who own no interest in any reserve or lands of which the legal title is vested in the Crown, who possess no common fund managed by the Government of Canada, or who have not had any treaty relations with the Crown. Irregular Band.

3, The term "Indian" means Indians.

First. Any male person of Indian blood reputed to belong to a particular band;

Secondly.

on the notion that Indian cultures and societies were clearly inferior to settler society.

The transition from tribal nation in the tripartite imperial system to legal incompetent in the bilateral federal/provincial system was now complete. While protection remained a policy goal, it was no longer collective Indian tribal autonomy that was protected: it was the individual Indian recast as a dependent ward—in effect, the child of the state. Moreover, protection no longer meant maintaining a more or less permanent line between Indian lands and the settler society; it meant the very opposite. By reducing the culture of distance through civilizing and assimilating measures that would culminate in enfranchisement of Indians and reduction of the reserve land base in 50-acre chunks, it was hoped Indian lands would in this piecemeal fashion soon lose their protected status and become part of the provincial land regime.

In keeping with the clear policy of assimilation, the *Indian Act* made no reference to the treaties already in existence or to those being negotiated at the time it was passed. The absence of any significant mention of the treaty relationship continues in the current version of the *Indian Act*. It is almost as if Canada deliberately allowed itself to forget the principal constitutional mechanism by which the nation status of Indian communities is recognized in domestic law....

The Indian Act of 1876 created an Indian legislative framework that has endured to the present day in essentially the terms in which it was originally drafted. Control over Indian political structures, land holding patterns, and resource and economic development gave Parliament everything it appeared to need to complete the unfinished policies inherited from its colonial predecessors. Indian policy was now clear and was expressed in the alternative by the minister of the interior, David Laird, when the draft act was introduced in Parliament: "[t]he Indians must either be treated as minors or as white men." There was to be no middle road.[71]

Under the provisions of the Indian Act, the federal government was authorized to contract with the provinces and churches to establish boarding schools for Indigenous education. The Indian Act empowered the minister of Indian affairs to enrol and place all Indigenous children (though excluding, for some years, the Métis) in school. What began as funding and agreements with churches to run schools for Indigenous children soon became the residential school system.

HECTOR-LOUIS LANGEVIN, ONE OF THE "FATHERS" OF CONFEDERATION AND A LEADING POLITICIAN, DESCRIBING THE NECESSITY TO ESTABLISH RESIDENTIAL SCHOOLS

In order to educate the children properly we must separate them from their families. Some people may say that this is hard but if we want to civilize them we must do that.[72]

The fact is that if you wish to educate the children you must separate them from their parents during the time they are being taught. If you leave them in the family they may know how to read and write, but they will remain savages, whereas by separating them in the way proposed, they acquire the habits and tastes . . . of civilized people.[73]

ANNUAL REPORT OF THE DEPARTMENT OF THE INTERIOR, 1876

Our Indian legislation generally rests on the principle, that the aborigines are to be kept in a condition of tutelage and treated as wards or children of the State. . . . the true interests of the aborigines and of the State alike require that every effort should be made to aid the Red man in lifting himself out of his condition of tutelage and dependence, and that is clearly our wisdom and our duty, through education and every other means, to prepare him

Kamloops Indian Residential School, 1937

for a higher civilization by encouraging him to assume the privileges and responsibilities of full citizenship.[74]

PRIME MINISTER SIR JOHN A. MACDONALD, DESCRIBING THE POLICY TO ESTABLISH RESIDENTIAL SCHOOLS, 1883

When the school is on the reserve the child lives with its parents, who are savages; he is surrounded by savages, and though he may learn to read and write his habits, and training and mode of thought are Indian. He is simply a savage who can read and write. It has been strongly pressed on myself, as the head of the Department, that Indian children should be withdrawn as much as possible from the parental influence, and the only way to do that would be to put them in central training industrial schools where they will acquire the habits and modes of thought of white men.[75]

SESSIONAL REPORT FROM THE INDIAN COMMISSIONER, DESCRIBING THE PURPOSE OF THE RESIDENTIAL SCHOOL SYSTEM, 1897

This branch of the Indian service has ever been recognized as one of the most, if not perhaps the most, important feature of the extensive system which is operating towards the civilization of our native races, having its beginning in small things—the first step being the establishment of reserve day-schools of limited scope of influence, the first forward step toward the founding of boarding schools both on and off the reserves. The beneficent effect of these becoming at once apparent, an impetus was thus given to the movement in the direction of Industrial training, which was at once entered upon the establishment of our earlier industrial institutions until to-day the Dominion has had at its command a system which provides for its Indian wards as practical course of industrial training, fitting for useful citizenship the youth of a people who one generation past were practically unrestrained savages.[76]

Thomas Moore Keesick, from Muscowpetung Saulteaux First Nation, images taken years apart at the Regina Indian Industrial School, published in 1897 for the Department of Indian Affairs 1896 annual report

<<<< >>>>

The Raven is about change, about the shifting that can occur in our lives and our world. And because change is an inevitable and intrinsic part of our existence, we are always, in a sense, the Raven. Where there is stasis, little of life can be maintained.

So, as we move up the pole, we should not envision ourselves as moving past the Raven. Rather, the Raven is moving with us as other forms of change come to the foreground. Some of the chaos and confusion experienced during dark times will now be met with a more present and public push for change. This is the ascendancy of the Wolf.

PART 3

Wolf

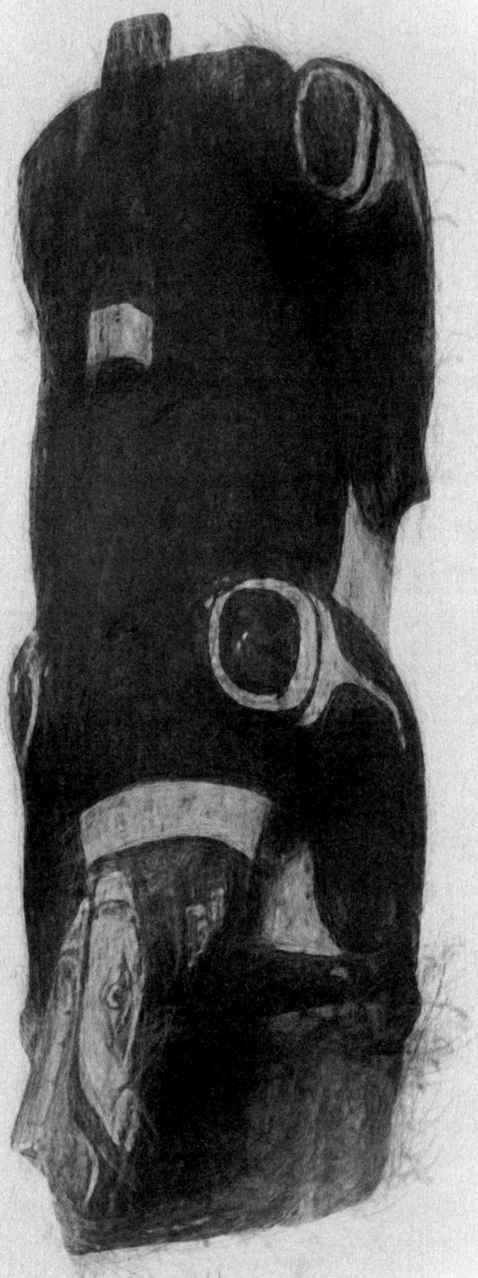

The Wolf stares down at the Raven with an almost menacing glare. It is as if we can hear the Wolf calling—demanding—for the mischief and the trouble to stop.

The Wolf has always been present, moving forward, and encouraging us to do the same.

Since contact, there has never been a moment in which Indigenous Peoples have not been working to govern their lands and peoples, uphold their legal orders and apply their laws, express and advance their teachings and culture, and care for the well-being of their children, families, and communities. We have always worked to resist colonial intrusion and the harm it causes, and to maintain our ways of being. We have already heard some Indigenous voices advocating for this change, and as we continue to tell the story of Canada, we will hear many more.

The howl of the Wolf is loud and uncompromising. It demands our attention, and when it comes, we cannot help but respond. But wolves are also relatively quiet creatures, often moving and hunting with stealth. The sounds wolves do make, in addition to the howl, are varied. Wolves bark, growl, and snarl.

When we seek out the voices of Indigenous people working for justice and change throughout history, all of the sounds of the Wolf are in evidence. This includes the Wolf's silence.

Colonization meant that much of this work of the Wolf had to be done in the shadows, hidden from view. This was true in the early days, before and after Confederation, and it has remained true in more recent times. For that reason, there are voices we are not able to hear today, and voices that will forever remain distant and faint. We continue to do our best to recover what we can and preserve them for posterity. But we also have to accept that the work of the Wolf, the work of our ancestors, often had to be stealth.

The Wolf in the shadows is how I understand the work of my grandmother, and countless others like her. The story of my grandmother that I come back to time and again is of how she and others preserved the traditions of our Big House, our ways of governing, hidden from view. The Big House, and other systems of First Nations government, was outlawed under the Indian Act as part of the federal government's drive to assimilate. This law, and many others like it, was enforced in multiple ways, including by Indian agents from the federal government, as well as the Royal Canadian Mounted Police (RCMP). As my granny recounted, when they were doing their work in the Big House, they would switch from that work to singing Christian hymns as the Indian agent got closer. Doing so was, effectively, a matter of survival. It was one expression of the work of the Wolf.

Today, we see the results of this work in the shadows. The Big House remains. The Indian agents, at least in their past incarnation, are gone.

There are many other illustrations of the power of the Wolf's work in the shadows. For years, the Survivors of the residential "school" system had to work and advocate for justice with almost no public awareness or acknowledgement of what they had endured. Undertaking this advocacy involved different types of sacrifice and harm, ranging from retraumatization to threats and ostracization. These harms continue today. We can see them in the various forms of denialism about aspects of the residential school reality present in some segments of society despite the testimony, lived experiences, documents and records, and physical findings that exist. Yet the Survivors persevered, a measure of justice was achieved, and a bright light has been cast on this indelible and deplorable part of Canada's history.

Yes, it is an unfortunate truth that there are countless voices we cannot recover in these pages because they had to show their strength in ways others would not notice. But we have tremendous evidence of what they accomplished, of their success. That evidence is us: the Indigenous Peoples who are here today, the generations that we know are yet to come, and the fact that so many of us from all backgrounds, across Canada, are working toward true reconciliation and confronting the legacy of colonization.

Yes, it has taken a long time—too long—to get here. And yes, we still have a long way to go. But I always remind myself that wolves hunt mostly through endurance and not ambush, and that they move forward with reliance on others, understanding there are distinct roles and responsibilities that must be played by different people. We will see more and more of that as we read on.

This has been our way—out of necessity, more than anything else—of finding justice. Our people, over many generations, have advocated for change to the systems and structures imposed on us. We have done this with courage and strength, and with risk to ourselves, much like wolves hunting down prey. As we will see, as colonization took its fullest form in the decades after Canada came into being, the responses of Indigenous Peoples intensified. And, over time, we were heard and seen more.

<<<< >>>>

In the years before and after Confederation, Indigenous Peoples constantly and continuously raised the alarm about the mounting harms, dispossession, and violence they were subjected to. As time passed, the concerns only deepened.

KJISAKAMOW [CHIEF] LOUIS-BENJAMIN PEMINUIT PAUL, PETITION TO QUEEN VICTORIA OVER THE TAKING UP OF LAND, 1841

My people are in trouble. I have seen upwards of a Thousand Moons. When I was young I had plenty: now I am old, poor and sickly too. My people are poor. No Hunting Grounds—No Beaver—no Otter—no nothing. Indians poor—poor for ever. No Store—no Chest—no Clothes. All these Woods once ours. Our fathers possessed them all. Now we cannot cut a tree to warm our Wigwam in Winter unless the White Man please. . . . Pity your poor Indians in Nova Scotia. . . . Let us not perish.[1]

MI'KMAW CHIEFS, PETITION TO THE GOVERNOR OF NOVA SCOTIA ON THEIR DECLINE, 1849

A long time ago our fathers owned and occupied all the lands now called Nova Scotia. . . . Tired of a war that destroyed many of our people, almost ninety years ago our Chief made peace and buried the hatchet forever. When that peace was made, the English governor promised us protection, as much land as we wanted, and the preservation of our fisheries and game. These we now very much want. . . .

Good and Honorable Governor, be not offended at what we say. . . . But your people . . . came and killed many of our tribe and took from us our country. You have taken from us our lands and trees and have destroyed our game. The Moose yards of our fathers, where are they . . . . You have put ships and steamboats upon the waters and they scared away the fish. You have made dams across the rivers so that the Salmon cannot go up and your laws will not permit us to spear them.

In old times our wigwams stood in the pleasant places along the sides of the rivers. These places are now taken from us, and we are told to go away. Upon our camping grounds you have built towns, and the graves of our fathers are broken by the plow and harrow. Even the ash and maple are growing scarce. We are told to cut no trees upon the farmer's ground, and the land you have given us is taken away every year.[2]

COAST SALISH CHIEFS TO GOVERNOR SEYMOUR, PETITIONS FOR CHANGE, 1860S AND '70S

We know the good heart of the Queen for the Indians. You bring that good heart with you, so we are happy to welcome you. We wish to become good Indians, and to be friends with the white people. . . . Please to protect our land, that it will not be small for us: many are well pleased with their reservations, and many wish that their reservations be marked out for them.

[10 years later] For many years we have been complaining of the land left to us being too small. We have laid our complaints before the Government officials nearest to us: they sent us to some others; so we had no redress up to the present; and we have felt like men being trampled on, and are commencing to believe that the aim of the white men is to exterminate us as soon as they can, although we have always been quiet, obedient, kind, and friendly to the whites.

The white men have taken our land and no compensation has been given us, though we have been told many times that the great Queen was so good she would help her distant children the Indians. White men have surrounded our Villages so much as in many instances especially on Fraser River but a few acres of Land have been left us.

We are now obliged to clear heavy timbered land, all prairies having been taken from us by white men. We see our white neighbors cultivate wheat, peas, &c., and raise large stocks of cattle on our pasture lands, and we are giving them our money to buy the flour manufactured from the wheat they have grown on same prairies.

What have we received for our good faith, friendliness and patience? . . . They have stolen our lands and everything on them and continue to use same for their own purposes . . . We demand that our land question be settled . . . We desire that every matter of importance to each tribe be a subject of treaty, so we may have a definite understanding with the government on all questions of moment between us and them.

We have also learned lately the British Columbia government claims absolute ownership of our reservations which means that we are practically landless. We only have a loan of those reserves in life rent, or at the option of the B.C. government. Thus we find ourselves without any real home in this our own country.[3]

CHIEF DAVID MACKAY OF THE NISGA'A, DESCRIBING HOW THE LAND WAS TAKEN, 1887

What we don't like about the Government is their saying this: "We will give you this much land." How can they give it when it is our own? We cannot understand it. They have never bought it from us or our forefathers. They have never fought and conquered our people and taken the land in that way, and yet they say now that they will give us so much land—our own land. These chiefs do not talk foolishly, they know the land is their own; our forefathers for generations and generations past had their land here all around us; chiefs have had their own hunting grounds,

> their salmon streams, and places where they got their berries; it has always been so. It is not only during the last four or five years that we have seen the land; we have always seen and owned it; it is no new thing, it has been ours for generations. If we had only seen it for twenty years and claimed it as our own, it would have been foolish, but it has been ours for thousands of years. If any strange person came here and saw the land for twenty years and claimed it, he would be foolish. We have always got our living from the land; we are not like white people who live in towns and have their stores and other business, getting their living in that way, but we have always depended on the land for our food and clothes; we get our salmon, berries, and furs from the land.[4]

Resistance has always been a major element of Métis life and identity. The Métis Resistance of 1870 and the Northwest Resistance of 1885 arose as the Métis, who constituted most of the area's population, became increasingly marginalized. While some Métis objectives were achieved in 1870, including those that resulted in the formation of the Province of Manitoba, Métis nationality continued to be ignored, and the suffering and disenfranchisement of the Métis people endured. Louis Riel and other Métis leaders were in exile to the United States, but they continued to drive for recognition and change, including through the 1885 resistance. When Riel returned to Canada, the Métis passed the Revolutionary Bill of Rights in March 1885 and proclaimed a provisional government. Riel was the president of this provisional government, and Batoche, in central Saskatchewan, was its capital. In May 1885, at the Battle of Batoche, Canada defeated the resistance. Riel surrendered and the provisional government fell apart. Louis Riel was executed by hanging in November 1885.

Louis Riel with councillors of the provisional government, c. 1869. L-R back row: Tom Laroque; Pierre Delorme; Thomas Bunn; Xavier Page; Andre Beauchemin; Baptiste Beauchemin; Thomas Spence. L-R middle row: Pierre Poitras; John Bruce; Louis Riel; W.B. O'Donoghue; Francois Dauphinais. L-F front row: Bob O'Lone; Paul Prue.

LOUIS RIEL, DESCRIBING THE ROOTS OF THE 1885 RESISTANCE

When I came into the Northwest in July, the 1st of July 1884, I found the Indians suffering. I found the half-breeds eating the rotten pork of the Hudson Bay Company and getting sick and weak every day. Although a half-breed, and having no pretension to help the whites, I also paid attention to them. I saw they were deprived of responsible government, I saw that they were deprived of their public liberties. I remembered that half-breed meant white and Indian and while I paid attention to the suffering Indians and the half-breeds I remembered that the greatest part of my heart and blood was white and I have directed my attention to help the Indians, help the half-breeds and to help the whites to the best of my ability. We have made petitions, I have made petitions with others to the Canadian government asking to relieve the condition of this country.[5]

GABRIEL DUMONT, MÉTIS LEADER, RECOUNTING WHAT RIEL SAID AT THE FOUNDING OF THE PROVISIONAL GOVERNMENT

It has been 15 years since I gave my heart to my country. I am ready to give it again now.[6]

Métis sash

CLAUDE ADAMS, REFLECTING ON THE BATTLE OF BATOCHE IN HIS POEM "MÉTIS SACRED GROUND"

My Grandpa came to get me
When I was just a boy
As we rode in a buggy
On his face I saw no joy
—

And this was so unusual
He always wore a smile
He told a sad, sad story
As we went mile by mile

"The Battle at Batoche" he said
"Is something you must hear!"
He talked on till we came upon
The battle site so near
I did not know its meaning
I learned to my surprise
As we walked to the trenches
There were tears in Grandpa's eyes

He showed me where the men dug in
While on the Métis side
A small boy stood right on the ground
Where brave young Métis died

I had respect for Grandpa
As he stood hat in hand
Right then I knew that this man felt
He stood on sacred land

The silence then was broken
As he began a prayer
He spoke their names so proudly
As if each man was there
A little boy stood so impressed
A promise he would keep
That once each year he'd come to pray
Where Métis heroes sleep

—

So many years have passed now
But something draws me there
I walk to see old trenches
And pray that Métis care

This I know that younger folk
Must pass tradition on
I know they'll build a better world
Where Peace and Love will dawn

I pray, like me, they understand
The reason I have found
To wear no hat when I walk on
Batoche's Sacred Ground.[7]

LOUIS RIEL, 1885

I am more convinced everyday that without a single exception I did right. And I have always believed that, as I have acted honestly, the time will come when the people of Canada will see and acknowledge it.[8]

I have nothing but my heart, and I have given it long ago to my country.[9]

PRIME MINISTER SIR JOHN A. MACDONALD ON LOUIS RIEL, 1885

He shall hang here though every dog in Quebec (shall) bark in his favour.[10]

PRIME MINISTER PIERRE ELLIOTT TRUDEAU ON LOUIS RIEL, 1968

Riel and his followers were protesting against the Government's indifference to their problems and its refusal to consult them on matters of vital interest. . . . Questions of minority rights have deep roots in our history; we must never forget that; in the long run, a democracy is judged by the way the majority treats the minority. Louis Riel's battle is not yet won.[11]

YVON DUMONT, PRESIDENT,
MANITOBA MÉTIS FEDERATION, 1993

The Metis believe that the right to a land and resource base naturally flows from the rights of the Metis Nation as set out in . . . the Manitoba Act . . . and the Constitution [of Canada]. . . . We hold the view that the quantum of land [to be given to us] must recognize and promote the social, cultural and economic development of the Metis Nation. . . .

Louis Riel referred to the Manitoba Act as a treaty between governments, and called upon Canada to respect [it]. Louis Riel has only recently received respect and recognition for his role in the creation of Canada, but his people have yet to receive respect and recognition for their rights [to land and self-government] for which he fought and died.[12]

In the decades after Confederation, the federal government also focused on expanding the reach of their authority over Indigenous Peoples. This meant looking west and looking north. A priority was placed on entering into treaties with First Nations as part of securing land surrenders from them and economic expansion for the government of Canada. Eleven numbered treaties were entered into between 1871 and 1921. The treaties covered a vast geographic area—between the Lake of the Woods and the Rocky Mountains, and to the Beaufort Sea.[13] *While the numbered treaties have distinctions, the common elements included payments (annuities), land reserves, rights to hunt and fish, and statements regarding land status.*

THE *FINAL REPORT OF THE TRUTH AND RECONCILIATION COMMISSION*, DESCRIBING TREATY-MAKING

At the Treaty 1 talks, [A.G.] Archibald [then lieutenant governor of Manitoba and the North-West Territories] said that although the Queen thought it best for her "red children" to "adopt the habits of the whites," she had "no idea of compelling you to do so. This she leaves to your choice, and you need not live like the white man unless you can be persuaded to do so of your own free will." This promise was at odds with the laws of the time, which limited First Nations participation in all aspects of Canadian society unless they went through the process of enfranchisement—which did require them to "live like the white man." In coming years, First Nations people would be compelled to send their children to residential schools, where those children would also be made to "live like the white man."

[Alexander] Morris [then lieutenant governor of Manitoba and the North-West Territories] also stressed the permanent nature of the government commitments, saying, "What I offer you is to be while the water flows and the sun rises." In 1876, Morris told the Cree, "What I trust and hope we will do is not for to-day and tomorrow only; what I will promise, and what I believe and hope you will take, is to last as long as the sun shines and yonder river flows." This concept of an agreement that lasts as long as the sun shines and the water flows was symbolized in the Treaty medals that were distributed at the signing of Treaty 3 through to Treaty 8. They showed a chief and an imperial officer shaking hands; a hatchet was buried in the ground and, in the background, the sun shone.

The First Nations negotiators demanded fair treatment. During the Treaty 3 talks, Chief Ma-we-do-pe-nais reminded Morris, "The white man has robbed us of our riches, and we don't wish to give them up again without getting something in their place."[14]

Treaty One Medal, 1873

EXCERPTS FROM TREATY 1, 1871

The Chippewa and Swampy Cree Tribes of Indians and all other the Indians inhabiting the district hereinafter described and defined do hereby cede, release, surrender and yield up to Her Majesty the Queen and successors forever all the lands . . . . To have and to hold the same to Her said Majesty the Queen and Her successors for ever; and Her Majesty the Queen hereby agrees and undertakes to lay aside and reserve for the sole and exclusive use of the Indians the following tracts of land, . . . as will furnish one hundred and sixty acres for each family of five, . . . reserving also a further tract enclosing said reserve to comprise an equivalent to twenty-five square miles of equal breadth, to be laid out round the reserve, it being understood, however, that if, at the date of the execution of this treaty, there are any settlers within the bounds of any lands reserved by any band, Her Majesty reserves the right to deal with such settlers as She shall deem just, so as not to diminish the extent of land allotted to the Indians.

And with a view to show the satisfaction of Her Majesty with the behaviour and good conduct of Her Indians parties to this treaty, She hereby, through Her Commissioner, makes them a present of three dollars for each Indian man, woman and child belonging to the bands here represented.

And further, Her Majesty agrees to maintain a school on each reserve hereby made whenever the Indians of the reserve should desire it.

Within the boundary of Indian reserves, until otherwise enacted by the proper legislative authority, no intoxicating liquor shall be allowed to be introduced or sold, and all laws now in force or hereafter to be enacted to preserve Her Majesty's Indian subjects inhabiting the reserves or living elsewhere from the evil influence of the use of intoxicating liquors shall be strictly enforced.

Her Majesty's Commissioner shall, as soon as possible after the execution of this treaty, cause to be taken an accurate census of all the Indians inhabiting the district above described, distributing them in families, and shall in every year ensuing the date hereof, at some period during the month of July in each year, to be duly notified to the Indians and at or near their respective reserves, pay to each Indian family of five persons the sum of fifteen dollars Canadian currency, or in like proportion for a larger or smaller family, such payment to be made in such articles as the Indians shall require of blankets, clothing, prints (assorted colours), twine or traps, at the current cost price in Montreal, or otherwise, if Her Majesty shall deem the same desirable in the interests of Her Indian people, in cash.

And the undersigned Chiefs do hereby bind and pledge themselves and their people strictly to observe this treaty and to maintain perpetual peace between themselves and Her Majesty's white subjects, and not to interfere with the property or in any way molest the persons of Her Majesty's white or other subjects.[15]

INDIAN COMMISSIONER JOSEPH PROVENCHER, ON THE PURPOSE OF THE TREATIES FOR THE CANADIAN ADMINISTRATION, 1873

There are two modes wherein the Government may treaty the Indian nations who inhabit this territory. Treaties may be made with them simply with a view to the extinction of their rights, by agreeing to pay them a sum, and afterwards abandon them to themselves. On the other side, they may be instructed, civilised and led to a mode of life more in conformity with the new position of this country and accordingly made good industrious and useful citizens.[16]

Reflecting earlier practices of treaty-making prior to Confederation, First Nations understood treaty-making in accordance with their own cultures, traditions, and laws. This included the First Nation signatories understanding the numbered treaties as recognizing their systems of government and law and their relationship to their territories, and as part of a sacred and enduring relationship with the Crown. For them, the treaties were an opportunity to continue to uphold their sovereignty and preserve their way of life.

MAWE-DO-PE-NAIS TO LIEUTENANT GOVERNOR ALEXANDER MORRIS AND HIS FELLOW COMMISSIONERS, AS PART OF TREATY-MAKING, 1873

Now you see me stand before you all: what has been done here to-day has been done openly before the Great Spirit and before the nation, and I hope I may never hear any one say that this treaty has been done secretly: and now in closing this council, I take off my glove, and in giving you my hand I deliver over my birthright and lands: and in taking your hand I hold fast all the promises you have made, and I hope they will last as long as the sun rises and the water flows, as you have said.

. . .

[Lieutenant governor, taking up his hand, then said in reply:] I accept your hand and with it the lands, and will keep all my promises, in the firm belief that the treaty now to be signed will bind the red man and the white together as friends for ever.[17]

LIEUTENANT GOVERNOR ALEXANDER MORRIS TO THE PLAINS CREES AT FORTS CARLETON AND PITT, AS PART OF NEGOTIATING AND CONCLUDING TREATY 6

What I have offered does not take away your living, you will have it then as you have now, and what I offer now is put on top of it.

. . .

The instructions of the Queen are to treat the Indians as brothers, and so we ought to be. The Great Spirit made this earth we are on. He planted the trees and made the rivers flow for the good of all his people, white and red; the country is very wide and there is room for all.

. . .

Now the whole burden of my message from the Queen is that we wish to help you in the days that are to come, we do not want to take away the means of living that you have now, we do not want to tie you down.[18]

AN ACCOUNT OF CHIEF SWEETGRASS'S SPEECH UPON ACCEPTANCE OF TREATY 6 TERMS, 1876

I am glad to have you as a brother and friend who will help lift us up from our present condition. I thank you for your offer and I am not afraid. I accept gladly . . . I want you to commence to protect the buffalo. I myself will commence at once to prepare a piece of land and my kinsmen will do the same. Then placing one hand over the governor's heart and the other over his own he said, "May the white man's blood never be spilt on this earth. I am thankful that the white man and the Indian can live together. I hold your hand

Chief Sweetgrass, c. 1872–76

and touch your heart. Let us be one. Do your utmost to help my children that they may prosper."[19]

THE ELDERS IN TREATIES 4, 6, AND 8, DEFINING THE WORD *WITASKEWIN*

"Witaskewin" (a Cree word), in the context of treaty-making refers to nations who are strangers to one another entering into agreements for the purpose of sharing land and territory with each other.[20]

ELDER JACOB BILL, DESCRIBING THE MEANING OF TREATIES

We say it's our Father (wiyohtawinmaw); the White man says "our Father" in his language, so from there we should understand that he becomes our brother and we have to live harmoniously with him. There should not be any conflict, we must uphold the word "witaskewin," which means to live in peace and harmony with one another.[21]

ELDER ALMA KYTWAYHAT, DESCRIBING THE MEANING OF TREATIES

We were told that these treaties were to last forever. The government and the government officials, the Commissioner, told us that, as long as the grass grows, and the sun rises from the east and sets in the west, and the river flows, these treaties will last. . . .[22]

KITIGAN ZIBI ANISHINABEG ELDER CLAUDETTE COMMANDA, ON THE SPIRIT AND INTENT OF TREATIES

There is the spirit and intent of those treaties, the sharing and coexistence of the land and the natural resources. The treaties were based on our laws. They contain that spirit. They contain the spirit of our ancestors, the spirit of Creator, the spirit of our prayers. They contain life. And they contain that special relationship between First Nations and settlers.[23]

Despite stated feelings of kinship and promises of lasting friendship, the struggles and conflict over treaty implementation began almost immediately. There were concerns about whether the written text reflected the understandings reached, about the failure to uphold certain promises, and about the imposition of laws, policies, and practices that were inconsistent with treaty understandings. In the 1930s, Canada entered into agreements with Manitoba, Saskatchewan, and Alberta to give the provinces more control over natural resources. Known as the Natural Resources Transfer Agreements, these documents remain a point of conflict today, including over their impacts on the land and hunting rights in the numbered treaties.

ANNUAL REPORT BY THE DEPUTY SUPERINTENDENT GENERAL OF INDIAN AFFAIRS, 1908

So long as no particular harm nor inconvenience accrued from the Indians' holding vacant lands out of proportion to their requirements, and no profitable disposition thereof was possible, the department firmly opposed any attempt to induce them to divest themselves of any part of their reserves.

Conditions, however, have changed and it is now recognized that where Indians are holding tracts of farming or timber lands beyond their possible requirements and by doing so seriously impeding the grown of settlement, and there is such demand as to ensure profitable sale . . . it is in the best interests of all concerned to encourage such sales.[24]

FRANK OLIVER, MINISTER OF THE INTERIOR AND IN CHARGE OF INDIAN AFFAIRS, ON TREATIES, 1911

For while we believe that the Indian having a certain treaty right is entitled ordinarily to stand upon that right and get benefit of it, yet we believe that there are circumstances and conditions in which the Indian by standing on his treaty rights does himself an ultimate injury, as well as does an injury to the white people, whose interests are brought into immediate conjunction with the interests of the Indians.[25]

CHIEF POUNDMAKER OF THE PLAINS CREE, DESCRIBING THE CONNECTION TO THE LAND AND HOW TREATIES CANNOT DESTROY THAT

This is our land, not a piece of pemmican to be cut off and given in little pieces. It is ours and we will take what we want.[26]

ELDER DANNY MUSQUA, KEESEEKOOSE FIRST NATION (TREATY 4), ON THE HOPE AND STRUGGLE TO HAVE TREATIES HELP PROTECT THE LAND

Now the old people tell us the day will come when the land will be sick again and there will be a fever, you know, a fever in the world, a fever in this land because the ascending problems that are coming up upon it because the land is sick; the economies are falling flat because the land is sick.

As [Indigenous] people, we don't think much of money. We still think of using things to help us live, helping one another, and that's the reason why the treaties were a dual road.[27]

HUGH CROW EAGLE, THE PEIGAN NATION (TREATY 7), ON THE BREAKING OF TREATY PROMISES

The treaty is held to be very strong and can't be broken. Indian people have never broken their agreements to the making of the treaty as far as they understood it to be. However, the White government had continued to break their promises to the Indians. There is an important distinction why this happened. The White negotiators' intent on the making of treaty was represented by a physical being, the Queen; therefore, their intent was weak and that is why they broke promises. The Indian leaders' intent was represented through the Creator; therefore, it was strong and binding and can never be broken with.[28]

CHIEF PASCALL BIGHETTY, PUKATAWAGAN FIRST NATION (TREATY 6), ON THE FAILURE OF TREATIES TO PROTECT THE LAND

First Nations are nations. First Nations (treaty people) signed over 300 treaties with the Europeans during the 1700s and 1800s. The treaties agreed to share the lands and resources with the immigrants. . . . Under existing legislation, treaty people are "sovereign" nations. . . . The Indians surrendered over 9.9 million square kilometres of their land to the immigrants. Today, the sons of the immigrants have the largest treaty rights in Canada. The Indians have become the poorest peoples in Canada.[29]

OFFICE OF THE TREATY COMMISSIONER OF SASKATCHEWAN, DESCRIBING THE NATURAL RESOURCE TRANSFER AGREEMENT, 2007

Until 1930, the public land and natural resources of Saskatchewan (like those of Manitoba and Alberta) were controlled by the federal government. In that year, the Natural Resources Transfer Agreement attempted to place the three Prairie provinces on the same footing as the original provinces under section 109 of the Constitution Act, 1867. In doing so, the Government of Canada did not fully require the provincial governments to honour and implement the spirit and intent of the treaties. In fact, according to a decision of the Supreme Court of Canada, the Natural Resources Transfer Agreement expressly took away the important treaty right of commercial hunting.

Canada did not consult with the Treaty First Nations about the Natural Resources Transfer Agreement, which gave the provincial government enormous leverage to delay and frustrate the fulfillment of treaty rights to land as well as game and fish harvesting.[30]

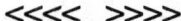

<<<< >>>>

I often remark that "words matter." This was instilled in me as I was growing up, both as a cultural teaching and as an important aspect of being a good person and having good character. Words cannot be taken back. When they are uttered, they affect the minds and hearts of those to whom they are directed.

Words can also have effects across time, impacting and influencing people who are completely removed from the original context in which the words were spoken or written. This book is a collection of such words. Except for the words that were written specifically for this book, and the contemporary interviews that appear in the final part, almost nothing here was written or spoken for you. These words were written and spoken by people in a different context, with different realities, preoccupations, and attitudes. In other words, the words in this book, with a few exceptions, were not spoken or written in order for you, for us, to understand the history of this country. They all had another purpose, and they had meaning in relation to that purpose. In fitting them within this history, as part of a telling of the story of Canada, and in having them be considered in relation to other statements and quotes, we are giving them another purpose and meaning.

As such, while we read, it is important to have in our mind, to ask ourselves about, what the original context and purpose of these words might have been. And, in doing that, to also have a degree of healthy skepticism about what some of them may convey.

This type of consideration and skepticism can be illustrated by some of the quotes that did not make it into this book. For example, consideration was given to including some statements from Chief Seattle that speak to issues of Indigenous worldviews and how they relate to caring for the land. But like some oft-quoted statements by historic Indigenous leaders, their veracity is suspect. In some instances, evidence suggests that these statements may have been written by settlers to fit a particular agenda. In other instances, evidence suggests that while the statement may have been spoken or written by the Indigenous leader, it has been rewritten and reshaped over time by non-Indigenous individuals and groups to meet their purposes.

In other words, some words from the past are, in effect, pretend. These words still matter, but they matter because of what they reveal about how perceptions and stories have been constructed to reinforce certain things about Indigenous people, and the relationship between peoples. They do not matter for what we originally thought them to be: a statement by an Indigenous leader about what they thought, felt, or believed.

We need to also be skeptical—or at least willing to question—for another reason.

There is no neutral telling of a story. As I described earlier, a story is always told from a vantage point, a perspective—in just the same way as we look at the totem pole from different angles and different perspectives. This book is grappling with stories of Canada told from different vantage points, and the quotations included here reflect those different vantage points. There is the colonizers' story. The stories of those who were here first. The stories of those who have sought change and justice. And, as noted, there are also the words that do not appear here: the missing voices, the missing stories, those words that cannot be recovered because of how they were not listened to, valued, or recorded.

From Wolf we learn that things cannot merely be taken at face value. Rather, we challenge. And in challenging, we are able to better see things for what they are, and to help others also see more of the truth.

As you move toward the end of the book, I encourage you to reflect on what you have read, and what you have yet to read, through the way of the Wolf. To ask yourself why different voices may have spoken as they have; to question how they may be trying to create a certain perception of themselves, and others; and to consider how the words mattered in their time and context, and not just in the context of this book as a telling of Canada's history.

And then I ask you to reflect on your reflections, to consider what it is about your own experience and perceptions that leads you to understand the words in those ways. To be a little self-critical about the understandings you are gaining.

When we do this, when we recognize that words matter, and, more so, recognize the different ways that they may have mattered in times and contexts, we move closer to an understanding of the truth. And as we do that, our capacity to contribute to the work of true reconciliation increases.

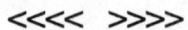

<<<< >>>>

Woman in an amauti with infant, cleaning a seal skin in fresh water, 1947 (Location listed as Rankin Inlet or Arviat)

After its creation in 1920, the RCMP began to play a larger role in the life of Indigenous Peoples across Canada. Often, the stated rationale for this overreach was that it was to "protect" Indigenous Peoples; rather, these actions were part of an extension of colonial social controls and law enforcement designed specifically with the goal of assimilation in mind.

This particular use of the RCMP originated most intensely in the North, where interactions between Inuit and Europeans in Inuit Nunangat were dramatically increasing. It extended south as well, with the police enforcing bans on First Nations governing systems, such as the Potlatch in parts of British Columbia, and with the Indian Act allowing for the appointment of RCMP officers as "truant officers" to enforce attendance at residential schools.

The RCMP also played a role in the forced relocation of Indigenous Peoples, such as moving Inuit from Inukjuak (in northern Quebec) and Mittimatalik (in what is now Nunavut) to form settlements in High Arctic islands.[31]

SPECIAL HOUSE OF COMMONS COMMITTEE, 1924

It is necessary to protect our rights against foreigners; to protect our fisheries, and to take care of our property generally. I think it is wise for us to exercise some oversight over the Canadian tribes, because . . . if you do not protect them, the traders who are not particularly anxious about the welfare of the native Eskimo, get in amongst them and debauch them, carry in liquor and exercise an evil influence among the tribes, and then the responsibility is ours. The Eskimo problem is beginning to be a rather serious one for us to handle, and we are establishing police posts at various points along the coast to protect the Eskimo and preserve their game.[32]

INDIAN AGENT WILLIAM MAY HALLIDAY, DESCRIBING THE REASONS TO HAVE THE RCMP ENFORCE A BAN OF THE POTLATCH, 1935

[The Potlatch is a] particularly wasteful and destructive custom, and [*sic*] created ill-feeling, jealousy and in most cases great poverty. . . . [T]he good obtained from it was small, and the evils associated with it were so great.[33]

HARRY ASSU, FROM CAPE MUDGE, DESCRIBING THE SHUTTING DOWN OF THE POTLATCH BY THE RCMP

The scow came around from the cannery and put in at the village to pick up the big pile of masks and headdresses and belts and coppers—everything we had for potlatching. I saw it pull out across Discovery Passage to the Campbell River side where more stuff was loaded on the Princess Beatrice for the trip to Alert Bay. Alert Bay was where the potlatch gear was gathered together. It came mainly from our villages around here and from Alert Bay and Village Island. It was sent to the museums in Ottawa from Alert Bay by the Indian agent. Our old people who watched the barge pull out from shore with all their masks on it said: "There is nothing left now. We might as well go home." When we say "go home" it means to die.[34]

Rynee Flaherty, right, the eldest survivor of the Grise Fiord Exiles, examines Pijamini's monument to the High Arctic relocation after its unveiling, 2010

LARRY AUDLALUK, REFLECTING ON BEING ONE OF EIGHTY-SEVEN INUIT TAKEN FROM INUKJUAK TO GRISE FIORD, RESOLUTE BAY IN 1953, WHEN HE WAS TWO YEARS OLD

My parents, I know, felt trapped for many years . . . We were actually on what we called "Prison Island" . . . you were left to your resources, alone, and [no one] worried about you running away because you're so far away. . . . It was awful for them. They had to learn to get ready for the dark season and they had to learn to get ready for very short warm sunny days, with very few vegetation in the land . . .

My family, the older generation, were used to having lots of different kinds of birds and then shore creatures like clams and oysters . . . There were none here.

It killed my father . . . He lasted ten months, and he was only 56 years old.

[Recalling his mother crying and crying] You know how that makes a little boy feel? You're vulnerable . . . It shaped much of my attitude towards the government. I was very angry.[35]

ELIYAH KOPALIE, SPEAKING ABOUT THE EXPERIENCE OF BEING RELOCATED FROM KIVITOO TO QIKIQTARJUAG IN 1963

All our belongings, we had to take only what we can carry, that is what we brought here. Winter came, my father went back to Kivitoo to pick up our belongings, there was nothing left. Not one little bit. They tried to get their belongings, even my father's guns, everything was bulldozed to the ground . . . everything we had in the qarmaq.[36]

First Nations, Métis, and Inuit advocacy continued to increase in an effort to stop these mounting harms, including with respect to lands and resources. What would come to be referred to as the "Indian Land Question," or what we often refer to today as the issue of "title," became a focal point in parts of Canada where few treaties existed, such as British Columbia. Elsewhere, the systematic violation of treaty land provisions was a deepening concern. The Allied Tribes of British Columbia, a political organization formed by the Nisga'a and the Interior Tribes in 1927, was a major force in this push to press the Indian Land Question. In 1926, they petitioned the Special Joint Committee of the Senate and House of Commons to Inquire into the Claims of the Allied Tribes of British Columbia, arguing that their title to their territories continued to exist.

FEDERAL INDIAN AGENT OF THE NAAS AGENCY, DESCRIBING TENSIONS AROUND LAND, 1913

The management of nearly all the bands in this agency, as is the case with many other bands in British Columbia, has become much more difficult of recent years owing to the great agitation that has been going on, a claim being made that the Indians do not own merely the reserves they have been assigned, but the whole province. Many of the bands object to control of their affairs by the government, benign under the impression that to acknowledge the authority of the government would be to surrender their alleged rights to land.[37]

ALLIED TRIBES OF BRITISH COLUMBIA, PETITION TO THE SPECIAL JOINT COMMITTEE, 1926

2. When British Columbia entered Confederation Section 109 of the British North America Act was made applicable to all public lands with certain specific exceptions, By virtue of the application of this Section it was enacted that the public lands belonging to the Colony of British Columbia should belong to the new Province. By virtue of the application of the same Section as explained by the Minister of Justice in January, 1875, all territorial land rights claimed by the Indian Tribes of the Province were preserved and it was enacted that such rights should be an "interest" in the public lands of the Province. The Indian Tribes of British Columbia claim

The Allied Tribes of British Columbia, 1927

actual beneficial ownership of their territories, but do not claim absolute ownership in the sense of ownership excluding the title of the Crown. It is recognized by the Allied Tribes that there is in respect of all the public lands of the Province an underlying title of the Crown, which title at least for the present purposes it is not thought necessary to define.[38]

JOHN CHILIHITZA, AN INTERIOR CHIEF, TO THE SPECIAL JOINT COMMITTEE ON THE CROWN'S PROMISE TO RESPECT THE TITLE OF FIRST NATIONS, 1926

I am going to refer to the time when Sproat came as a messenger from the Queen. . . . The Indians were told by Sproat that the Queen would not touch their Indian rights and their rights would include the right to keep their native titles. Sproat told a lot of things to the Indians of what the Queen said, but I will not speak about that, as it will take too much time, but the Indians have kept in mind what Sproat told them concerning the white man.[39]

Indigenous advocacy included seeking to use the courts domestically as well as seeking out international venues for change. Following the lead of some peoples subject to British colonization in other parts of the world, attempts were made by some First Nations in British Columbia to advance their rights in the courts in London. As well, the Privy Council made rulings related to Indigenous peoples even where Indigenous peoples were not present or a party.

Attempts were also made to use the League of Nations (which would later evolve into the United Nations) in this capacity. Deskaheh, the Chief of the Iroquois League representing the Six Nations of the Iroquois Confederacy, left Canada for Switzerland, looking to be heard by the League of Nations. They refused. As well, on the rare occasions when Indigenous peoples were able to access these international forums, it often further revealed the racist attitudes of the day.

ARGUMENT MADE BY THE ATTORNEY GENERAL OF ONTARIO IN *ST. CATHARINES MILLING AND LUMBER CO. V. R*, 1887

To maintain their position the appellants must assume that the Indians have a regular form of government, whereas nothing is more clear than that they have no government and no organization, and cannot be regarded as a nation capable of holding lands. . . .

It is a rule of the common law that property is the creature of the law and only continues to exist while the law that creates and regulates it subsists. The Indians had no rules or regulations which could be considered laws.[40]

DESKAHEH, CHIEF OF THE IROQUOIS LEAGUE, WRITING TO SIR J.E. DRUMMOND, SECRETARY-GENERAL OF LEAGUE OF NATIONS ON THE CLAIM OF THE IROQUOIS, 1923

The constituent members of the State of the Six Nations of the Iroquois, that is to say, the Mohawk, the Oneida, the Onondaga, the Cayuga, the Seneca and the Tuscarora, now are, and have been for many centuries, organised and self-governing peoples, respectively, within domains of their own, and united in the oldest League of Nations, the League of the Iroquois.[41]

As political advocacy intensified, so too did the response of the federal government. In 1926, a Special Joint Committee of the House of Commons and Senate on Indian Affairs was formed. The committee heard representations from Indigenous Peoples. As part of the federal government's response to these advocacy efforts, the Indian Act was amended in 1927 to make it illegal for "Indians" to obtain funds or legal counsel to advance rights. Other amendments targeted First Nations governance. Advocacy was increasingly forced to move underground.

SPECIAL JOINT COMMITTEE OF THE HOUSE OF COMMONS, 1927

[T]he claims of the Indians were not well founded, and that no Aboriginal title, as alleged, had ever existed.[42]

INDIAN ACT, 1927, SECTION 141

Every person who, without the consent of the Superintendent General expresses in writing, receives, obtains, solicits or requests from any Indian any payment or contribution for the purpose of raising a fund or providing money for the prosecution of any claims which the tribe or band of Indians to which such Indian belongs, or of which he is a member, has or is represented to have for the recovery of any claim or money for the benefit of the said tribe or band, shall be guilty of an offence and liable upon summary conviction for each such offence to a penalty not exceeding two hundred dollars and not less than fifty dollars or to imprisonment for any term not exceeding two months.[43]

When the Second World War broke out in September 1939, many Indigenous people voluntarily participated in the war effort, as they had in other wars, both abroad as soldiers and at home. In addition to participating in combat in Europe and Asia, which saw more than two hundred Indigenous soldiers lose their lives, Indigenous people worked in wartime factories, helped raise money, and provided moral support to victims. These sacrifices in defence of Canada were made when most Indigenous people lacked citizenship and other fundamental rights and privileges.

AMBROSE REID, SPOKESMAN OF THE NATIVE BROTHERHOOD OF BRITISH COLUMBIA

It is our duty as patriotic citizens to put aside our personal claims or claims of our brotherhood and aid our country in this time of stress . . . our country is at war so we the Native Brotherhood are at War.[44]

Pte Mary Greyeyes, 1942

TOMMY PRINCE, FIRST NATIONS VETERAN

As soon as I put on my uniform I felt a better man.[45]

Sergeant Tommy Prince (R), M.M., 1st Canadian Parachute Battalion, with his brother, Private Morris Prince, at an investiture at Buckingham Palace, 1945

LEROY LITTLEBEAR, FIRST NATIONS VETERAN

I was working. I was a sawer in the sawmill in Flatbush. All of my friends and people I know were joining the army so, I wasn't going to be left behind.[46]

GILBERT MONTURE, FIRST NATIONS VETERAN

It's a long way from a two-roomed cabin on the Six Nations Reserve shared with eight brothers and sisters to the position of world citizen.[47]

ANONYMOUS FIRST NATIONS VETERAN

We were Canadian Native soldiers . . . warriors in a proud tradition stretching back over the thousands of years into the dim past. We travelled by ship, by plane . . . and mostly on foot. In a dozen places—we raised our flags, and were buried in those foreign soils.[48]

DR. HAROLD MCGILL, DIRECTOR OF THE INDIAN AFFAIRS BRANCH OF THE DEPARTMENT OF MINES AND RESOURCES, COMMENTING ON THE RESPONSE OF INDIGENOUS PEOPLES AND COMMUNITIES ACROSS CANADA IN THE WAR EFFORT, 1936

They were not slow to come forward with offers of assistance in both men and money. About one hundred Indians had enlisted . . . and the contribution of the Indians to the Red Cross and other funds amounted to over $1300.[49]

Indians are very loyal.[50]

Due to growing public scrutiny, shifts began to occur in government policy and practice after the war. One example: During the war, the American military had built a system of airfields in the North, which had the effect of accelerating changes to Inuit life. This included a separation from their land due to relocation to settlements. Around the same time, laws and policies were also being introduced that interfered more and more with their Inuit way of life. Dogs, which were critical for transportation, hunting, and economy, were culled, and limitations were put on their use. This changing reality in the North brought the challenges faced by Inuit more "forcefully to the attention of the Government and the country as a whole."[51] In response, Prime Minister Louis St. Laurent announced in 1953 that the government would create a Department of Northern Affairs and Natural Resources. Jean Lesage was the first minister to head the new department.

ONE INUIT INFORMANT, TO AN ANTHROPOLOGIST, 1958

The [government] didn't want Eskimos to have dogs any more. Eskimos sometimes have dogs untied, they get hungry and run around looking for food. . . . The Eskimos can't feed them regularly because the hunting around Frobisher Bay is no longer good. Everyone is working so no dog meat can be hunted for. But they need the dogs for hunting in the winter.[52]

AKEESHOO JOAMIE, DESCRIBING THE INCREASE IN NON-INUIT

In the '40s, there was a whole bunch of Qallunaat [people who are not Inuit]; that is when we really came in contact with Qallunaat. We would come into a community to seek some work for the summer. Perhaps for about three months, as part of the wage economy, during the re-supply season, we would come to work during the summer time. In October, we would go back to our wintering camps. We travelled by boat; it was the only way to get back to our camps.[53]

SAMMY JOSEPHEE, DESCRIBING THE INCREASE IN NON-INUIT

There was a bunch of Inuit moved to an island so that they could make room for the Americans. There were no more Inuit in Iqaluit. They wanted us out of the way to make room for the army.[54]

JEAN LESAGE, MINISTER OF NORTHERN AFFAIRS AND NATURAL RESOURCES, DESCRIBING SOME OF THE POLICY FOR THE NORTH

It is pointless to consider whether the Eskimo was happier before the white man came, for the white man has come and time cannot be reversed. . . . [it is government's responsibility to help the Inuit] climb the ladder of civilization.[55]

With the growing public awareness of human rights issues after the Second World War, including the development of the UN's Universal

Declaration of Human Rights, as well as some recognition of the sacrifices of Indigenous people in the war effort, several changes in law and policy were advanced. A joint Senate and House of Commons committee was formed in 1946 to examine the general administration of Indian affairs. The mandate and outcomes of the committee were quite narrow and continued to reflect the policy of assimilation. Nonetheless, a few important amendments to the Indian Act were made in 1951. These included removing the provision limiting the hiring of lawyers, lifting the bans on ceremonies, reducing the discretionary power of the minister, and increasing some of the powers of the Band Councils permitted by the Indian Act.[56]

MANDATE OF THE SPECIAL JOINT SENATE AND HOUSE OF COMMONS COMMITTEE, 1946–48

[To] examine and consider the Indian Act . . . , 1927, and amendments thereto and suggest such amendments as they deem advisable, with authority to investigate and report on Indian administration in general and, in particular, the following matters:

1) Treaty rights and obligations.
2) Band membership.
3) Liability of Indians to pay taxes.
4) Enfranchisement of Indians both voluntary and involuntary.
5) Eligibility of Indians to vote at dominion elections.
6) The encroachment of white persons on Indian reserves.
7) The operation of Indian day and residential Schools.
8) Any other matter or thing pertaining to the social and economic status of Indians and their advancement which . . . should be incorporated in the revised Act.[57]

D.F. BROWN, SPECIAL COMMITTEE CO-CHAIRMAN, EARLY IN THE FIRST YEAR OF HEARINGS, 1946

And I believe that it is a purpose of this Committee to recommend eventually some means whereby Indians have rights and obligations equal to those of all other Canadians. There should be no difference in my mind, or anybody else's mind, as to what we are, because we are all Canadians.[58]

DIAMOND JENNESS, ANTHROPOLOGIST AND SENIOR FEDERAL CIVIL SERVANT, OFFERING HIS THOUGHTS ON NEEDED POLICY CHANGES TO THE COMMITTEE, 1947

[T]o abolish, gradually but rapidly, the separate political and social status of Indians (and Eskimos); to enfranchise them and merge them into the rest of the population on an equal footing.[59]

JOHN BLACKMORE, LETHBRIDGE MP, EXPRESSING AN IDEA OF THE PUBLIC'S REVIVED INTEREST IN INDIAN AFFAIRS, 1947

The Indians now have confidence we are really going to do something for them, the Canadian people as a whole are interested in the problem of Indians; they have become aware that the country has been neglected in the matter of looking after the Indians and they are anxious to remedy our shortcomings. Parliament and the country is "human rights" conscious. This is clearly shown, as we all know, by discussions in the House of Commons at the present time.[60]

WALTER HARRIS, THE MINISTER RESPONSIBLE FOR INDIAN AFFAIRS, IN A SPEECH TO THE HOUSE OF COMMONS, SUMMARIZING THE LONG-TIME AIMS OF INDIAN AFFAIRS POLICY, 1950

The underlying principles of Indian legislation through the years have been protection and advancement of the Indian population. In the earlier period the main emphasis was on protection. But as the Indians become more self-reliant and capable of successfully adapting themselves to modern conditions, more emphasis is being laid on greater participation and responsibility by Indians in the conduct of their own affairs. Indeed, it may be said that ever

> since Confederation the underlying purpose of Indian administration has been to prepare the Indians for full citizenship with the same rights and responsibilities as enjoyed and accepted by other members of the community . . . .
>
> The ultimate goal of our Indian policy is the integration of the Indians into the general life and economy of the country. It is recognized, however, that during a temporary transition period of varying length, depending upon the circumstances and stage of development of different bands, special treatment and legislation are necessary.[61]

During this postwar period, there were also debates regarding and subsequent changes to voting rights; Inuit, for example, were granted the right to vote in federal elections in 1950. However, the ability to exercise this right was severely limited as there was literally nowhere to vote in most Inuit communities until 1962, when ballot boxes were finally provided. In 1960, First Nations people subject to the Indian Act were granted the same right to vote. However, this was not without controversy. Historically, after Confederation, enfranchisement of Indigenous Peoples (at that time meaning males) has been considered as part of the efforts to assimilate and remove what was distinct and diverse about Indigenous Peoples. Given this history—with enfranchisement of Indigenous Peoples masking a policy linked to assimilation and the denial of status as an Indigenous person—there was suspicion of government motivations in extending these rights. As well, at various times, all provinces except Nova Scotia and Newfoundland had legislation that in various ways disqualified status Indians from voting. After the Second World War, this changed in all provinces—though in Quebec, for example, this did not occur until as late as 1969.

PRIME MINISTER JOHN DIEFENBAKER, DESCRIBING AMENDMENTS TO THE INDIAN ACT REGARDING VOTING, 1960

The other measure, the provision to give Indians the vote, is one of those steps which will have an effect everywhere in the world—for the reason that wherever I went last year on the occasion of my trip to Commonwealth countries, it was brought to my attention that in Canada the original people within our country, excepting for a qualified class, were denied the right to vote. I say that so far as this long overdue measure is concerned, it will remove everywhere in the world any suggestion that color or race places any citizen in our country in a lower category than the other citizens of our country.

I say this to those of the Indian race that in bringing forward this legislation the Minister of Citizenship and Immigration (Mrs. Fairclough) will reassure, as she has assured to date, that existing rights and treaties, traditional or otherwise, possessed by the Indians shall not in any way be abrogated or diminished in consequence of having the right to vote. That is one of the things that throughout the years has caused suspicion in the minds of many Indians who have conceived the granting of the franchise as a step in the direction of denying them their ancient rights.[62]

ELLEN L. FAIRCLOUGH, SUPERINTENDENT GENERAL OF INDIAN AFFAIRS AND MINISTER OF CITIZENSHIP AND IMMIGRATION, DESCRIBING AMENDMENTS TO THE INDIAN ACT REGARDING VOTING, 1962

I should like to state for the record, so there will be no possibility of misunderstanding on the point, that the rights of Indians under treaty and the rights of Indians not under treaty are not in any way diminished or affected by the legislation passed in 1960 which conferred on persons of Indian status the right to vote in federal elections. The legislation in question takes nothing at all away from the Indians; instead, it confers an additional right or benefit, the right to vote in exactly the same way as any other citizen of Canada.

I would now like to give you my personal assurance that none of your rights will be affected by your voting and I urge you to exercise this privilege of citizenship.[63]

JAMES SINCLAIR, LIBERAL MP FOR VANCOUVER NORTH, 1947

I feel that one of the great incentives in the way of getting the Indians off the reserves, so that they might live as the rest of Canadians do under normal circumstances, would be to say to them, "If you cease being wards of the government, if you move out of the reserve and live as other Canadians live, you will get the vote." That would be a great incentive to the Indians.[64]

BILL ERASMUS, NATIONAL CHIEF OF THE DENE NATION, DESCRIBING WHY GRANTING OF VOTING RIGHTS WAS SOMETIMES SEEN AS PART OF A PLAN FOR ASSIMILATION, 2010

That's what the whole exercise was about. It was to make us Canadians, and we never had a discussion about that.[65]

The Indian Act amendments in 1951 also had some provisions regarding First Nations women. One undeniable reality of colonization is that Indigenous women have always been subject to differential and subordinate treatment in laws, policies, and practices. For First Nations women, the Indian Act had disparate and destructive impacts. In addition to displacing the traditional and public roles of women in First Nations cultures, societies, and laws, the Indian Act prevented women from running and voting in Band Council elections. Further, if a First Nations woman married a non–First Nations man, she lost her ability to be registered as an "Indian" under the Indian Act. Changes to these laws, policies, and practices have been slow in coming. In 1951, a few small steps were taken, but fundamental forms of discrimination remained. In 1985, after decades of Indigenous women and others forcefully advocating to fix the problem, the Indian Act was again amended to address the outstanding discrimination. In 2019, the federal government claimed to have fixed the problems, but Indigenous women have continued to point to discrimination in the act. Some of those who led the fight to end gender discrimination in the Indian Act include Mary Two-Axe Earley, Yvonne Bedard, Jeannette Corbiere Lavell, Sandra Lovelace Nicholas, and Sharon McIvor.

INDIAN ACT, 1876, DEFINITION OF AN 'INDIAN"

Any male person of Indian blood.[66]

INDIAN ACT, 1951, SECTION 12(B), CHANGING THE DEFINITION OF "INDIAN" FROM BEING BASED ON BLOOD TO BEING BASED ON REGISTRATION

[An Indian] woman who married a person who is not an Indian . . . [is] not entitled to be registered.[67]

ELSIE MARIE KNOTT, REFLECTING ON BEING THE FIRST ELECTED FEMALE CHIEF UNDER THE INDIAN ACT IN 1954

When I went in by a real big landslide, it never dawned on me that I was making history.[68]

MARY TWO-AXE EARLEY, ON HER MARRIAGE TO A NON-INDIGENOUS PERSON

Who thought about status? We were in love.[69]

MARY TWO-AXE EARLEY, SPEAKING TO THE ROYAL COMMISSION ON THE STATUS OF WOMEN ON THE DISCRIMINATION FIRST NATIONS WOMEN FACE, 1968

We are afraid. We can't voice our opinions on the reservation because the band council could tell us to get out. We're not sure we're going to have a home when we get back.[70]

Mary Two-Axe Earley, 1983

THE ROYAL COMMISSION ON THE STATUS OF WOMEN IN CANADA, 1970

[T]here is a special kind of discrimination under the terms of the Indian Act which can affect Indian women upon marriage.

. . . Indian women and men should enjoy the same rights and privileges in matters of marriage and property as other Canadians.[71]

MARY TWO-AXE EARLEY, IN A PUBLIC LETTER, 1985

When the Canadian government restores Indian women and their children to their rightful place in their Indian culture, Canada's own honor will be restored.[72]

JUSTICE HARVEY GROBERMAN, *MCIVOR V. CANADA*, 1985

[4] Prior to the coming into force of the current legislation in 1985, the Indian Act treated women and men quite differently. An Indian woman who married a non-Indian man ceased to be an Indian. An Indian man who married a non-Indian woman, on the other hand, remained an Indian; his wife also became entitled to Indian status.

[5] Children who were the product of a union of an Indian and a non-Indian were non-Indian if their father was non-Indian.

On the other hand, the legitimate children of an Indian father were Indian, subject only to the "Double Mother Rule," which provided that if a child's mother and paternal grandmother did not have a right to Indian status other than by virtue of having married Indian men, the child had Indian status only up to the age of 21.

[6] The old provisions had been heavily criticized prior to 1985, and there was a strong movement to amend them. Unfortunately, there was considerable controversy over what ought to replace them. With the coming into force of s.15 of the Charter on April 17, 1985, the need to amend the law took on new urgency, as it was clear that the then-existing regime discriminated on the basis of sex.[73]

NATIONAL INQUIRY INTO MISSING AND MURDERED INDIGENOUS WOMEN AND GIRLS (MMIWG), DESCRIBING THE CONNECTION BETWEEN DISCRIMINATION IN THE INDIAN ACT AND THE CURRENT CRISIS OF MMIWG

The truths shared in these National Inquiry hearings tell the story—or, more accurately, thousands of stories—of acts of genocide against First Nations, Inuit and Métis women, girls, and 2SLGBTQQIA people. This violence amounts to a race-based genocide of Indigenous Peoples, including First Nations, Inuit, and Métis, which especially targets women, evidenced notably by the *Indian Act*, the Sixties Scoop, residential schools, and breaches of human and Inuit, Métis, and First Nations rights, leading directly to the current increased rates of violence, death, and suicide in Indigenous populations.[74]

These abuses and violations have resulted in the denial of safety, security, and human dignity. They are the root causes of the violence against Indigenous women, girls, and 2SLGBTQQIA people that generate and maintain a world within which Indigenous women, girls, and 2SLGBTQQIA people are forced to confront violence on a daily basis, and where perpetrators act with impunity.[75]

While there were incremental shifts, such as through the amendments to the Indian Act in 1951, fundamental harms and forms of oppression carried on. Foremost amongst these were, of course, the residential schools that continued to operate in full force. The Canadian government's efforts to eradicate and assimilate Indigenous Peoples remained focused on taking control of the lives of Indigenous children, often with disastrous and violent impacts. There were more than 130 Indian residential schools in Canada. The first one opened in 1831, and the last one did not close its doors until 1996.

GERONIMO HENRY, MOHAWK, ATTENDED MOHAWK INSTITUTE, BRANTFORD, ONTARIO

They tried to convert me in there. They took away my ceremonies, my rituals and my language. They tried to assimilate us. They told us our religion and rituals were the devil's work. My father put me in there in 1942. He assumed it was a good place because I was going to get an education but they took away my language, my own spiritual beliefs, and my culture. Not for a minute would he have sent me there if he had known.[76]

BEV SELLARS, XATŚŪLL FIRST NATION, ATTENDED ST. JOSEPH'S MISSION INDIAN RESIDENTIAL SCHOOL, WILLIAMS LAKE, BRITISH COLUMBIA

I wasn't allowed to be a normal child . . . to grow and experience things and question things and whatever . . .

We couldn't say anything, we couldn't think for ourselves, we weren't allowed to think for ourselves and that was just awful . . . We were programmed to self-destruct, we weren't programmed to succeed . . .

Group of female students [7th from left is Josephine Gillis (nee Hamilton), 8th from left is Eleanor Halcrow (nee Ross) and a nun (Sister Antoine)] in a classroom at Cross Lake Indian Residential School, Cross Lake, Manitoba, 1940

They controlled us with fear and the strap. . . . We were so scared to do anything. For little kids, always being threatened with the strap, that has a traumatic effect on you. They treated us like we weren't human.[77]

The schools robbed us of our traditional ways of life, robbed us of the closeness that families should have, robbed us of the securities a child should have, robbed us of knowing our family members and robbed us of much of our adult lives trying to get over the destructive teachings of the schools.[78]

BERTHA FONTAINE, OJIBWE, ATTENDED FORT ALEXANDER RESIDENTIAL SCHOOL AND ASSINIBOIA RESIDENTIAL SCHOOL, MANITOBA

My daughter asked, "If there were 250 children in the school and only four supervisors, why didn't you rebel and take over the school?" I told her "They had so much control over us that people couldn't stop them if they tried." At Fort Alexander school, we were far from home, at least five miles (eight kilometers). When I was in high school in Winnipeg, we wrote letters to our family, but they never got mailed.[79]

They sewed the boys' pockets shut so they couldn't put their hands in their pockets. When my brother came home for the summer, he was amazed that he had pockets on his pants.[80]

EDMUND METATAWABIN, FORT ALBANY FIRST NATION, ATTENDED ST. ANNE'S INDIAN RESIDENTIAL SCHOOL, FORT ALBANY, ONTARIO

I looked out the little window and saw my dad walking by, head down, looking really sad. I hear, "Come out of there, that's enough,

Cree students at their desks with their teacher in a classroom, All Saints Indian Residential School, Lac La Ronge, Saskatchewan, 1945

your daddy's not here to protect you no more!" As soon as I opened the door, she grabbed my shoulder, gave me a vicious slap across the face from behind. And I hit the wall on the other side.[81]

ANGIE CRERAR, MÉTIS, ATTENDED FORT RESOLUTION INDIAN RESIDENTIAL SCHOOL, NORTHWEST TERRITORIES

We were ridiculed. We were punished for things we didn't do. We were called savage. I struggled, and struggled, and struggled, for many years to get back my Métis identity, to bring back my pride, to get my spirit going again, and make sure my children will never have to go through what I went through.[82]

JOHN JONES, NANOOSE FIRST NATION, ATTENDED ALBERNI INDIAN RESIDENTIAL SCHOOL, BRITISH COLUMBIA

The only important thing to a child is to play and be loved. That's what my life was like before residential school.

The physical abuse was every day . . . And being assaulted verbally—if I didn't do things the way that they wanted me to do, I was called a dirty, stupid Indian that would be good for nothing.[83]

LINA SCHOTT GALLUP, CREE/DENE, ATTENDED THE ST. BERNARD MISSION SCHOOL, GROUARD, ALBERTA

My two sisters and I were picked up by dog sled. The Northwest Mounted Police took us from Fort McKay to Fort McMurray (in Alberta), then by train to Edmonton. Before we took another train to Grouard, the nuns put us in a tub filled with hot water. We thought they were going to cook us! Our trip to school was 867 kilometres. We never went back home. We lost our language because we weren't allowed to speak it.[84]

FRANCES ROBINSON, OKANAGAN, ATTENDED ST. MARY'S INDIAN RESIDENTIAL SCHOOL, CRANBROOK, BRITISH COLUMBIA

When I arrived, the nuns took everything out of my luggage. One nun told me, "Don't even bother crying."[85]

RONALD E. IGNACE, SECWÉPEMC, ATTENDED THE KAMLOOPS INDIAN RESIDENTIAL SCHOOL, BRITISH COLUMBIA

I was in a state of shock or in awe about the school when I was first brought there. I gave out a type of scream that I had never given out in my life. I learned that there is a type of name for that kind of scream. It's called a primal scream. That is a cry a person gives, a cry of distress that comes from the centre of the soul.[86]

ROSEMARY PAUL, MI'KMAW, ATTENDED SHUBENACADIE INDIAN RESIDENTIAL SCHOOL, NOVA SCOTIA, REFLECTING ON POPE FRANCIS' S APOLOGY TO SURVIVORS

He never did nothing for me, except make me hate the Catholic Church . . . I was taught I had to say the rosary every day, every day go to church . . . and (it) never made no sense to me . . . I don't have faith in the Catholic Church at all, I'm sorry.

We never made it up . . . We all had our stories, some worse than others. I would just like the people to know what really happened there, and accept that wrongdoings that were done to us really happened. I am thankful I survived.[87]

DONALD TWIN, CREE, ATTENDED ST. BRUNO INDIAN RESIDENTIAL SCHOOL, JOUSSARD, ALBERTA

We were always called savages. Any traditional and cultural beliefs were belittled and said to be the work of the devil. Only by relating our residential school experiences can we begin to heal our wounds. Throughout all this, the residential school system could not break the spirit of our people.[88]

PHIL FONTAINE, OJIBWE, ATTENDED FORT ALEXANDER RESIDENTIAL SCHOOL, MANITOBA

In my grade three class, if there were 20 boys, every single one of them would have experienced what I experienced. They would have experienced some aspect of sexual abuse.[89]

ROBERT JOSEPH, KWAKWAKA'WAKW, ATTENDED ST. MICHAEL'S INDIAN RESIDENTIAL SCHOOL, ALERT BAY, BRITISH COLUMBIA

Early on in the healing movement, "spiritual" wasn't a driving word. Yet. But that's what the residential school issue is about—the destruction of our most inner sense of self.[90]

St. Michael's Indian Residential School, Alert Bay, c. 1987

EVELYN KORKMAZ, FORT ALBANY FIRST NATION, ATTENDED ST. ANNE'S INDIAN RESIDENTIAL SCHOOL, FORT ALBANY, ONTARIO

I didn't know what was going on at St Anne's . . . Even though I saw things when I was a kid, I didn't realize what I was seeing. For example, when we would line up for lunch or line up for class, one of the missionaries would come in, grab a kid by the arm, and take them out of the line. I just thought that they were misbehaving or talking in the lineup or whatever. Later, I found out that they were taken to a room where a priest would be sexually abusing them. As an adult, now I can see that very clearly, but as a kid, that's not the way you think.[91]

CHARLOTTE MARTEN, CREE/OJIBWE, ATTENDED POPLAR HILL DEVELOPMENT SCHOOL, RED LAKE, ONTARIO

I always remember walking into the place and all these toothbrushes are all lined up on the wall with the numbers. And I was told, this is gonna be your number, it's gonna be 63. They gave us the rules. We were not allowed to speak our language, and this is what's gonna happen if we do, and so forth.[92]

RAYMOND J. TUCCARO, CREE, ATTENDED BISHOP PICHÉ SCHOOL AS A DAY STUDENT, FORT CHIPEWYAN, ALBERTA

I'm the third generation affected by residential school. Three generations who could not show love or caring. I'm learning to show love now. If I don't, I will always be lonely.[93]

ROGER ELLIS, NORTHERN TUTCHONE, ATTENDED CARCROSS INDIAN RESIDENTIAL SCHOOL AND YUKON HALL, YUKON

All through my school years, I heard, "You're dumb. You're never going to amount to much." I heard this every day from the teachers. After 15 years at school, they told me to get out. I had to scramble to know where to go. I ended up an alcoholic, on the streets for 20 years. The drinking took my pain away. One day I woke up and realized, this is not me. I'm going to prove those guys wrong. I went back to school in my early forties, got a good education, had a career. I wanted to help my people and I do that in my work today. I'm married with four grandchildren. I've never been happier.[94]

MEDICAL INSPECTOR P.H. BRYCE, REPORTING ON FILE HILLS INDIAN RESIDENTIAL SCHOOL, BALCARRES, SASKATCHEWAN, 1922

Seventy-five per cent of the children at File Hills were dead at the end of the 16 years since the school opened.[95]

Children in class at the Roman Catholic-run Fort George Catholic Indian Residential School, Fort George, Quebec, 1939

SCHOOL INSPECTOR J.W. BREAKY, REPORTING TO MEDICAL DIRECTOR OF INDIAN AFFAIRS P.E. MOORE, 1953

Children at the Brandon Indian Industrial School are not being fed properly to the extent that they are garbaging around in the barns for food that should only be fed to the barn occupants.[96]

In addition to the imposition of the residential school system, there were other policies and actions that also caused irreparable harm and suffering for Indigenous children and families. The 1951 amendments to the Indian Act involved the provinces in on-reserve child welfare and protection. This has contributed to an enduring crisis of Indigenous children in care, disconnected from family, community, and culture. For example, while Indigenous children make up less than 8 percent of those under the age of fifteen in Canada, they are grossly overrepresented in the child protection system—more than 50 percent of children in foster care are Indigenous. At the same time, the amount of funding and support spent on caring for an Indigenous child has amounted to less than for children of other backgrounds—a matter that is now being addressed after relentless advocacy by many, including Dr. Cindy Blackstock.

The "Sixties Scoop" is the name given to a series of policies that saw the large-scale apprehension of Indigenous children for the purpose of putting them up for adoption to non-Indigenous families, often without consent. The harms and impacts of these policies and practices on Indigenous children and families have, in many instances, been catastrophic, and include cultural dislocation, loss of family connection, denial of adequate support systems, violence and abuse, and even death. For these reasons, the current child welfare systems across Canada are referred to by some as the new residential school system.

CHIEF MARCIA BROWN MARTEL, ON HOW THE SIXTIES SCOOP ROBBED HER OF HER CULTURAL IDENTITY

There is a sadness to me . . . There truly is a sadness to me, not to have been able to speak to my mother in her own language, to have great dialogue with her, not to be able to speak to my grandmother, who had such knowledge. Those are the regrets that I have.[97]

"NO QUIET PLACE," REPORT OF THE REVIEW COMMITTEE ON INDIAN AND MÉTIS ADOPTIONS AND PLACEMENTS, 1984

Cultural genocide has been taking place in a systematic, routine manner.[98]

ONTARIO ASSOCIATION OF CHILDREN'S AID SOCIETIES, ACKNOWLEDGING THE DAMAGE OF THE SIXTIES SCOOP IN ITS OFFICIAL APOLOGY, 2017

We acknowledge that we, as the Children's Aid Societies, were aware of, or should have been aware of, the damage and trauma created first by residential schools, then carried forward by our participation in the Sixties Scoop. . . . We saw the broken and devastated communities and were complacent in the belief that the fault was all yours. It was not. The actions we participated in clearly led you to this point.[99]

JANE PHILPOTT, MINISTER OF INDIGENOUS SERVICES, ON THE CRISIS IN INDIGENOUS CHILD WELFARE, 2019

We are facing a humanitarian crisis in this country where Indigenous children are vastly disproportionately over-represented in the child welfare system.[100]

CINDY BLACKSTOCK, ADVOCATE AND CHAMPION FOR INDIGENOUS CHILDREN, AND EXECUTIVE DIRECTOR OF FIRST NATIONS CHILD AND FAMILY CARING SOCIETY

Words don't change children's lives. Real action by the government and equality would.[101]

Cindy Blackstock, 2021

MARY TEEGEE, EXECUTIVE DIRECTOR OF CARRIER SEKANI FAMILY SERVICES, ON THE GOAL OF THE CHANGES BEING MADE TODAY

We're in a pivotal time where we can make fundamental change so not another generation of children will have to go into care, not another generation will have to be discriminated against.[102]

CANADIAN HUMAN RIGHTS TRIBUNAL ORDER, IN *FIRST NATIONS CHILD AND FAMILY CARING SOCIETY OF CANADA ET AL. V. ATTORNEY GENERAL OF CANADA*, 2019

[2] This Panel recognizes the shame and the pain and suffering experienced by children, families and communities who were deprived of this vital right to live in their families and communities as a result of colonization, racism and racial discrimination.

[3] This shame is not for you to bear, it is one for the entire Nation of Canada to bear, in the hope of rebuilding together and achieving reconciliation.[103]

<<<< >>>>

One of the realities of colonial systems is that their effects and impacts are everywhere. For those subject to colonial control, there is no sphere or facet of life that is left untouched. From the most private spaces (family relations) to the most public spaces (law and governance), there are forces of government oppression at work.

For this reason, it has been necessary to similarly bring the fight for justice to every sphere of life. One cannot address the legacy of colonialism by leaving it intact in one form or another, or in one space or another. It must be confronted in full. There should be no tolerance for the acceptance of some, or less, colonization, just as we cannot tolerate or accept the existence of some, or less, racism or misogyny. Yes, there are paths and steps that have to be taken to get to that full form of justice; the shift does not occur all at once or in a moment. But we must never confuse the taking of a mere step with the end goal, and we must always ensure that we do not get complacent through the advancement of half-measures.

To say it another way, colonialism is all-encompassing; as such, the response to it must be similarly comprehensive.

It effectively took more than a century after the formation of Canada for Indigenous Peoples to have the opportunity to begin to be thorough in their efforts to address the legacy of colonialism—to take their struggle for justice into all the necessary forums and spaces where it had to be present.

As we have seen, from the earliest days following Confederation, there was Indigenous grassroots advocacy for change, and efforts to appeal to Canada's elected leaders. But it was not until the 1960s that the courts, and the political system as a whole, could truly begin to be accessed by Indigenous Peoples as they pushed for change. And it would take even more years for the media, and public life and opinion generally, to gain the necessary awareness to become effectively engaged with the challenges faced by Indigenous Peoples.

Perhaps the greatest challenge on this journey to justice is the endurance and resilience that it requires. Thinking about this challenge evokes the lessons of the Wolf, and brings to mind all of the work that the Wolf does before reaching its goal and achieving success.

The way of the Wolf is also evident in another aspect of the shifts that occurred around the 1960s. A Wolf is part of a pack, and as such, the work of the Wolf does not happen alone or in isolation.

Ever since the arrival of Europeans, there have been some examples of friendship, allyship, and partnership between Indigenous and non-Indigenous people. There were non-Indigenous partners who were visible and public in their efforts, while others toiled in the shadows, alongside Indigenous people, to try to support progress.

But for much of Canada's history, these partnerships have been limited in scope and scale. This, too, is an effect of colonization's reach, and it kept generations of non-Indigenous Canadians largely ignorant of the reality and circumstances Indigenous people faced.

Over time, however, this has changed, and it continues to change today. More and more non-Indigenous peoples have become involved in the work of reconciliation, including seeking out learning and understanding that can help them take meaningful action.

As we move through the 1960s and toward more contemporary times in the history of Canada, we see evidence of these positive shifts in non-Indigenous people's awareness and actions. The struggle for justice is moving into the light, and into more spaces. In particular, we see this playing out in the courts, as well as in national political processes, including in discussions about the Constitution—which, of course, was shaped without the input of Indigenous people. Increasingly, there is an understanding by non-Indigenous Canadians of the issues Indigenous people face, and an understanding that they may have a role to play in addressing them. Increasingly, there are Canadians who look at the Totem Pole and see their own responsibility reflected back at them. They too have a role to play in the work of the Wolf. Achieving justice is everyone's calling, and no one's burden alone.

<<<< >>>>

In the 1960s, with the limitations on the hiring of lawyers removed from the Indian Act, Indigenous Peoples began to access the courts. One of the earliest Indigenous rights cases involved hunting, wherein two men, Clifford White and David Bob, were charged under the British Columbia Game Act with hunting deer out of season. In response to the charges, White and Bob claimed that a pre-Confederation treaty had been entered into in 1854 with James Douglas, the first governor of the Colony of Vancouver Island and the Hudson Bay Company's chief factor, which protected their right to hunt. The judge at their trial balked at their assertion. Indeed, Canada, British Columbia, and the entire justice system apparently had no knowledge or memory that a treaty—one of fourteen signed up and down Vancouver Island prior to Confederation—had ever been entered into. The British Columbia Court of Appeal, however, accepted that the treaty existed and that it protected the right to hunt. The Supreme Court of Canada agreed and affirmed the treaty and its protection of rights. The young lawyer who acted for White and Bob—Thomas Berger—would go on to be a lifelong advocate for the recognition of Indigenous rights, and decades of lawyers fighting alongside Indigenous people began.

CLIFFORD WHITE AND DAVID BOB, IN ANSWER TO THE CHARGE OF HUNTING OUT OF SEASON, 1963

The peace treaty signed years ago between the crown and the Indians, gives us the right to hunt and fish any time of the year.[104]

HIS WORSHIP MAGISTRATE L. BEEVOR-POTTS, EXPRESSING FRUSTRATION AT THE CLAIM THAT A TREATY EXISTED AND PROTECTED HUNTING RIGHTS

You have had ample opportunity, two and a half months, nearly three months to bring material cause forward in this matter. Nothing was done so Counsel retired from the case. We had no information whatsoever and I now hold, it is too late and I hold that the alleged Treaty as read by Mr. Elliot, does not apply to this case. You are both found guilty as charged. It is on the face, pure pigishness. You could have permits for a reasonable amount. You go out and get six deers.[105]

THOMAS BERGER, REFLECTING ON *WHITE AND BOB* AND THE BEGINNING OF THE ROLE OF LAWYERS IN ADVOCATING FOR INDIGENOUS RIGHTS

In the mid-1960s, I argued early cases dealing with Aboriginal rights, which led my career, unexpectedly, down a lengthy road . . .

I had a small walk-up law office. I practiced by myself and the rent was $120 a month. I had a secretary and my mother, Perle, acted as my bookkeeper. From that pocket-sized office, the land claims industry developed . . .

The case [*White and Bob*] did not sound like an important case. But it was to be the first shot fired by the Aboriginal peoples of Canada in their campaign to reclaim Aboriginal and treaty rights . . . Thus did I become a lifelong defender of Aboriginal causes.[106]

The Nisga'a brought their long-standing claims to the court under the leadership of Frank Calder, who would go on to become the first Indigenous person elected to a legislature in the Commonwealth, and the first to hold a Cabinet post. The 1973 Calder decision of the Supreme Court of Canada was the first time the court acknowledged the existence of Aboriginal title

Dr. Frank Calder, Ottawa, November 1999

at the time of the Royal Proclamation of 1763. The court was split three to three in its judgment on the issue of whether the Nisga'a's claims to hold title were valid.

As part of the response to the Calder decision, the federal government adopted the Comprehensive Claims Policy that stated the government's intention to settle rights claims of Indigenous Peoples, including those related to land. In 1982, the federal government also adopted the Specific Claims Policy, and in 1995 the recognition of the Inherent Right of Self-Government Policy. While some elements of these policies and the way they were described by governments and politicians made them sound attractive, they came with severe limitations and restrictions, including typically that they were not grounded in the recognition of the existence of Indigenous rights, governments, and laws. Though fiercely criticized by Indigenous Peoples for these and other reasons, these policies would remain the foundation of government negotiations regarding Indigenous land and governance issues for decades.

For some Indigenous peoples, settlements were reached. The first modern land claim agreement was completed with the James Bay Cree in 1975. But the pace of settling claims would remain glacially slow. The Nisga'a finally completed a treaty with the federal government and the Province of British Columbia in 2000. It took 113 years for the Nisga'a to settle their land claim.

DR. JOHN BORROWS, LEGAL SCHOLAR AND PROFESSOR, DESCRIBING THE IMPORTANCE OF THE CALDER DECISION

[The Calder case made it clear that] the Crown has legally binding obligations towards Aboriginal peoples in Canada.[107]

PRIME MINISTER PIERRE ELLIOTT TRUDEAU, IN REACTION TO THE CALDER DECISION AND INDIGENOUS CLAIMS

Perhaps you had more legal rights then we thought you did . . . but it will take us a decade to define what they are.[108]

JEAN CHRÉTIEN, MINISTER OF INDIAN AFFAIRS AND NORTHERN DEVELOPMENT, DESCRIBING THE ADOPTION OF THE COMPREHENSIVE CLAIMS POLICY

The present statement is concerned with claims and proposals for the settlement of long-standing grievances. These claims come from groups of Indian people who have not entered into Treaty relationship with the Crown. They find their basis in what is variously described as "Indian Title," "Aboriginal Title," "Original Title," "Native Title," or "Usufructuary Rights." In essence, these claims relate to the loss of traditional use and occupancy of lands in certain parts of Canada where Indian Title was never extinguished by treaty or superseded by law.

The Government has been fully aware that the claims are not only for money and land, but involve the loss of a way of life. Any settlement, therefore, must contribute positively to a lasting solution of cultural, social and economic problems that for too long have kept the Indian and Inuit people in a disadvantaged position within the larger Canadian society.

It is basic to the position of the Government that these claims must be settled and that the most promising avenue to settlement is through negotiation. It is envisaged that by this means agreements will be reached with groups of the Indian and Inuit people concerned and that these agreements will be enshrined in legislation, enacted by Parliament, so that they will have the finality and binding force of law.

The Government is now ready to negotiate with authorized representatives of these native peoples on the basis that where their traditional interest in the lands concerned can be established, an agreed form of compensation or benefit will be provided to native peoples in return for their interest. . . .

The Government views this claims policy in the context of other policies intended and designed to remove the sense of grievance and injustice which impedes the relationship of the Indian and

Inuit peoples with the governments concerned and with their fellow Canadians.[109]

CHIEF DR. BILLY DIAMOND, CREE NATION OF WASKAGANISH, ON THE JAMES BAY AND NORTHERN QUEBEC AGREEMENT

I was negotiating with Cree rights and Cree title that had been recognized by the courts, and it was my vision that these rights would never again be questioned or I never want to see another government official sit across the table from my children or grandchildren and state that they have no rights, but just privileges that can be taken away at any time. I wanted to succeed so that the Cree rights must be put into provincial legislation after the James Bay and Northern Quebec Agreement. Therefore, when the Agreement was signed in 1975 the Cree rights were also rights in the Agreement, and when the provincial and federal legislation came into force, then those Cree rights also became legislative rights.[110]

Billy Diamond, Grand Chief of the Grand Council of the Crees of Quebec, Ottawa, December 1976

JOE CLARK, LEADER OF THE OPPOSITION IN THE HOUSE OF COMMONS, ON THE PASSAGE OF THE JAMES BAY AND NORTHERN QUEBEC AGREEMENT IMPLEMENTATION LEGISLATION, 1976

The Crees were hauled down to Montreal and forced to deal, being people accustomed to a very different way of life, with the accumulated might of Crown corporations, the government of Quebec and other agencies.

[I]t was clear from the outset, certainly to them, that if they did not come to an agreement . . . a settlement would be imposed on them . . . The native people were negotiating under the gun of a deadline to which they had to adhere. If they did not adhere, they and their people would suffer serious consequences. . . .

[T]hey were forced to negotiate under the gun of extraordinary conditions, conditions to which people of a different kind of background would probably not have been subjected . . . [for example] conditions which denied in advance their right to invoke social impact factors of proposed future hydroelectric projects. . . .

It is very clear that as hard as the Grand Council of the Crees worked throughout this, it is highly likely that the agreement we are dealing with today would have been very different if the native people involved were not forced to meet deadlines of the sort imposed on them under the threat of imposition of conditions.[111]

GRAND CHIEF MATTHEW COON COME, SUBMISSION TO THE ROYAL COMMISSION ON ABORIGINAL AFFAIRS, 1993

We negotiated the James Bay and Northern Quebec Agreement because we did not have a choice.[112]

CHIEF DR. BILLY DIAMOND, CREE NATION OF WASKAGANISH, DESCRIBING NEGOTIATING THE JAMES BAY AND NORTHERN QUEBEC AGREEMENT

History was being made and history does not necessarily pick you, but you pick the time and place to change history. You can change history with boldness and fortitude if you know where you want to go and what you want to achieve. When I look back now there was a time when we couldn't use some terminology such as Aboriginal, First Nation, Cree Nation, Nation building, but over time these words became synonymous with the Land Claims policy.[113]

FRANK CALDER, DESCRIBING THE NISGA'A TREATY

Under the [Nisga'a] Treaty, we will no longer be wards of the state. We will no longer be beggars in our own lands. We will own our own lands, which now far exceed the postage stamp reserves that were begrudgingly set aside for us by colonial governments. We will once again govern ourselves by our institutions, in the context of Canadian law. We will be allowed to make our own mistakes, to savour our own victories, to stand on our own feet.[114]

The government's perpetual focus on studies regarding the conditions of Indigenous Peoples, and the seeking of new policies, would continue. Some earlier reports after the Second World War, such as the Hawthorn–Tremblay Report[115]—which looked at the contemporary situation of the Indians of Canada with a view to understanding the difficulties they faced in overcoming some pressing problems—introduced the idea of Indigenous Peoples being "citizens plus," in the face of continuing and growing Indigenous advocacy for recognition of their rights and self-government. The report stated, "Indians should be regarded as 'citizens plus'; in addition to the normal rights and duties of citizenship, Indians possess certain additional rights as charter members of the Canadian community."[116]

In 1969, Prime Minister Pierre Elliott Trudeau took a different approach, issuing the "White Paper," which called for an end to Indian status. The White Paper created an immediate and harsh backlash and deepened the bitter and ongoing legacy of intense suspicion and questioning of the federal government's true policy agenda.

STATEMENT OF THE GOVERNMENT OF CANADA ON INDIAN POLICY (THE WHITE PAPER)

The policies proposed recognize the simple reality that the separate legal status of Indians and the policies which have flowed from it have kept the Indian people apart from and behind other Canadians. The Indian people have not been full citizens of the communities and provinces in which they live and have not enjoyed the equality and benefits that such participation offers.

[A] separate road cannot lead to full participation, to equality in practice as well as theory. . . . [T]he Government has outlined a number of measures and a policy which it is convinced will offer another road for Indians, a road that would lead gradually away from different status to full social, economic and political participation in Canadian life. This is the choice. Indian people must be persuaded, must persuade themselves, that this path will lead them to a fuller and richer life.[117]

PRIME MINISTER PIERRE ELLIOTT TRUDEAU, DESCRIBING THE WHITE PAPER

We have set the Indians apart as a race. We've set them apart in our laws. We've set them apart in the ways the governments will deal with them. They're not citizens of the province as the rest of us are. They are wards of the federal government. They get their services from the federal government rather than from the provincial or municipal governments. They have been set apart in law. They have been set apart in the relations with government and they've been set apart socially too . . .

We can go on treating the Indians as having a special status. We can go on adding bricks of discrimination around the ghetto in which they live and at the same time perhaps helping them preserve certain cultural traits and certain ancestral rights. Or we can say you're at a crossroads—the time is now to decide whether the Indians will be a race apart in Canada or whether [they] will be Canadians of full status.

. . . well one of the things the Indian bands often refer to are their aboriginal rights and in our policy, the way we propose it, we say we won't recognize aboriginal rights. We will recognize treaty rights. We will recognize forms of contract which have been made with the Indian people by the Crown and we will try to bring justice in that area and this will mean that perhaps the treaties shouldn't go on forever. It's inconceivable, I think, that in a given society one section of the society to have a treaty with the other section of the society. We must be all equal under the law and we must not sign treaties among ourselves and many of these treaties, indeed, would have less and less significance in the future anyhow but things that in the past were covered by the treaties like things like [*sic*] so much twine or so much gun powder and which haven't

Prime Minister Pierre Trudeau and his cabinet with a delegation of about 200 Indigenous leaders at Parliament Hill, Ottawa, June 4, 1970

been paid this must be paid. But I don't think that we should encourage Indians to feel these treaties should last forever within Canada so that they be able to receive their twine or their gun powder. They should become Canadians as all other Canadians.[118]

JEAN CHRÉTIEN, MINISTER OF INDIAN AFFAIRS AND NORTHERN DEVELOPMENT, IN THE STATEMENT OF THE GOVERNMENT OF CANADA ON INDIAN POLICY (THE WHITE PAPER)

Indian relations with other Canadians began with special treatment by government and society, and special treatment has been the rule since Europeans first settled in Canada. Special treatment has made the Indians a community disadvantaged and apart.

Obviously, the course of history must be changed.[119]

EXCHANGE BETWEEN "GRANDMOTHER FROM SIX NATIONS RESERVE" AND JEAN CHRÉTIEN

[Grandmother] When did we lose our identity?
[Jean Chrétien] When you signed the treaties.
[Grandmother] How can you come here and ask us to become citizens when we were here long before you?[120]

HAROLD CARDINAL, CREE WRITER AND LEADER, IN RESPONSE TO THE WHITE PAPER

[The White paper is] a thinly disguised programme of extermination through assimilation.

In spite of all government attempts to convince Indians to accept the white paper, their efforts will fail, because Indians understand that the path outlined by the Department of Indian Affairs through its mouthpiece, the Honourable Mr. Chrétien, leads directly to cultural genocide. We will not walk this path.[121]

We do not want the Indian Act retained because it is a good piece of legislation. It isn't. It is discriminatory from start to finish. But it is a lever in our hands and an embarrassment to the government, as it should be. No just society and no society with even pretensions to being just can long tolerate such a piece of legislation, but we would rather continue to live in bondage under the inequitable Indian Act than surrender our sacred rights.[122]

PRIME MINISTER PIERRE ELLIOTT TRUDEAU, IN RESPONSE TO CRITICISMS OF THE WHITE PAPER

We'll keep them in the ghetto as long as they want.[123]

GEORGE MANUEL, FIRST PRESIDENT OF THE WORLD COUNCIL OF INDIGENOUS PEOPLES, ON AGENDA INDIGENOUS PEOPLES SHOULD FOLLOW

Organize and unify around a clear set of objectives. Battle against all the forces of assimilation and try to build your nations economically, culturally and politically. Consult the people, politicize the people and never get too far ahead of them, because when all is said and done, they are your masters.[124]

The 1960s saw the emergence of new national Indigenous political organizations—and for many of them the White Paper became a rallying cry. While there had been efforts to establish such organizations as far back as 1919, and various initiatives in this direction over the years, it was in 1961 that the National Indian Council (NIC) was formed. In 1968, the NIC split into the National Indian Brotherhood and the Canadian Métis Society. In 1971, the Inuit Tapirisat of Canada (ITC) created a united advocacy voice for Inuit.

The National Indian Brotherhood became the Assembly of First Nations in 1982. The Métis National Council was formed in 1993. The ITC changed its name to "Inuit Tapiriit Kanatami" in 2001. The Congress of Aboriginal Peoples, representing urban and non-status Indians, was formed in 1993.

All of these organizations continue today as national political advocacy bodies for Indigenous Peoples.

CHARTER OF THE ASSEMBLY OF FIRST NATIONS

SO, WE HAVE RESOLVED TO CONFINE OUR EFFORTS TO ACCOMPLISH COMMON AIMS.

ACCORDINGLY, our respective Governments, through their Chiefs assembled in the City of Penticton in 1982, agreed to establish a national organization known as the Assembly of First Nations (AFN) and now agree in the City of Vancouver in 1985 to the Charter of the Assembly of First Nations.[125]

INUIT TAPIRIIT KANATAMI, DESCRIBING THEIR FOUNDING

Inuit Tapiriit Kanatami, formerly the Inuit Tapirisat of Canada, was founded at a meeting in Toronto in February 1971 by seven Inuit community leaders. The impetus to form a national Inuit organization evolved from shared concern among Inuit leaders about the status of land and resource ownership in Inuit Nunangat. Industrial encroachment into Inuit Nunangat from projects such as the then proposed Mackenzie Valley pipeline in the Northwest Territories and the James Bay Project in Northern Québec, spurred community leaders to action.

They agreed that forming a national Inuit organization was necessary to voice their concerns about these and related issues, choosing the name Inuit Tapirisat of Canada ("Inuit will be united") for the new organization. The first ITC conference was held in Ottawa later that year.[126]

MÉTIS NATIONAL COUNCIL, DESCRIBING THEIR HISTORY

Since 1983, the MNC has represented the Métis Nation nationally and internationally. It receives its mandate and direction from the democratically elected leadership of Métis governments in

Ontario, Saskatchewan, Alberta, and British Columbia, the MNC Governing Members. Specifically, the MNC reflects and moves forward on the desires and aspirations of these Métis governments at the national and international levels.[127]

Conflicts over resource development also continued to intensify in various parts of the country. This was seen in action on the ground by Indigenous Peoples to oppose particular projects; in an increasing use of the courts to challenge certain use of lands and resources; as well as in the growth of political action and advocacy. These conflicts included struggles over mining, hydroelectric dams, pipeline development, and forestry, among others. Underlying all were the unresolved issues of Indigenous land rights and broken treaty promises.

The increasing focus on the North proceeded unabated into the 1970s as resource development continued to grow, including proposals for a natural gas pipeline in the Mackenzie Valley. To examine these proposals, the federal government launched a commission of inquiry chaired by politician and jurist Thomas Berger. The Berger Commission assessed the impacts of the potential pipelines. A tragedy underlined the importance of the inquiry—two days after testifying, Nelson Small Legs Jr. committed suicide, leaving a note that condemned the treatment of Indigenous Peoples. Berger would end up recommending a ten-year ban on any pipeline development until land claims were settled. The federal government accepted the recommendation.

DENE CHIEF FRANK T'SELEIE TO THE BERGER COMMISSION, DESCRIBING OPPOSITION TO PIPELINE DEVELOPMENT, 1974

You are coming to destroy a people that have a history of thirty thousand years. Why? For twenty years of gas? Are you really that insane? The original General Custer was exactly that insane. You still have a chance to learn. A chance to be remembered by history as something other than a fool bent on destroying everything he

Dene Chief Frank T'selei, Fort Good Hope, 1974

touched. You still have a chance, you have a choice. Are you a strong enough man to really exercise your freedom and make that choice. You can destroy my nation, Mr. Blair [a prominent Calgary oilman whose company had applied for pipeline rights as a part of a consortium, who attended the hearings], or you could be a great help to give us our freedom. Which choice do you make, Mr. Blair? Which choice do you make for your children and mine?

It seems to me that the whole point in living is to become as human as possible. To learn to understand the world and to live in it. To be part of it. To learn to understand the animals, for they are our brothers and they have much to teach us. We are a part of this world. We are like the river that flows and changes, yet is always the same. The river cannot flow too slow and it cannot flow too fast. It is a river and it will always be a river, for that is what it was meant to be.

We are like the river, but we are not the river. We are human. That is what we were meant to be. We were not meant to be destroyed and we were not meant to take over other parts of the world. We were meant to be ourselves. To be what it is our nature to be.

Our Dene Nation is like this great river. It has been flowing before any of us can remember. We take our strength and our wisdom and our ways from the flow and direction that has been established for us by ancestors we never knew, ancestors of a thousand years ago. Their wisdom flows through us to our children and our grandchildren to generations we will never know. We will live out our lives as we must and we will die in peace because we will know that our people and this river will flow on after us.

We know that our grandchildren will speak a language that is their heritage, that has been passed on from before time. We know they will share their wealth and not hoard it, or keep it to themselves. We know they will look after their old people and respect them for their wisdom.

We know they will look after this land and protect it and that five hundred years from now someone with skin my colour and moccasins on his feet will climb up the Ramparts and rest and look over the river and feel that he too has a place in the universe, and he will thank the same spirits that I thank, that his ancestors have looked after his land well and he will be proud to be a Dene.

It is for this unborn child, Mr. Berger, that my nation will stop the pipeline. It is so that this unborn child can know the freedom of this land that I am willing to lay down my life.[128]

GEORGES ERASMUS, DENE NATION LEADER, DESCRIBING TESTIMONY AT THE BERGER COMMISSION

We were simply stating the same position that our people have always had. Our people have never given up the right to govern themselves. Our people have never given up the right to this land.[129]

THOMAS BERGER, DESCRIBING THE COMMISSION FINDINGS

It is my conviction that the social impact on the native people will be devastating. I think the economic benefits, to northerners generally, will be limited.[130]

The North is a frontier, but it is a homeland too. . . . And it is a heritage, a unique environment that we are called upon to preserve for all Canadians. . . .

The decisions we have to make are not, therefore, simply about northern pipelines. They are decisions about the protection of the northern environment and the future of northern peoples.[131]

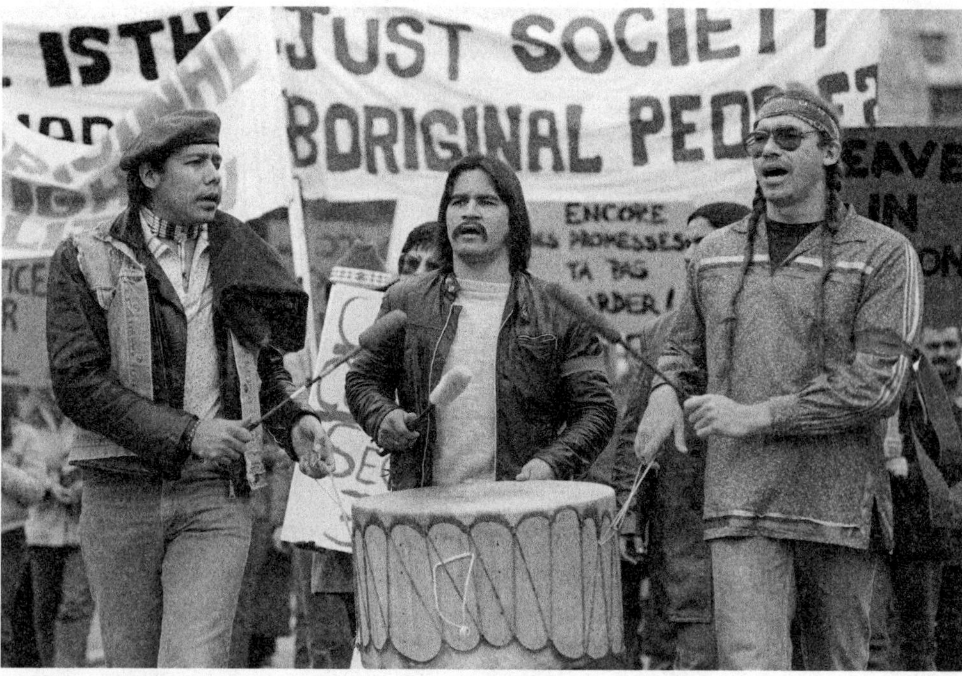

Indigenous people march on Parliament Hill, Ottawa, November 16, 1981

Since the 1920s, there had been dialogue and debate about repatriating and amending the Constitution. This focus intensified in the late 1970s, leading to formal efforts in this regard by the Trudeau government in the early 1980s. Major issues being considered were the potential inclusion of a charter of individual rights and freedoms, and the ongoing threat of Quebec separation. There were a range of reactions from Indigenous people regarding this development. Some had fears about severing ties with Great Britain and what constitutional repatriation would mean for treaties signed with the Crown, as well as other rights. These concerns increased in 1980 when Indigenous leaders learned that the proposed constitutional amendments would not include a reference to Indigenous Peoples or protection of their treaties, title, and rights. A legal case was brought forward by Indigenous Peoples of Alberta, New Brunswick, and Nova Scotia seeking responsibility to be left with the British Crown. Direct action was also taken by Indigenous Peoples, including what was called the "Constitution Express"—a movement organized in 1980 and 1981 to protest the lack of recognition of Aboriginal rights in the proposed patriation of the Canadian Constitution.

ACTIVISTS ERIC ROBINSON AND HENRY BIRD QUINNEY, DESCRIBING HOW CONSTITUTIONAL REFORM THREATENS SELF-DETERMINATION AND SELF-GOVERNMENT

During early colonialism, infested blankets were used to wipe out entire Tribes and Nations of the Original Peoples of this land now called Canada. . . . Today in a 1980's [*sic*] style of colonialism, Canada is trying to blanket the First Nations with the 1982 Canada Act. It is infested with colonialism and the death of Indian Nationhood. Today, Indian Nations must not trade off our Sovereign Nationhood for this modern form of genocide.[132]

George Manuel, 1970

UNION OF BRITISH COLUMBIA INDIAN CHIEFS (UBCIC), DESCRIBING THE POSITION OF THE CHIEFS OF BRITISH COLUMBIA ON CONSTITUTIONAL REFORM

[T]he convention gives full mandate to the UBCIC to take the necessary steps to ensure that Indian Governments, Indian Lands, Aboriginal Rights and Treaty Rights are entrenched in the Canadian Constitution.[133]

GEORGE MANUEL, PRESIDENT OF THE UNION OF BRITISH COLUMBIA INDIAN CHIEFS, DESCRIBING CONCERNS WITH CONSTITUTIONAL REFORM

I would rather pass onto my grandchildren the legitimacy of the struggle than to leave them with a settlement they can't live with.[134]

The Constitution was repatriated in 1982 and included provisions—section 35—regarding the collective rights of Indigenous Peoples.

CONSTITUTION ACT, 1982

35 (1) The existing aboriginal and treaty rights of the aboriginal peoples of Canada are hereby recognized and affirmed.

(2) In this Act, "aboriginal peoples of Canada" includes the Indian, Inuit and Métis peoples of Canada.[135]

It was unclear what the protections of Indigenous rights in section 35(1) meant. There was a promise to hold constitutional conferences to address the matter. Four conferences did occur—in 1983, 1984, 1985, and 1987—and while some amendments were made to the Constitution in 1983, regarding modern land claims agreements and gender equality, the conferences failed to address the core issues about the protection of Indigenous rights, including the right of self-government. The inaction led directly to a further intensification of Indigenous Peoples turning to the courts for answers. In court, and effectively in law, policy, and practice, the federal and provincial governments adopted a position that section 35(1) meant very little; those Indigenous rights had been largely extinguished or surrendered. In the years ahead, the courts clearly and consistently, in decision after decision, disagreed with the Crown, and affirmed that Indigenous rights are real, meaningful, and must be upheld.

BILL WILSON, FIRST NATIONS LEADER AND VICE-PRESIDENT OF THE NATIVE COUNCIL OF CANADA, ON THE CONSTITUTIONAL CONFERENCES

The constitution of the country was finally patriated and the native Indian people held out a great deal of hope that this patriation would once again restore them to the position they had enjoyed before contact. These conferences that were held unfortunately reduced themselves to little more than dancing around the table.[136]

EXCHANGE BETWEEN CHIEF JAMES GOSNELL (NISGA'A) AND PRIME MINISTER PIERRE ELLIOTT TRUDEAU AT THE FEDERAL-PROVINCIAL CONFERENCE OF FIRST MINISTERS ON ABORIGINAL CONSTITUTIONAL MATTERS, 1983

[Gosnell:] It has always been our belief, Mr. Chairman, that when God created this whole world he gave pieces of land to all races of people throughout this world, the Chinese people, Germans and you name them, including Indians, so at one time our land was this whole continent right from the tip of South America to the North Pole. . . . It has always been our belief that God gave us the land . . . and we say that no one can take our title away except He who gave it to us to begin with.

. . .

[Trudeau:] Going back to the Creator doesn't really help very much. So He gave you title, but you know, did He draw on the land where your mountains stopped and somebody else's began . . . ? God never said that the frontier of France runs along the Rhine or somewhere west of Alsace-Lorraine where the German-speaking people of France live. . . . I don't know any part of the world where history isn't constantly rewritten by migrations and immigrants and fights between countries changing frontiers and I don't think you can expect North America or the whole of the Western Hemisphere to settle things differently than they have been settled everywhere else, hopefully peacefully here.

. . .

[Trudeau:] [Y]ou have to sit down and discuss with someone what that [Aboriginal] title is.

[Gosnell:] [W]e are the true owners of the land, lock, stock and barrel.[137]

BILL WILSON, ADDRESSING PRIME MINISTER PIERRE ELLIOTT TRUDEAU AT THE FEDERAL-PROVINCIAL CONFERENCE OF FIRST MINISTERS ON ABORIGINAL CONSTITUTIONAL MATTERS, 1983

Mr. Chairman . . . we must stop viewing it [Aboriginal title and rights] from the point of view of the dominant society if we are ever going to understand what the Indian people, the Inuit people and the Metis people want.

. . .

You, Mr. Chairman, and your people, have been involved in nation-building for some 115 or some 116 years. My people from the coast of British Columbia have been involved in nation-building for 30,000 years on the same piece of land. If it takes us another 30,000 years to make this the kind of nation that is suitable for our people, we commit ourselves to that task, as I am sure that you in your desire to bring the constitution home to our country have committed yourself to the task to make sure our rights are protected and the people's rights in Canada are protected.

I think one of the things the public should understand, and you, sir, should certainly understand, is that despite efforts intended or otherwise to divide and conquer us, even in these discussions, that we stand here united with the other people at the table representing Metis, Inuit and Indian groups because it is our belief that no group individually can exercise rights unless all people have those same rights.

We know that it would be very easy for governments, as they have sometimes in the past, to play off individual groups against each other by giving certain people benefits. We have no desire to become involved in that kind of process.

. . .

I want to talk to you, Mr. Chairman, about what I believe to be the essence of nation building and it is very simple. It is as simple as making sure that you have mutual respect and dignity for all

B.C. Chief Bill Wilson at 1983 Constitutional conference

1983 Constitutional conference

of the people that you talk to and deal with. The unfortunate reality is that mutual respect and dignity becomes clouded with considerations of power and who exercises it and perhaps in your discussions about openness and frankness that is one thing that we should be open and frank about. I know that there are people here at this table who are more concerned with protecting the power they have, the jurisdictions they have, than making sure that the laws of Indian, Inuit and Metis people across this country is improved. . . .

We have the ten Premiers and yourself, the Prime Minister of this country. We have leaders from the two territories as well as the leaders of the native Indian, Inuit and Metis communities across the country and we have thousands of years of history. You have some 200 years of history on our land and we have allowed ourselves, unfortunately, to see that 200-year history erased to a large extent. What the Great Spirit put here in this country for us to exercise, our right to our own languages, our own cultures, our own traditions, our own religions, our own relationship to the land and our own way of doing things and we must make the commitment as you have said to restoring that, not only in economic terms, because dollars are not going to solve this problem. A change in attitude among all Canadians must solve this problem and if that change in attitude can begin here at this table and filter out across the country, perhaps then we won't have the problems that we have in this country somewhere down the road. The native Indian, Metis and Inuit people of this great land provided the land and the resources that allowed you people to develop. It all belonged to us and we shared it.[138]

JOHN AMAGOALIK, INUIT LEADER, AT THE FIRST MINISTERS' CONFERENCE ON ABORIGINAL CONSTITUTIONAL MATTERS, 1987

The theme of this Conference is the completing of the circle of Confederation. This nation is incomplete, this nation is not whole. It is our duty to complete the circle of Confederation.

I love this nation for two main reasons. First, because I have seen others, because I have studied others, and I love this nation. The people of this country are tolerant and generous people. It is unfortunate that this is not always interpreted into the policy of governments.

Secondly, I love this nation because one third of it is the Inuit homeland. I ask you to dig deep into your hearts and find the courage to do the right thing.

As the Prime Minster [Brian Mulroney] has said, it is time to move on to a new plateau. It is time to write a new chapter in Canada's history. When we have done this we will have changed the fundamental fabric of this nation, and the nation will be the better for it.[139]

JIM SINCLAIR, MÉTIS NATIONAL COUNCIL, AT THE CONCLUSION OF THE FIRST MINISTERS' CONFERENCE ON ABORIGINAL CONSTITUTIONAL MATTERS, 1987

We came to set a foundation for the liberation and justice for our people. That is the purpose of coming to this conference. We are not disappointed because we have lost. We are not disappointed in the stand that we took—the right to land, the right to self-government, and the right to self-determination. Those causes are right in any society.

I am disappointed that some of the Premiers who made a stand, and I have to say they made a stand against us, for reason that I consider were invalid.

Premier Vander Zalm [British Columbia], you pointed out to us

President Jim Sinclair at 1987 Constitutional conference

that you came from Holland in 1949. You said that you met Indian and native troops from Canada who went into your country and died for your country and for your people. We have them buried all over Europe and Asia. They went out to die for this country even though they were not even recognized when they stepped off the train to come home to this country.

It is a shame, that, when you can come here and in a few years become the premier of one of the largest provinces in Canada, you will not recognize the rights of our people here in this country of their origin.

. . .

We have struggled hard to make a deal. We have kept our end of the bargain . . . . One thing I want to say, as we leave this meeting: I am glad that we stuck together on a right that is truly right for our people, right for all of Canada, and right within international law throughout the world. . . . We have the right to self-government, to self-determination and land. . . . This is not an end. It is only the beginning. . . . Do not worry, Mr. Prime Minister and Premiers of the provinces . . . our people will be back.[140]

The primary focus of constitutional debates was Aboriginal self-government. In 1983, the Report of the House of Commons Special Committee on Indian Self-Government, also known as the Penner Report, recommended that First Nations be recognized as a constitutionally protected distinct order of government within Canada. Despite some statements that seemed to endorse Aboriginal self-government, the Constitutional Conferences would not succeed in achieving any constitutional amendments about self-government. In the decades since, Indigenous Peoples continue to advocate for principled and proper laws, policies, and practices that uphold self-government, while trying to negotiate and complete self-government arrangements. Currently, twenty-nine Indigenous groups have completed self-government agreements with Canada, while work to change laws, policies, and practices continues.

PENNER REPORT ON INDIAN SELF-GOVERNMENT, 1983

While the committee has concluded that the surest way to lasting change is through constitutional amendments, it encourages both the federal government and Indian First Nations to pursue all processes leading to the implementation of self-government, including the bilateral process.[141]

PRIME MINISTER PIERRE ELLIOTT TRUDEAU, OPENING REMARKS AT THE FEDERAL-PROVINCIAL CONFERENCE OF FIRST MINISTERS ON ABORIGINAL CONSTITUTIONAL MATTERS, 1984

There is nothing revolutionary or threatening about the prospect of aboriginal self-government. Aboriginal communities have rightful aspirations to have more say in the management of their affairs, to exercise more responsibility for discussions affecting them. . . . The Government of Canada remains committed to the establishment of aboriginal self-government and it is my impression that the provinces are very much of the same mind. And so, we are not here to consider whether there should be institutions of self-government, but how these institutions should be brought into being; what should be their jurisdictions, their powers; how they should fit into the interlocking system of jurisdictions by which Canada is governed.[142]

PRIME MINISTER BRIAN MULRONEY, OPENING REMARKS AT FIRST MINISTERS' CONFERENCE ON THE ABORIGINAL CONSTITUTIONAL MATTERS, 1985

The Canada we are building for the twenty-first century must have room for self-governing aboriginal peoples. Where our ongoing arrangements have failed to leave room for aboriginal peoples to control their own affairs, we must find room. Canada is big enough for us all. We need to rethink our understanding of Canada, so that the aboriginal peoples too will have their own space in our own time.

. . .

In Canada, we assume that we can participate in the charting of our destinies, in determining how we are represented, in holding our representatives accountable. But the Indian, Inuit, and Metis peoples do not feel they have the same degree of participation.

In Canada, we assume that our cultural and linguistic backgrounds and traditions will be respected, even cherished and enhanced. But Indian, Inuit, and Metis peoples do not have this assurance, or the power to determine their own cultural development. In fact, there were times when aspects of their cultures were subject to legal sanctions and suppression.

The key to change is self-government for aboriginal peoples within Canadian federation. We are a cautious people and self-government is a term which is worrisome to some of us. But self-government is not something that I fear. It is not an end in itself, but rather a means to reach common goals. It is the vehicle, not the destination. The challenge and satisfaction is in the journey itself.

. . .

As a Canadian and as a prime minister, I fully recognize and agree with the emphasis that the aboriginal peoples place on having their special rights inserted into the highest law of the land, protected from arbitrary legislative action. Constitutional protection for the principle of self-government is an overriding objective because it is the constitutional manifestation of a relationship, an unbreakable social contract between aboriginal peoples and their governments.[143]

CHIEF STAN DIXON, SHÍSHÁLH NATION, ABOUT WHY SHÍSHÁLH NEGOTIATED CANADA'S FIRST SELF-GOVERNMENT AGREEMENT, 1986

The Indian Act is like a prison, with four walls around you, and with a warden and guards.[144]

REPORT OF THE ROYAL COMMISSION ON ABORIGINAL PEOPLES, ON THE INHERENT RIGHT OF SELF-GOVERNMENT, 1996

This authority is not something bestowed by other governments. It is inherent in their identity as peoples. But to be fully effective, their authority must be recognized by other governments.[145]

Efforts continued to confirm the scope and nature of Indigenous rights, including self-government, protected in Canada's Constitution. The Meech Lake Accord, proposed in 1987, was the result of a political process to amend the Constitution that, amongst other things, would have recognized Quebec as a distinct society and enhanced the powers of the provinces. Indigenous Peoples were not formally involved in its negotiation,

"[T]his wonderful country is at a crucial, and very fragile, juncture in its history. . . . [A]ny process of change or reform in Canada—whether constitutional, economic or social—should not proceed, and cannot succeed, without aboriginal issues being an important part of the agenda."

—The Right Honourable Brian Dickson, Report of the Special Representative respecting the Royal Commission on Aboriginal Peoples (1991) *and critical issues, such as the inherent right of self-government, were not addressed. As it happened, Elijah Harper, a First Nations' member of the Legislative Assembly of Manitoba, was a central force in the defeat of the Meech Lake Accord in 1990.*

ELIJAH HARPER, DESCRIBING HIS OPPOSITION TO THE MEECH LAKE ACCORD

Well I was opposed to the Meech Lake Accord because we weren't included in the Constitution. We were to recognize Quebec as a distinct society, whereas we as Aboriginal people were completely left out. We were the First Peoples here—First Nations of Canada—we were the ones that made treaties with the settlers that came from Europe. These settler people and their governments didn't recognize us as a Nation, as a government and that is why we opposed the Meech Lake Accord.

Elijah Harper

We need to let Canadians know . . . that we have been shoved aside. We're saying that Aboriginal issues . . . should be put on the priority list. We want to be a part of the Canadian society . . . and to contribute toward . . . the development of this Country.[146]

PRIME MINISTER BRIAN MULRONEY, IN REFERENCE TO ELIJAH HARPER'S OPPOSITION

Aboriginals are not to blame for Meech Lake's failure despite Elijah Harper's stupidity. . . . He turned down a sweetheart deal.[147]

LOUIS "SMOKEY" BRUYERE, PRESIDENT OF THE NATIVE COUNCIL OF CANADA, DESCRIBING ATTITUDES TO THE MEECH LAKE ACCORD

Aboriginal peoples' view on the [Meech Lake] Accord can be summarized in four words: It abandons aboriginal peoples. It does this by being silent about the uniqueness and distinctiveness of aboriginal peoples.[148]

PHIL FONTAINE, OJIBWE AND GRAND CHIEF OF THE ASSEMBLY OF MANITOBA CHIEFS, DESCRIBING THE STOPPING OF THE MEECH LAKE ACCORD

[Meech Lake] was a turning point in history for indigenous people. . . . We came to the realization very quickly that our voice mattered. We could make history, we could change the course of history. We knew and understood what was possible.[149]

The 1992 Charlottetown Accord was the result of another political process to amend the Constitution that again would have recognized Quebec as a distinct society, decentralized certain powers from the federal government to the provinces, and, this time, would have included provisions recognizing Indigenous self-government. In 1992, the accord was rejected by Canadians in a referendum.

CHARLOTTETOWN ACCORD, FINAL TEXT

2\. (1) The Constitution of Canada, including the Canadian Charter of Rights and Freedoms, shall be interpreted in a manner consistent with the following characteristics:

. . .

(b) the Aboriginal peoples of Canada, being the first peoples to govern this land, have the right to promote their languages, cultures and traditions and to ensure the integrity of their societies, and their governments constitute one of the three orders of government in Canada

. . .

41\. The Inherent Right of Self-Government

The Constitution should be amended to recognize that the Aboriginal peoples of Canada have the inherent right of self-government within Canada. This right should be placed in a new section of the Constitution Act, 1982, section 35.1(1).

The recognition of the inherent right of self-government should be interpreted in light of the recognition of Aboriginal governments as one of three orders of government in Canada.

A contextual statement should be inserted in the Constitution, as follows:

The exercise of the right of self-government includes authority of the duly constituted legislative bodies of the Aboriginal peoples, each within its own jurisdiction:

(a) to safeguard and develop their languages, cultures, economies, identities, institutions and traditions; and,

(b) to develop, maintain and strengthen their relationship with their lands, waters and environment so as to determine and control their developments as peoples according to their own values and priorities and ensure the integrity of their societies.

Before making any final determination of an issue arising from the inherent right of self-government, a court or tribunal should take into account the contextual statement referred to above, should enquire into the efforts that have been made to resolve the issue through negotiations and should be empowered to order the parties to take such steps as are appropriate in the circumstances to effect a negotiated resolution.

. . .

60. Aboriginal Consent

There should be Aboriginal consent to future constitutional amendments that directly refer to the Aboriginal peoples. Discussions are continuing on the mechanism by which this consent would be expressed with a view to agreeing on a mechanism prior to the introduction in Parliament of formal resolutions amending the Constitution.[150]

With constitutional issues still at the forefront, in the summer of 1990 the so-called Oka Crisis took place between the Mohawk People of Kanesatake and the town of Oka, northwest of Montreal. The seventy-day conflict was triggered by the proposed expansion of a golf course onto Mohawk lands, which a court had allowed to proceed. Some members of the Mohawks erected a barricade, and eventually tensions escalated as police advanced on them and a police officer was killed. The blockade expanded. The RCMP and the armed forces—some four thousand soldiers—were deployed, and the blockades were removed.

OKA CHIEF, 1869, FORESHADOWING ANGER IN 1990

This land was given you in trust for the tribe to whom it belongs; and how have you betrayed that trust? By . . . filling your treasury with the proceeds of stolen property. This land is ours—ours by right of possession; ours as a heritage. . . . We will die on the soil of our fathers, and our bleaching skeletons shall be a witness to nations yet unborn.[151]

Ellen Gabriel (front middle) and a group of land defenders at Oka, 1990

GEORGES ERASMUS, NATIONAL CHIEF OF THE ASSEMBLY OF FIRST NATIONS, ON SELF-GOVERNMENT AND IN RESPONSE TO OKA, 1990

We have come to a fork in the road, where if we are going to continue to be immersed in a status quo, we're just not going to be together very much longer. Or else we are going to be so disgruntled across this country we're not going to be able to live with each other. We have the ability to create a country that will be envied. We have the potential, but we also have the potential to fragment and create many smaller states, and that's absolutely not necessary. What we have here is the ability to bring together two European peoples, complemented by cultures from all around the world, with an indigenous population that has been here for tens of thousands of years. We have the ability to create a culture that will be different from others because we will take from each other and we will give to each other, but we will not have to crush each other. We will not have to make beggars of any of us. We will have to make people orphans from their culture. . . .

. . .

The time is here. We must now be sincere. Native people are not a threat to this country. We are not a threat to the sovereignty of Canada. We actually want to reinforce the sovereignty of Canada. We want to walk away from the negotiating table with an agreement that Canada feels good about and Native people feel good about, where we can say that we have strengthened the sovereignty of Canada . . . we're not a threat. We are only a threat if we continue to be ignored and taken lightly. We are only a threat if people don't understand that it is impossible for people to maintain the frustration level without the kind of actions that we've seen this summer [at Oka]. . . .

We're not trying to get out of Confederation. We never were a part of it. We're still knocking on the door. Let's hope we get a wonderful reception when the door is open.[152]

PRIME MINISTER BRIAN MULRONEY, IN RESPONSE TO OKA, 1990

The summer's events must not be allowed to over-shadow the commitment that my government has made to addressing the concerns of aboriginal people. . . . These grievances raise issues that deeply affect all Canadians and therefore must be resolved by all Canadians working together. . . . The government's agenda responds to the demands of aboriginal peoples and has four parts: resolving land claims; improving the economic and social conditions on reserves; defining a new relationship between aboriginal peoples and governments; and addressing the concerns of Canada's aboriginal peoples in contemporary Canadian life. Consultation with aboriginal peoples and respect for the fiduciary responsibilities of the Crown are integral parts of the process. The federal government is determined to create a new relationship among aboriginal and non-aboriginal Canadians based on dignity, trust and respect.[153]

Oka, 1990

Oka was not an isolated event. There were demonstrations and protests across the country in support of the crisis and the issues it raised. They reflected the serious ramifications of the continuing failure to address Indigenous land rights and the underlying conflict that denial had created. Prior to Oka, realities existed across the country in which Indigenous Peoples felt their only option to advance recognition of their relationship with their lands was to take direct action.

These realities continue to exist today, and challenges continue to arise—including national rail blockades in response to pipeline development in Wet'suwet'en and Gitanyow territory and the conflict between Six Nations of the Grand River and the Government of Canada regarding the development of a sub-division in Caledonia, referred to now as 1492 Land Back Lane, to name but a few.

One of the responses to the Oka Crisis and the failure of the Meech Lake Accord was the formation of the Royal Commission on Aboriginal Peoples in 1991. The commission undertook the most comprehensive study ever completed on the state of Indigenous Peoples in this country. Its identification of the challenges to be addressed, and the solutions to be implemented, was clear, compelling, and specific. Nonetheless, to this day its recommendations remain almost completely unimplemented by successive governments.

ROYAL COMMISSION ON ABORIGINAL PEOPLES, STATING SOME OF ITS RECOMMENDATIONS, 1996

Our vision of a renewed relationship is based on four principles: mutual recognition, mutual respect, sharing and mutual responsibility.

These principles define a process that can provide solutions to many of the difficulties afflicting relations among Aboriginal and non-Aboriginal peoples. Again, we have chosen a circle to represent this process because a circle has no beginning and no end; the process is continuous. As we move through the cycle represented by the four principles, a better understanding is gradually achieved. As the cycle is repeated, the meanings associated with each principle change subtly to reflect this deeper level of understanding. In other words, no single, all-encompassing definition can be assigned to any of these principles. They take on different meanings, depending on the stage we have reached in the process. When taken in sequence, the four principles form a complete whole, each playing an equal role in developing a balanced societal relationship. Relations that embody these principles are, in the broadest sense of the word, partnerships.

. . . The Commission recommends that a renewed relationship between Aboriginal and non-Aboriginal people in Canada be established on the basis of justice and fairness.

The Commission recommends that

1.16.1 To begin the process, the federal, provincial and territorial governments, on behalf of the people of Canada, and national Aboriginal organizations, on behalf of the Aboriginal peoples of Canada, commit themselves to building a renewed relationship based on the principles of mutual recognition, mutual respect, sharing and mutual responsibility; these principles to form the ethical basis of relations between Aboriginal and non-Aboriginal societies in the future and to be enshrined in a new Royal Proclamation and its companion legislation. . . .

2.3.2 All governments in Canada recognize that Aboriginal peoples are nations vested with the right of self-determination.[154]

JANE STEWART, MINISTER OF INDIAN AFFAIRS, ONE YEAR AFTER THE RELEASE OF REPORT OF THE ROYAL COMMISSION ON ABORIGINAL PEOPLES, REGARDING THE FEDERAL GOVERNMENT'S RESPONSE, 1997

We are not quite ready.[155]

JANE STEWART, MINISTER OF INDIAN AFFAIRS, ON BEHALF OF THE FEDERAL GOVERNMENT, FORMALLY RESPONDING TO THE ROYAL COMMISSION ON ABORIGINAL PEOPLES WITH THE RELEASE OF *GATHERING STRENGTH: CANADA'S ABORIGINAL ACTION PLAN*, 1998

Gathering Strength can best be described as a framework for new partnerships with First Nations, Inuit, Métis and non-status Indians. . . . The Action Plan responds to the Royal Commission and sets directions for a new course based on greater cooperation with Aboriginal groups and provinces.[156]

Royal Commission on Aboriginal Peoples logo by Joseph Sagaj[157]

The use of the courts by Indigenous Peoples continued to expand, and the courts continued to uphold Indigenous rights. Dozens upon dozens of cases have reached the Supreme Court of Canada, with the large majority confirming the existence of Indigenous rights, clarifying constitutional obligations of the Crown, and highlighting the need for governments to negotiate and address issues of Indigenous rights. There are core themes in these court decisions: that a just reconciliation is required between Indigenous Peoples and the Crown; that Indigenous title and rights are inherent—meaning they exist because Indigenous Peoples were here, had governments, and were sovereigns before the arrival of Europeans; that the Crown must act honourably in all dealings with Indigenous Peoples; that acting honourably imposes many legal obligations on the Crown, including to consult and accommodate; and that treaties must be diligently implemented. These decisions also encouraged the necessity of political negotiations to resolve these matters. As the law progressed, the court system has also been challenged to hear more, and learn more, about Indigenous laws, governance, societies, and culture.

GISDAY'WAY (ALFRED JOSEPH), OPENING STATEMENT, *DELGAMUUKW V. BRITISH COLUMBIA*, BRITISH COLUMBIA SUPREME COURT, 1987

The Chief is responsible for ensuring that all the people in his House respect the law, respect the land, and all living things. When a Chief directs his House properly and the laws are followed, then original power can be recreated. That is the source of a Chief's authority.[158]

DELGAMUUKW (KEN MULDOE), OPENING STATEMENT, *DELGAMUUKW V. BRITISH COLUMBIA*, BRITISH COLUMBIA SUPREME COURT, 1987

My power is carried in my House's histories, songs, dances and the crests. It is recreated at the feast when the histories are told, the songs and the dances performed and the crests displayed.

With the wealth that comes from respectful use of the territory, the House feeds the name of the Chief in the feast hall. In this way, the law, the Chief, the territory and the feast become one. The unity of the Chief's authority and his House's ownership of its territory are witnessed and thus affirmed by other Chiefs at the feast.[159]

'Ksan Historical Village

GWIIS GYEN (STANLEY WILLIAMS), ON AYOOKW, OR GITXSAN LAW

[The ayooxw] is like an ancient tree that has grown the roots right down into the ground. This is the way our law works. It's sunk. This big tree's roots are sunk deep into the ground, and that's how our land is.

The strength of our law is passed on from generation to generation, and each generation makes it stronger, right to this day where I am now.

I've taken the name that I have now since I was 10 years old and I'm 80 now, and our law was always the same and it's the same today. Every time we put this law into action, it becomes stronger and stronger. Each day our people use our law, they make it stronger, and it still goes on today.[160]

CHIEF JUSTICE ANTONIO LAMER, SUPREME COURT OF CANADA DECISION, *DELGAMUUKW V. BRITISH COLUMBIA*, 1997

Finally, this litigation has been both long and expensive, not only in economic but in human terms as well. By ordering a new trial, I do not necessarily encourage the parties to proceed to litigation and to settle their dispute through the courts. As was said in Sparrow . . . s. 35(1) "provides a solid constitutional base upon which subsequent negotiations can take place". Those negotiations should also include other aboriginal nations which have a stake in the territory claimed. Moreover, the Crown is under a moral, if not a legal, duty to enter into and conduct those negotiations in good faith. Ultimately, it is through negotiated settlements, with good faith and give and take on all sides, reinforced by the judgments of this Court, that we will achieve what I stated in Van der Peet . . . to be a basic purpose of s. 35(1)—"the reconciliation of the pre-existence of aboriginal societies with the sovereignty of the Crown". Let us face it, we are all here to stay.[161]

Protesters laid hundreds of blankets representing land and security on the front lawn of the Supreme Court of Canada, Ottawa, 2001

CHIEF JUSTICE BEVERLEY MCLACHLIN, IN *HAIDA NATION V. BRITISH COLUMBIA (MINISTER OF FORESTS)*, 2004

The government's duty to consult with Aboriginal peoples and accommodate their interests is grounded in the principle of the honour of the Crown, which must be understood generously. While the asserted but unproven Aboriginal rights and title are insufficiently specific for the honour of the Crown to mandate that the Crown act as a fiduciary, the Crown, acting honourably, cannot cavalierly run roughshod over Aboriginal interests where claims affecting these interests are being seriously pursued in the process of treaty negotiation and proof. The duty to consult and accommodate is part of a process of fair dealing and reconciliation that begins with the assertion of sovereignty and continues beyond formal claims resolution. The foundation of the duty in the Crown's honour and the goal of reconciliation suggest that the duty arises when the Crown has knowledge, real or constructive, of the potential existence of the Aboriginal right or title and contemplates conduct that might adversely affect it. Consultation and accommodation before final claims resolution preserve the Aboriginal interest and are an essential corollary to the honourable process of reconciliation that s. 35 of the Constitution Act, 1982, demands.[162]

JUSTICE IAN BINNIE, IN *MIKISEW CREE FIRST NATION V. CANADA (MINISTER OF CANADIAN HERITAGE)*, 2005

The fundamental objective of the modern law of aboriginal and treaty rights is the reconciliation of aboriginal peoples and non-aboriginal peoples and their respective claims, interests and ambitions. The management of these relationships takes place in the shadow of a long history of grievances and misunderstanding. The multitude of smaller grievances created by the indifference of some government officials to aboriginal people's concerns, and the lack of respect inherent in that indifference has been as destructive of the process of reconciliation as some of the larger and more explosive controversies.[163]

*The courts have also played a role in clarifying some of the distinctions between First Nations, Inuit, and Métis. For example, in two seminal decisions—*R. v. Powley *and* Daniels v. Canada (Indian Affairs and Northern Development)*—the Supreme Court of Canada confirmed specific approaches to determining and understanding Métis rights, as well as federal government responsibilities to Métis. Additionally, in* Manitoba Métis Federation Inc. v. Canada (Attorney General), *the unique historic circumstances of the Red River Métis and their role in the history of Canada was recognized.*

SUPREME COURT OF CANADA, IN *R V. POWLEY*, ON THE IMPORTANCE AND DISTINCTIVE NATURE OF MÉTIS RIGHTS, 2003

[13] The inclusion of the Métis in s. 35 is based on a commitment to recognizing the Métis and enhancing their survival as distinctive communities. The purpose and the promise of s. 35 is to protect practices that were historically important features of these distinctive communities and that persist in the present day as integral elements of their Métis culture.[164]

CHIEF JUSTICE BEVERLEY MCLACHLIN AND JUSTICE ANDROMACHE KARAKATSANIS, IN *MANITOBA MÉTIS FEDERATION INC. V. CANADA (ATTORNEY GENERAL)*, ADDRESSING A WRONG FROM THE TIME OF CONFEDERATION, 2013

[4] The government policy with respect to the Métis population—which, in 1870, comprised 85 percent of the population of what is now Manitoba—was less clear. Settlers began pouring into the region, displacing the Métis' social and political control. This led to resistance and conflict. To resolve the conflict and assure peaceful annexation of the territory, the Canadian government entered into negotiations with representatives of the Métis-led provisional government of the territory. The result was the *Manitoba Act, 1870*, S.C. 1870, c. 3 ("*Manitoba Act*"), which made Manitoba a province of Canada.

[5] This appeal is about obligations to the Métis people enshrined in the *Manitoba Act*, a constitutional document. These promises represent the terms under which the Métis people agreed to surrender their claims to govern themselves and their territory, and become part of the new nation of Canada. These promises were directed at enabling the Métis people and their descendants to obtain a lasting place in the new province. Sadly, the expectations of the Métis were not fulfilled,

and they scattered in the face of the settlement that marked the ensuing decades.

[6] Now, over a century later, the descendants of the Métis people seek a declaration in the courts that Canada breached its obligation to implement the promises it made to the Métis people in the *Manitoba Act*.[165]

JUSTICE ROSALIE ABELLA, IN *DANIELS V. CANADA (INDIAN AFFAIRS AND NORTHERN DEVELOPMENT)*, ON CROWN REFUSAL TO TAKE RESPONSIBILITY FOR THE MÉTIS, 2016

[13] Both federal and provincial governments have, alternately, denied having legislative authority over non-status Indians and Métis. As the trial judge found, when Métis and non-status Indians have asked the federal government to assume legislative authority over them, it tended to respond that it was precluded from doing so by s. 91(24). And when Métis and non-status Indians turned to provincial governments, they were often refused on the basis that the issue was a federal one.

[14] This results in these Indigenous communities being in a jurisdictional wasteland with significant and obvious disadvantaging consequences.[166]

Contrary to hopes that the resolution of issues regarding Indigenous rights and settling claims would accelerate, progress remained slow. Even with the advances made by Indigenous Peoples in the courts, which includes strong encouragement to negotiate and settle these issues; the climate of growing conflict; and the insights and guidance of the Royal Commission on Aboriginal Peoples, it would take decades for a number of land claims agreements to finally be reached in the North, including the founding of Nunavut in 1999.

John Amagoalik, "Father of Nunavut"

JOHN AMAGOALIK, INUIT LEADER SOMETIMES CALLED THE "FATHER OF NUNAVUT," DESCRIBING SOME OF THE PROCESS OF CREATING NUNAVUT

When we first presented our Nunavut proposal to the Government of Canada, they indicated that they did not want to deal with political development at the land claims table. They very much wanted to negotiate land claims and to leave political development on "another track." Those were their words. The Inuit wanted to keep the two things together. We made it very clear that we could not sign any agreement that did not include the commitment to create Nunavut. At that point we agreed to disagree. But we agreed to start negotiating the details of the land claims agreement while we were pursuing Nunavut through the political arena. We made it clear that when the land claims agreement was ready to be signed, the creation of Nunavut would have to be brought in, if it was ready to be part of the land claims agreement. In the twenty years that it took to negotiate the land claims settlement, the two went along parallel lines. We were negotiating the claims here, and we were pursuing Nunavut through other means.[167]

In 1993, after the Oka Crisis, the tripartite treaty process began in British Columbia among many Indigenous Peoples, the federal government, and the provincial government with the goal of settling the "Indian Land Question" across the province in five years. The B.C. treaty process was guided by the 1991 Report of the British Columbia Claims Task Force, which is the blueprint for the made-in-B.C. treaty process. Approximately three decades later, only four Final Agreements (modern treaties) have been completed through this process.[168] *The Nisga'a Final Agreement was negotiated outside of the B.C. treaty process. Across other parts of the country, the Treaty Land Entitlement process was created to address the fact that First Nations did not receive all the land that they were entitled to under treaties signed in the past. The process of settling Treaty Land Entitlement issues has been slow, hampered by the availability of adequate land as well as policy and practice restrictions in the federal government.*

CHIEF JOE MATHIAS OF THE SQUAMISH NATION AT THE FOUNDING OF THE BRITISH COLUMBIA TREATY PROCESS

Negotiations, in our view, will not be based on that tired old notion of extinguishment. We will not tolerate the extinguishment of our collective Aboriginal rights.[169]

DOUGLAS EYFORD, IN A REVIEW OF THE MODERN TREATY NEGOTIATIONS CONDUCTED IN 2015 ON BEHALF OF THE FEDERAL GOVERNMENT

There is a conspicuous lack of urgency in negotiations and in many cases there are sharp differences between the parties about the core elements of a modern treaty.[170]

Dr. Joseph Gosnell, president of the Nisga'a Tribal Council, arrives in the Senate chamber on Parliament Hill, Ottawa, 1999

NOEL STARBLANKET, ON TREATY LAND ENTITLEMENT

When my grandfather and great grandfather signed the Treaty, they were talking about me and now I've got to talk about my grandchildren and the youth, and so that's the kind of process we're trying to continue in this whole Treaty-making process and that's what we try to remember when we work in TLE [Treaty Land Entitlement], to think about the future and make sure that we provide for the future. . . .

It means trying to do the best we can, often making compromises between ourselves and the various levels of government, federal and provincial, municipal, and also having to work with white society as a whole, trying to understand them, trying to work with them, and yet at the same time educating them to understand us. . . .

There are those who will never understand it and don't want to, and never will. On the other hand, there's a whole lot of good people out there who want to and will understand it. There will be benefits coming out of it for those people, and it's happening now. All of that bodes well for the coming together of a people.[171]

While some incremental shifts were occurring in government policy regarding self-government, lands, and resources, the social challenges faced by Indigenous Peoples have in many respects continued or even deepened—including housing, drinking-water access, suicide, addiction, and poverty. Further, in addition to the enduring challenges facing Indigenous children and families, there has also been a deepening crisis of Indigenous people being grossly overrepresented in the criminal justice system. For example, in 2017–18, Indigenous youth made up 43 percent of those admitted to correctional services while representing about 8 percent of the Canadian youth population. In the same year, 42 percent of the women admitted into custody were Indigenous.

For decades, study after study has identified the forces, including systemic racism, that have contributed to the overpolicing and overincarceration of Indigenous people, and the need for transformative change, including more Indigenous control over their own criminal justice systems. In 1999, in R v. Gladue, *the Supreme Court of Canada recognized the significant problem of overincarceration and established a framework to help address it—which they have reiterated in subsequent decisions. In recent years, governments and the public have grown increasingly aware of the massive challenges involving Indigenous people and the justice system. One high-profile example was the case of Colten Boushie, who was shot and killed by Gerald Stanley while on Stanley's property. Stanley was charged, and acquitted, of second-degree murder and manslaughter.*

JUSTICE PETER CORY AND JUSTICE FRANK IACOBUCCI, IN *R. V. GLADUE*, ON THE CRIMINAL JUSTICE SYSTEM AND HOW IT HAS FAILED INDIGENOUS PEOPLE, 1999

61 Not surprisingly, the excessive imprisonment of aboriginal people is only the tip of the iceberg insofar as the estrangement of the aboriginal peoples from the Canadian criminal justice system is concerned. Aboriginal people are overrepresented in virtually all aspects of the system. As this Court recently noted in *R. v. Williams*, [1998] 1 S.C.R. 1128, at para. 58, there is widespread bias against aboriginal people within Canada, and "[t]here is evidence that this widespread racism has translated into systemic discrimination in the criminal justice system."

62 Statements regarding the extent and severity of this problem are disturbingly common. In *Bridging the Cultural Divide*, *supra*, at p. 309, the Royal Commission on Aboriginal Peoples listed as its first "Major Findings and Conclusions" the following striking yet representative statement:

> The Canadian criminal justice system has failed the Aboriginal peoples of Canada—First Nations, Inuit and Métis people, on-reserve and off-reserve, urban and rural—in all territorial and governmental jurisdictions.

> The principal reason for this crushing failure is the fundamentally different world views of Aboriginal and non-Aboriginal people with respect to such elemental issues as the substantive content of justice and the process of achieving justice.

63 To the same effect, the Aboriginal Justice Inquiry of Manitoba described the justice system in Manitoba as having failed aboriginal people on a "massive scale," referring particularly to the substantially different cultural values and experiences of aboriginal people: *The Justice System and Aboriginal People*, *supra*, at pp. 1 and 86.

64 These findings cry out for recognition of the magnitude and gravity of the problem, and for responses to alleviate it. The figures are stark and reflect what may fairly be termed a crisis in the Canadian criminal justice system. The drastic overrepresentation of aboriginal peoples within both the Canadian prison population and the criminal justice system reveals a sad and pressing social problem.[172]

B.C. FIRST NATIONS JUSTICE STRATEGY, DESCRIBING THE LEGACY OF COLONIALISM IN THE JUSTICE SYSTEM, 2021

Among the most damaging of colonial patterns has been efforts to marginalize and dismantle First Nations legal orders and governance institutions, including as it relates to criminal justice. Concurrent with this has been the imposition of a common law justice system that has long reflected and struggled with racist and outdated perspectives, policies and practices regarding Indigenous peoples. The end result is a contemporary reality where Indigenous peoples in British Columbia, and across Canada, are disproportionately and negatively impacted by the justice system, often with devastating consequences for individuals, families, communities, Nations, and society at large.

BC First Nations Justice Council logo by Jamin Zuroski [173]

Throughout the history of the colonial interaction of First Nations with the justice system, rarely, if ever, has there been the commitment, will, support and vision, for systematic, joint efforts to transform these harmful realities. While constructive and important efforts have been made over many decades to improve the reality of the relationship of Indigenous peoples with the justice system, and some important steps taken, these efforts and achievements have never been comprehensive or transformative in scope and intent.[174]

DEBBIE BAPTISTE, MOTHER OF COLTEN BOUSHIE, AT A NEWS CONFERENCE AFTER THE ACQUITTAL OF GERALD STANLEY, 2021

I miss my son so much. . . . I come here with a heavy heart today. I hope and pray for change within the justice system. . . . He deserved a life. . . . He had dreams, and they were cut short. . . . I would like everybody to remember Colten. He was a victim, not a criminal.[175]

The enduring challenges and threats faced by Indigenous women also continued, and in many ways deepened. While there was some progress on other fronts, Indigenous women continued to raise the alarm about the specific forms of violence and oppression they were confronting. Until quite recently, these issues went largely ignored by governments, police, and the court system. In 2017, after decades of advocacy by families and communities calling for justice, the National Inquiry into Missing and Murdered Indigenous Women and Girls was formed. The inquiry issued its final report in 2019.

CHIEF COMMISSIONER MARION BULLER, IN THE PREFACE TO MMIWG REPORT, 2019

The violence against Indigenous women, girls, and 2SLGBTQQIA people is a national tragedy of epic proportion. . . .

As a nation, we face a crisis: regardless of which number of missing and murdered Indigenous women and girls is cited, the number is too great. The continuing murders, disappearances and violence prove that this crisis has escalated to a national emergency that calls for timely and effective responses.[176]

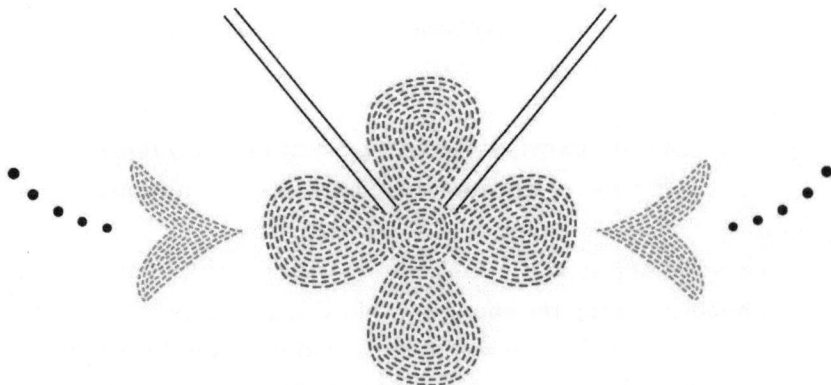

The National Inquiry into Missing and Murdered Indigenous Women and Girls logo by Meky Ottawa[177]

DANIELLE E, IN HER TESTIMONY TO THE NATIONAL INQUIRY

I have hope that something good will come out of this, that as an Indigenous woman, I don't have to walk on the street and be afraid because, today, when I go somewhere, I'm afraid, and it's a fear that we all carry every day and you get so used to it that it's like it's part of you, and it shouldn't have to be because not everybody in society today has to walk around and be afraid the way Indigenous women are and girls. I have seven daughters and lots of granddaughters that I worry about constantly all day. I don't want them to become a statistic.[178]

PAM PALMATER, ON THE CONTEXT OF HISTORIC DISCRIMINATION AGAINST INDIGENOUS WOMEN AND THE REALITY OF MISSING AND MURDERED INDIGENOUS WOMEN AND GIRLS

If you speak to Indigenous women today, they will tell you that the crisis is far from over. The Indian Act still discriminates against Indigenous women and their descendants in the transmission of Indian status and membership in First Nations. Indigenous women suffer far greater rates of heart disease and stroke; they have higher rates of suicide attempts; they disproportionately live in poverty as single parents; their overincarceration rates have increased by 90% in the last decade; and 48% of all children in foster care in Canada are Indigenous. With this list of harrowing statistics, is it any wonder that thousands of our sisters are missing or murdered?[179]

MELANIE D, ON CONCERNS OVER WHETHER THE INQUIRY CAN LEAD TO CHANGE

My biggest question is what is the government planning to do after this Inquiry?

Like, what is the action plan? Because I hope it's not like another RCAP [Royal Commission on Aboriginal Peoples] report.

> I hope it's not 94 Calls to Action where we have roundabout circle talks about reconciliation. . . . And I'm not just placing that on to the government, but . . . what is Canada, all of Canada going to do?[180]

As awareness of the need for transformative shifts to address the enduring and harsh social, economic, and cultural reality of Indigenous people grew, non-Indigenous governments began contemplating possible responses. One initiative was the Kelowna Accord, in 2002, which was led by Prime Minister Paul Martin, the provinces and territories, and Indigenous leaders. The accord would have included $5 billion in the first five years to improve Indigenous health care and education, and another $5 billion in the subsequent five years. Five days after the Kelowna Accord was signed, Martin's minority Liberal government fell. The new Conservative government of Stephen Harper did not follow through on the mandates laid out in the accord, providing only a fraction of the funding committed.

PRIME MINISTER PAUL MARTIN, REFLECTING ON HIS APPROACH TO THE KELOWNA ACCORD

> The position that I took [with Indigenous leaders] was to say to them, look, I'm going to call a federal-provincial conference and we are going to work with you.
>
> You tell us what you believe the issues are, so it's going to be your agenda. And they said to us the issues are health care, education, and those things which follow, child welfare being one of them. . . .
>
> Ultimately my goal was the elimination of the Indian Act and its replacement by self-government dealing with all of these issues, beginning with health care and education, and child welfare.[181]

PRESIDENT CLÉMENT CHARTIER, MÉTIS NATIONAL COUNCIL, DESCRIBING THE IMPORTANCE OF THE KELOWNA ACCORD

The Kelowna Accord will mean the difference between continuing the cycle of poverty and desperation to one of real hope. The agreement will help to bring our people out of poverty by creating jobs, securing health care and education opportunities.[182]

<<<< >>>>

While totem poles may appear linear and hierarchical from one perspective, this is not typical of the meanings they intend to convey. While variations between poles, cultures, and artists do, of course, exist, totem poles are not meant to express how one part leads to another, and then another. Instead, they express the enduring and living connections and relationships between all that is portrayed.

To say it another way, the whole is always greater than the sum of its parts.

As such, in using the parts of the totem pole as a metaphor and symbol, as we have in this book, we must constantly strive to understand what we see through the perspective of the whole. This is especially important as we move upward to the Thunderbird. From one vantage point, Thunderbird is a reflection of strength and re-emergence, of the work of decolonization and reconciliation. But Thunderbird is also calling us to try to view, in transformative ways, the real connections between all of us—everyone—and how we must build foundations rooted in those connections. In other words, the Thunderbird, while sitting atop the pole, is also about how we understand the pole's foundation, and everything in between.

PART 4

Thunderbird

The wings of the Thunderbird are open and spread out. When I look at her, she appears ready to take flight.

This is how I think of my people, of Indigenous Peoples, at this moment in time. The challenges remain great. But what we are now bearing witness to is the taking flight of Indigenous Peoples in contemporary Canada. The vibrancy of our young people. The creative explosion of our arts and culture. The energy of sport and the determination of our athletes. The emergence of our people as leaders in politics and business. The accomplishments of our Indigenous professionals. The rebuilding of our nations and governments, and revitalization of our Indigenous laws and legal orders.

This is also how I think about Canada and our potential as a country. No country is perfect, and all societies can, and must, continue to evolve, change, and improve. While the changes needed vary from place to place, there are commonalities that we see. Every country has its own history of oppression and exclusion of certain peoples, and experiences forms of conflict, marginalization, and uncertainty as a result. At a minimum, striving with seriousness and purpose to address these histories of oppression and exclusion is always necessary to continue to build and maintain social cohesion, stability, and growth. In some places, however, failure to address these histories can lead to more disastrous outcomes, whether it be violence and even war or, in some instances, the collapse and disassembling of countries themselves.

On these lands, the effects of Canada's history of oppression and exclusion of Indigenous Peoples are still visible all around us, with significantly increased rates of poverty, suicide, and addictions, and reduced educational and employment outcomes. In spite of some improvements, there is a socio-economic gap between Indigenous and non-Indigenous Canadians that has endured throughout the history of Canada, and stubbornly continues today. What this reveals, in effect, is that the well-being of all Indigenous Peoples and the well-being of Canada as a whole is indivisible. If we want to be a stronger, happier, and healthier country, with greater environmental and economic sustainability and stability, and deeper social peace and cohesion, we must confront and address the legacy of oppression and exclusion of Indigenous Peoples. To say it another way, if Canada is to secure its future and reach its full potential, we must rise to the challenge of reconciliation.

So, what do we need to do?

One aspect of our history is that we have identified with specificity, time and again, what needs to be done to confront the effects of colonization. As we have seen in these pages, year after year, for many decades, these effects have been measured, analyzed, and documented through studies and reports. Between 1965 and 1996, a period of thirty years, almost nine hundred reports on Indigenous policy were completed, with well over one hundred of these being considered "major."[1] In the years since 1996, there have been many, many more—far beyond the famous ones, such as the Truth and Reconciliation Commission and the National Inquiry into Missing and Murdered Indigenous Women and Girls. Literally, there are now thousands of reports on what has caused the challenges facing Indigenous Peoples and how to address them.

Some of these reports and studies are essential and important, and document things that were not previously recorded. But to be blunt, many just repeat or retread ground that has already been covered. In my more cynical moments (and I have a few—though hope predominates), both when I was within and outside of government, I have thought, and said out loud, that another report or study was being commissioned just to delay taking real action.

The reality is, however, that we know full well what the solutions are. They have been articulated and advocated over a period of many generations, such as by the Royal Commission on Aboriginal Peoples. The Royal Commission was asked to do a lot: to investigate the evolution of the relationship among Indigenous Peoples (Indian, Inuit, and Métis), the Canadian government, and Canadian society as a whole, and to offer solutions. The commission did its job, and in 1996 issued a final report including 440 sweeping recommendations for change and a twenty-year timeline for the implementation.

Most of those recommendations have been ignored by successive governments. Meanwhile we have continued to generate studies and reports about what the problems are and what needs to be done.

But it's at this moment in time that we are starting to see movement from words to action. We see action in the acceleration and intensification of non-Indigenous people advocating alongside Indigenous people. We see action in the long overdue work of making changes to laws, policies, and practices, such as the adoption of the United Nations Declaration on the Rights of Indigenous Peoples as the framework for reconciliation. We see this in how First Nations, Inuit, and Métis are advancing the work of rebuilding their governments and upholding their own laws.

At this moment in time, we are witnessing the growing presence of Indigenous people in the forefront of Canadian society. Indigenous writers and artists are shaping and reshaping what we understand about the traditions and future of literature, film, painting, and other art forms in this country, and there are more and more Indigenous athletes on the national stage. Indigenous leaders are, though still few in numbers, moving from the world of Indigenous politics into mainstream Canadian politics, and bringing with them worldviews, teachings, and practices that can challenge and change for the better some of our conventional ways of doing things. Indigenous young people, though still experiencing the intergenerational trauma of the residential "school" system and other wrongs, are making their voices heard in all dimensions of Canada's public life.

This movement we see is a result of the underlying reality that the voices in this book illustrate. The relentless drive among Indigenous people to keep marching forward, preserving our knowledge, culture, and ways of life, and helping to secure a better future for the generations to come.

This relentlessness is the way of the Thunderbird. In diverse ways in the teachings and stories of many First Nations, the Thunderbird fights the underworld and the forces of darkness that exist within it. Thunder and lightning are used in this fight, to stop creatures that will cause destruction. The Thunderbird helps maintain the light, even if at times it is just a glimmer, until it is able to shine more fully again.

The shifts we are seeing today are a result of the light shining a bit brighter and stronger.

The Thunderbird, like the sound of thunder itself, is loud. The voices in this part of the book are similarly loud. They are in the shadows no more. There are more of them, too, and they are more representative of everyone. We hear women, children, and youth. We hear "grassroots." We hear partners and allies, and, as I have referred to some people, inbetweeners. We hear the colonizers, the Crown, trying to find a new voice. We hear the change that has come about from the relentless efforts of so many.

<<<< >>>>

Through significant efforts among survivors, including organizing to bring lawsuits in the 1980s and '90s, progress was made in addressing the impacts of residential schools. This vital work resulted in the 2006 financial settlement agreement, an apology from Prime Minister Stephen

Harper in the House of Commons in 2008, and the creation of the Truth and Reconciliation Commission. The voices of survivors attest to the importance of these steps.

INDIAN RESIDENTIAL SCHOOLS SETTLEMENT, SCHEDULE N, 2006

There is an emerging and compelling desire to put the events of the past behind us so that we can work towards a stronger and healthier future. The truth telling and reconciliation process as part of an overall holistic and comprehensive response to the Indian Residential School legacy is a sincere indication and acknowledgement of the injustices and harms experienced by Aboriginal people and the need for continued healing. This is a profound commitment to establishing new relationships embedded in mutual recognition and respect that will forge a brighter future. The trust of our common experiences will help set our spirits free and pave the way to reconciliation.[2]

PRIME MINISTER STEPHEN HARPER, IN HIS APOLOGY FOR THE RESIDENTIAL SCHOOL SYSTEM, 2008

I stand before you today to offer an apology to former students of Indian residential schools. The treatment of children in these schools is a sad chapter in our history. For more than a century, Indian residential schools separated over 150,000 aboriginal children from their families and communities.

. . .

Two primary objectives of the residential school system were to remove and isolate children from the influence of their homes, families, traditions and cultures, and to assimilate them into the dominant culture.

These objectives were based on the assumption that aboriginal cultures and spiritual beliefs were inferior and unequal.

Indeed, some sought, as it was infamously said, "to kill the Indian in the child."

Today, we recognize that this policy of assimilation was wrong, has caused great harm, and has no place in our country.

. . .

The government recognizes that the absence of an apology has been an impediment to healing and reconciliation.

. . .

To the approximately 80,000 living former students and all family members and communities, the Government of Canada now recognizes that it was wrong to forcibly remove children from their homes, and we apologize for having done this.

We now recognize that it was wrong to separate children from rich and vibrant cultures and traditions, that it created a void in many lives and communities, and we apologize for having done this.

We now recognize that in separating children from their families, we undermined the ability of many to adequately parent their own children and sowed the seeds for generations to follow, and we apologize for having done this.

We now recognize that far too often these institutions gave rise to abuse or neglect and were inadequately controlled, and we apologize for failing to protect you.

Not only did you suffer these abuses as children, but as you became parents, you were powerless to protect your own children from suffering the same experience, and for this we are sorry.

The burden of this experience has been on your shoulders for far too long. The burden of this experience is properly ours as a government, and as a country. There is no place in Canada for the attitudes that inspired the Indian residential schools system to ever again prevail.

There is no place in Canada for the attitudes that inspired the Indian residential schools system to ever again prevail.

You have been working on recovering from this experience for a long time, and in a very real sense we are now joining you on this journey. The Government of Canada sincerely apologizes and asks the forgiveness of the aboriginal peoples of this country for failing them so profoundly.

We are sorry.[3]

NATIONAL CHIEF PHIL FONTAINE, ASSEMBLY OF FIRST NATIONS, IN RESPONSE TO THE APOLOGY, 2008

[F]or all of the generations which have preceded us, this day testifies to nothing less than the achievement of the impossible.

. . .

[T]he significance of this day is not just about what has been but, equally important, what is to come. Never again will this House consider us the Indian problem just for being who we are.

National Chief Phil Fontaine, Assembly of First Nations, House of Commons, Ottawa, June 11, 2008

We heard the Government of Canada take full responsibility for this dreadful chapter in our shared history. We heard the Prime Minister declare that this will never happen again. Finally, we heard Canada say it is sorry.

Brave survivors, through the telling of their painful stories, have stripped white supremacy of its authority and legitimacy. The irresistibility of speaking truth to power is real.

Today is not the result of a political game. Instead, it is something that shows the righteousness and importance of our struggle. We know we have many difficult issues to handle. There are many fights still to be fought.

What happened today signifies a new dawn in the relationship between us and the rest of Canada. We are and always have been an indispensable part of the Canadian identity.

Our peoples, our history, and our present being are the essence of Canada. The attempts to erase our identities hurt us deeply, but it also hurt all Canadians and impoverished the character of this nation.

We must not falter in our duty now. Emboldened by this spectacle of history, it is possible to end our racial nightmare together. The memories of residential schools sometimes cut like merciless knives at our souls. This day will help us to put that pain behind us.

But it signifies something even more important: a respectful and, therefore, liberating relationship between us and the rest of Canada.

Together we can achieve the greatness our country deserves. The apology today is founded upon, more than anything else, the recognition that we all own our own lives and destinies, the only true foundation for a society where peoples can flourish.

We must now capture a new spirit and vision to meet the challenges of the future.

. . . we are all part of one "garment of destiny." The differences between us are not blood or colour and "the ties that bind us are deeper than those that separate us." The "common road of hope" will bring us to reconciliation more than any words, laws or legal claims ever could.

We still have to struggle, but now we are in this together.

I reach out to all Canadians today in this spirit of reconciliation.

Meegwetch [thank you].[4]

WILLIE BLACKWATER, A SURVIVOR AND LEADER OF LEGAL ACTION ABOUT THE RESIDENTIAL SCHOOLS, IN RESPONSE TO THE APOLOGY, 2008

The apology makes a huge difference for me, because it will help . . . the pain and suffering I inflicted not only on my wife and daughter but also to my son . . . and his mother, because they felt the pain and they felt the atrocities too.[5]

CHARLIE THOMPSON, SURVIVOR, IN RESPONSE TO THE APOLOGY, 2008

Today I feel relief. I feel good. For me, this is a historical day.[6]

MARY SIMON, PRESIDENT OF INUIT TAPIRIIT KANATAMI, IN RESPONSE TO THE APOLOGY, 2008

I am one of these people that have dreamed for this day and there have been times in this long journey when I despaired that this would never happen. I am filled with hope and compassion for my fellow aboriginal Canadians. There is much hard work to be done. We need the help and support of all thoughtful Canadians and our governments to rebuild strong healthy families and communities. This can only be achieved when dignity, confidence and respect for traditional values and human rights once again become part of our daily lives and are mirrored in our relationships with governments and other Canadians.

I am also filled with optimism that this action by the Government of Canada and the generosity in the words chosen to convey this apology will help all of us mark the end of this dark period in our collective history as a nation. . . . Let us now join forces with the common goal of working together to ensure that this apology opens the door to a new chapter in our lives as aboriginal peoples and in our place in Canada. . . . I stand here today ready to work with you, as Inuit have always done, to craft new solutions and new arrangements based on mutual respect and mutual responsibility.[7]

PRESIDENT BEVERLY JACOBS OF THE NATIVE WOMEN'S ASSOCIATION OF CANADA, IN RESPONSE TO THE APOLOGY, 2008

Prior to the residential schools system, prior to colonization, the women in our communities were very well respected and honoured for the role that they have in our communities as being the life givers, being the caretakers of the spirit that we bring to mother earth. We have been given those responsibilities to look after our children and to bring that spirit into this physical world.

Residential schools caused so much harm to that respect and to that honour. There were ceremonies for young men and for young women that were taken away for generations in residential schools. Now we have our language still, we have our ceremonies, we have our elders, and we have to revitalize those ceremonies and the respect for our people not only within Canadian society but even within our own peoples. . . . [I]t is about making sure that we have strong nations again. . . .

We have given thanks to you for your apology. I have to also give you credit for standing up. I did not see any other governments before today come forward and apologize, so I do thank you for that.[8]

The findings of the Truth and Reconciliation Commission in 2015 and the National Inquiry into Missing and Murdered Indigenous Women and

Girls in 2019 brought vital awareness and education to the Canadian public about the depth of colonialism's impacts on children, families, women, and the LGBTQ+ community. They also made clear the pressing need for urgent change, and the various and far-reaching solutions that needed to be implemented. Throughout these studies and reports, Indigenous people and communities continued to push for more change, justice, and healing.

STATEMENT OF ELDERS GATHERED IN MUSQUEAM TERRITORY, 2012

As Canadians, we share a responsibility to look after each other and acknowledge the pain and suffering that our diverse societies have endured—a pain that has been handed down to the next generations. We need to right those wrongs, heal together, and create a new future that honours the unique gifts of our children and grandchildren.

How do we do this? Through sharing our personal stories, legends and traditional teachings, we found that we are interconnected through the same mind and spirit. Our traditional teachings speak to acts such as holding one another up, walking together, balance, healing and unity. Our stories show how these teachings can heal their pain and restore dignity. We discovered that in all of our cultural traditions, there are teachings about reconciliation, forgiveness, unity, healing and balance.

We invite you to search in your own traditions and beliefs, and those of your ancestors, to find these core values that create a peaceful harmonious society and a healthy earth.[9]

TRUTH AND RECONCILIATION COMMISSION, ON THE ACTIONS OF CANADA AND CULTURAL GENOCIDE, 2015

For over a century, the central goals of Canada's Aboriginal policy were to eliminate Aboriginal governments; ignore Aboriginal rights; terminate the Treaties; and, through a process of assimilation, cause Aboriginal peoples to cease to exist as distinct legal, social, cultural, religious, and racial entities in Canada. The establishment and operation of residential schools were a central element of this policy, which can best be described as "cultural genocide."

. . . *Cultural genocide* is the destruction of those structures and practices that allow the group to continue as a group. States that engage in cultural genocide set out to destroy the political and social institutions of the targeted group. Land is seized, and populations are forcibly transferred and their movement is restricted. Languages are banned. Spiritual leaders are persecuted, spiritual practices are forbidden, and objects of spiritual value are confiscated and destroyed. And, most significantly to the issue at hand, families are disrupted to prevent the transmission of cultural values and identity from one generation to the next.

In its dealing with Aboriginal people, Canada did all these things.[10]

Truth and Reconciliation Commission, Ottawa, 2015

TRUTH AND RECONCILIATION COMMISSION, DESCRIBING WHAT RECONCILIATION REQUIRES, 2015

Reconciliation is going to take hard work. People of all walks of life and at all levels of society will need to be willingly engaged.

Reconciliation calls for personal action. People need to get to know each other. They need to learn how to speak to, and about, each other respectfully. They need to learn how to speak knowledgeably about the history of this country. And they need to ensure that their children learn how to do so as well.

Reconciliation calls for group action. The 2010 Vancouver Olympics Organizing Committee recognized, paid tribute to, and honoured the Four Host First Nations at all public events it organized. Clubs, sports teams, artists, musicians, writers, teachers, doctors, lawyers, judges, and politicians need to learn from that example of how to be more inclusive and more respectful, and how to engage more fully in the dialogue about reconciliation.

Reconciliation calls for community action. The City of Vancouver, British Columbia, proclaimed itself the City of Reconciliation. The City of Halifax, Nova Scotia, holds an annual parade and procession commemorating the 1761 Treaty of Peace and Friendship. Speeches are delivered and everyone who attends is feasted. The City of Wetaskiwin, Alberta, erected a sign at its outskirts with the city's name written in Cree syllabics. Other communities can do similar things.

Reconciliation calls for federal, provincial, and territorial government action.

Reconciliation calls for national action.

The way we govern ourselves must change.

Laws must change.

Policies and programs must change.

The way we educate our children and ourselves must change.

The way we do business must change.

Thinking must change.

Walk for Reconciliation, Vancouver, 2013

The way we talk to, and about, each other must change.

All Canadians must make a firm and lasting commitment to reconciliation to ensure that Canada is a country where our children and grandchildren can thrive.[11]

CHIEF COMMISSIONER MARION BULLER, PREFACE TO THE FINAL REPORT OF THE NATIONAL INQUIRY INTO MISSING AND MURDERED INDIGENOUS WOMEN AND GIRLS, 2019

This report is also about hope. I believe, especially after witnessing the resilience of Indigenous families, survivors and communities, that change will happen. An Elder said, "We all have to get past the guilt and shame." This begins with recognizing the truth. For non-Indigenous Canadians, this means rethinking commonly held stereotypes, and confronting racism in every context. For Indigenous Peoples, this means using the truth to rebuild our lives, our families, our communities and Canada itself. And for governments, this means nothing less than a new and decolonized social order; it is an opportunity to transform and to rebuild in real partnership with Indigenous Peoples.[12]

While awareness was building across the country, international developments also increasingly began to influence Canada's policy toward Indigenous Peoples. In 2007, after approximately twenty-five years of efforts to draft a specific instrument dealing with the protection of the human rights of Indigenous Peoples around the world, the United Nations Declaration on the Rights of Indigenous Peoples was adopted. The declaration expresses established international human rights norms as applied in the specific context of Indigenous Peoples. The forty-six articles of the UN Declaration are understood to be the minimum standards for the "survival, dignity, and well-being" of Indigenous Peoples. Canada was one of four countries—the others being the United States, New Zealand, and Australia—that voted against the adoption of the declaration. In November 2010, Canada reversed its position and expressed support with "reservations." In 2016, Canada removed these reservations and fully endorsed the UN Declaration.

UNITED NATIONS DECLARATION ON THE RIGHTS OF INDIGENOUS PEOPLES, 2007

Article 3

Indigenous peoples have the right to self-determination. By virtue of that right they freely determine their political status and freely pursue their economic, social and cultural development.

Article 4

Indigenous peoples, in exercising their right to self-determination, have the right to autonomy or self-government in matters relating to their internal and local affairs, as well as ways and means for financing their autonomous functions.

Article 5

Indigenous peoples have the right to maintain and strengthen their distinct political, legal, economic, social and cultural institutions, while retaining their right to participate fully, if they so choose, in the political, economic, social and cultural life of the State.

. . .

Article 26

Indigenous peoples have the right to the lands, territories and resources which they have traditionally owned, occupied or otherwise used or acquired.

. . .

Article 27

States shall establish and implement, in conjunction with indigenous peoples concerned, a fair, independent, impartial, open and transparent process, giving due recognition to indigenous peoples' laws, traditions, customs and land tenure systems, to recognize and adjudicate the rights of indigenous peoples pertaining to their lands, territories and resources, including those which were traditionally owned or otherwise occupied or used. Indigenous peoples shall have the right to participate in this process.

Article 28

Indigenous peoples have the right to redress, by means that can include restitution or, when this is not possible, just, fair and equitable compensation, for the lands, territories and resources which they have traditionally owned or otherwise occupied or used, and which have been confiscated, taken, occupied, used or damaged without their free, prior and informed consent.

. . .

Article 33

1. Indigenous peoples have the right to determine their own identity or membership in accordance with their customs and traditions. This does not impair the right of indigenous individuals to obtain citizenship of the states in which they live.

. . .

Article 38

States in consultation and cooperation with indigenous peoples, shall take the appropriate measures, including legislative measures, to achieve the ends of the Declaration.[13]

UNITED NATIONS GENERAL ASSEMBLY PRESIDENT SHEIKHA HAYA RASHED AL KHALIFA, ON THE ADOPTION OF THE UN DECLARATION, 2007

The General Assembly today overwhelmingly backed protections for the human rights of indigenous peoples, adopting a landmark declaration that brought to an end nearly 25 years of contentious negotiations over the rights of native people to protect their lands and resources, and to maintain their unique cultures and traditions. By a vote of 143 in favour to 4 against (Australia, Canada, New Zealand and the United States), with 11 abstentions, the Assembly adopted the United Nations Declaration on the Rights of Indigenous Peoples, which sets out the individual and collective rights of the world's 370 million native peoples, calls for the maintenance and strengthening of their cultural identities, and emphasizes their right to pursue development in keeping with their own needs and aspirations.

The importance of this document for indigenous peoples and, more broadly, for the human rights agenda, cannot be underestimated.[14]

PRIME MINISTER STEPHEN HARPER, ON THE ADOPTION OF THE UN DECLARATION BY THE UNITED NATIONS GENERAL ASSEMBLY, 2007

We shouldn't vote for things on the basis of political correctness; we should actually vote on the basis of what's in the document.[15]

NATIONAL CHIEF PHIL FONTAINE, ASSEMBLY OF FIRST NATIONS, ON CANADA'S VOTE AGAINST THE UN DECLARATION, 2007

In our view, it's a stain on Canada's reputation internationally. . . . In this case, Canada is blowing against the very consistent position it has taken in the last few decades. . . . When they decided to go against the thing that they had supported for so long, it was inexplicable. . . . It's an aspirational document, neither convention nor treaty. . . . We're talking here about minimum standards that relate to our right to self-rule of our territories.[16]

MINISTER CAROLYN BENNETT, EXPRESSING CANADA'S FULL ENDORSEMENT OF THE UN DECLARATION, 2016

Today, we honour all of their work as we continue the journey. As the Minister of Justice indicated yesterday, our Prime Minister wrote to every Minister and indicated in their mandate letters, and I quote: "No relationship is more important to me and to Canada than the one with Indigenous peoples. It is time for a renewed relationship with Indigenous peoples based on recognition of rights, respect, cooperation and partnership."

All of these mandate letters were made public, and by doing so, the Prime Minister spoke to all Canadians. Today, we are addressing Canada's position on the UN Declaration on the Rights of Indigenous Peoples. I'm here to announce, on behalf of Canada, that we are now a full supporter of the Declaration without qualification.

We intend nothing less than to adopt and implement the declaration in accordance with the Canadian Constitution. Canada is in a unique position to move forward.[17]

Indigenous advocacy was also evolving, as women, young people, and grass-roots community members increasingly and publicly led calls for change. In 2012, the Idle No More movement captured the attention of Canadians for weeks. Thousands of Indigenous people and supporters called for change on the streets of Ottawa and around the country. At the same time, after expansive efforts to draw attention to the dire circumstances in her community, Attawapiskat Chief Theresa Spence went on a hunger strike on Victoria Island near the Parliament Buildings in Ottawa.

CHIEF THERESA SPENCE, SENDING A MESSAGE TO INDIGENOUS PEOPLES, CANADIANS AND GOVERNMENTS, 2011

We must go together and tell the government: This is our land, this is our life. We need to say enough is enough.[18]

IDLE NO MORE, STATEMENT OF VISION

Idle No More calls on all people to join in a peaceful revolution which honours and fulfills Indigenous sovereignty and which protects the land, the water, and the sky. Colonization continues through attacks to Indigenous rights and damage and harm to all our relations. We must repair these violations, live the spirit and intent of the treaty relationship, work towards justice in action, and protect Mother Earth.[19]

Idle No More

WAB KINEW, THEN A JOURNALIST, RECOUNTING THE "GRASSROOTS" RISE OF IDLE NO MORE IN THE *FREE PRESS*, 2012

"Tweeting up on Sunday, December 2, the #IdleNoMore event in Alberta. Lets get it trending! Here is the FB event . . ."

Tanya Kappo (@Nehiyawskwew) posted that on Nov. 30 to drum up support for an event she organized called "Idle No More." Her fellow organizers began using the "#idlenomore" hashtag . . . and so did their followers.

Kappo told me she expected her event to be "15 people in a room listening to what I thought about the legislation." Instead,

150 people descended on Louis Bull First Nation in Alberta to hear Kappo and her co-organizers speak against Bill C-45. . . .

At the Idle No More event last Sunday, Kappo says many people were upset their chiefs were not talking about the bill. "There was angst building against our leadership. People asked 'What's (the Assembly of First Nations) doing?' and 'What are the chiefs doing?'"

In the aftermath . . . Manitoba Grand Chief Derek Nepinak [said:] "As chiefs, we always watch what our young people are doing. . . . They're putting their words out on social media saying, 'What are the chiefs going to do?', 'We need to stand up now.' We are going to act and this is just the beginning of it."

Kappo says . . . "If there's going to be real and profound change, it's not only about the relationship with the feds, but also the relationship with ourselves."[20]

Cree youth walkers arrive in Ottawa, March 25, 2013

SYLVIA MCADAM, ONE OF THE FOUNDERS OF IDLE NO MORE, ON THE ROOTS OF THE MOVEMENT, 2013

After I graduated from law school, I returned to my father's traditional land near the Whitefish reserve and to the waters that I had been to when I was a child, and they were gone. The waters had dried up! It was a terrible thing to witness. When my father and I went back to his traditional hunting lands, his cabin was gone. There was just a huge burn mark on the ground. When my father saw it, he just stood there, so quiet, so upset. It was terrible to watch.

I started investigating, and I learned that the conservation officers had blocked hunting roads to keep the traditional indigenous hunters away, and the lands were being logged. I felt intensely protective of the land and the water, so I went around nailing boards on trees, saying, "No Trespassing. Treaty 6 Territory!"

When I read Bill C-45 [a budget bill of the Harper government with changes to the environmental legislation], I was horrified. I got into a chat on Facebook with Jessica [Gordon] and Nina [Wilson], and I started explaining to them the implications of C-45 for the environment, for the waters. I told them there's something in law called acquiescence. That means that if you're silent, then your silence is taken as consent. All of us agreed that we couldn't be silent, that grassroots people have a right to know.[21]

NATIONAL CHIEF SHAWN ATLEO, ASSEMBLY OF FIRST NATIONS, SPEAKING DURING IDLE NO MORE PROTESTS

This is a powerful moment. . . . There is no going back to the way it was before.

. . .

This is not something that we created as First Nations. It was thrust on us. The unilateral actions of others.

. . .

As I'm standing right here our spirit is not broken. Our spirit is strong. Our people are proud. Young people are leading the way. And Chiefs, we better make sure we follow the young people. Because they are the leaders not of tomorrow, they are the leaders right now.

. . .

We will not silently suffer without protest.[22]

Another shift that had been emerging over decades was the involvement of Indigenous people in provincial and federal politics, as well as other positions of prominence and power in public life. While Inuit participation in territorial politics, as well as in Parliament in Ottawa, had steadily increased, Métis and First Nations, with a few exceptions, had been relatively absent from the political sphere until quite recently.

JODY WILSON-RAYBOULD, MEMBER OF PARLIAMENT FOR VANCOUVER–GRANVILLE, TESTIMONY IN THE SNC-LAVALIN JUSTICE COMMITTEE HEARINGS, ON BEING INDIGENOUS AND IN CANADIAN POLITICS, 2019

My understanding of the rule of law has also been shaped by my experience as an indigenous person and an indigenous leader. The history of Crown-indigenous relations in this country includes a history of the rule of law not being respected. Indeed, one of the main reasons for the urgent need for justice and reconciliation today is that in the history of our country we have not always upheld foundational values, such as the rule of law, in our relations with indigenous peoples. I have seen first-hand the negative impacts for freedom, equality and a just society this can have, so when I pledged to serve Canadians as your Minister of Justice and Attorney General, I came to do so with a deeply ingrained commitment to the rule of law and the importance of acting independently of partisan, political and narrow interests in all matters. When we do not do that, I firmly believe, and know, we do worse as a society.[23]

Jody Wilson-Raybould being sworn in as the Minister of Justice and Attorney General of Canada, Rideau Hall, Ottawa, November 4, 2015

MUMILAAQ QAQQAQ, MEMBER OF PARLIAMENT FOR NUNAVUT, FAREWELL SPEECH IN THE HOUSE OF COMMONS, 2021

Mr. Speaker, every time I walk on to House of Common grounds, speak in these chambers, I'm reminded every step of the way I don't belong here.

I have never felt safe or protected in my position, especially within the House of Commons, often having pep talks with myself in the elevator or taking a moment in the bathroom stall to maintain my composure. When I walk through these doors, not only am I reminded of the clear colonial house on fire I am willingly walking into, I am already in survival mode. . . .

You see, Mr. Speaker, I don't belong here. But my presence, I hope, is starting to crack the foundations of this very federal institution that started colonizing Inuit barely 70 years ago. I realized that this is difficult for some members to hear. But it's the reality and the truth. This place was built on the oppression of Indigenous peoples. People like my grandfather, who were born and raised on the land, but forcibly relocated into settlement that was financed and built by the federal institution.[24]

MICHELLE O'BONSAWIN, THE FIRST INDIGENOUS JUSTICE OF THE SUPREME COURT OF CANADA, REFLECTING ON GROWING UP FIRST NATIONS, 2022

As an Abenaki woman, I have a deep appreciation of the realities of First Nation, Inuit and Métis Peoples. Growing up as a young First Nations person off reserve, my family experienced adversity. I had a memorable conversation with my father in approximately 1982 during which he asked me if other kids laughed at me because I was "native." I recall telling him that they laughed at my name, which was evidently much different from the others in our small predominantly French community. My father got a sad look in his eyes and told me that when he was a child, the kids in his school would laugh, point at him and say that he came from "that family," le "sauvage" who lived on Sunnybrae Street. One teacher told him, "tu as un dernier nom pour coucher dehors"[25] which was clearly insensitive and ignorant. The lack of respect shown to my father and our family affected me as I was growing up.[26]

WAB KINEW, CANADA'S FIRST FIRST NATIONS PREMIER OF MANITOBA, IN HIS ACCEPTANCE SPEECH AFTER BECOMING PREMIER-ELECT, 2023

I want to speak to young Neechees in particular. I was given a second chance in life, and I would like to think that I have made good on that opportunity, and you can do the same.[27]

Premier Wab Kinew, swearing-in ceremony, Winnipeg, October 18, 2023

SALENA STARLING, PRESIDENT OF COMMUNITY OF BIG HEARTS, ON THE HOPE INSPIRED BY KINEW'S ELECTION, 2023

We deserve to see this change, and we are so happy to finally see it happening. . . . For myself, being a foster care survivor, being 18 years old, getting to see this change happen, it gives me a sense of hope and especially the thousands of Indigenous youth across Canada, seeing the first First Nations Premier in Canadian history. It's crucial, it's incredible and it's a beautiful thing that has happened.[28]

The social and cultural presence of Indigenous people, including Indigenous artists, authors, and performers, has steadily grown. While Indigenous worldviews, teachings, culture, and art have always greatly influenced Canadian society, that influence is now being recognized and understood in new ways, including through the acknowledgement and celebration of individual achievements and contributions.

KENOJUAK ASHEVAK, INUIT CARVER

There is no word for art. We say it is to transfer something from the real to the unreal. I am an owl, and I am a happy owl. I like to make people happy and everything happy. I am the light of happiness and I am a dancing owl.[29]

Northern Flash, 2022 by Kyle Natkusiak Aleekuk, Toronto, ON

KENT MONKMAN, CREE ARTIST

History is a narrative; it's a collection of stories sanctioned by the ruling power, and reinforced through words and images that suit them. That was the whole point of taking on history painting: to authorize these moments that have been swept under the rug for generations.[30]

ALANIS OBOMSAWIN, ABENAKI FILMMAKER

I will never leave my people. Even if I was a millionaire, or even if I had all kinds of power, I would always think of making a better place for them.

It's because they are still there—there are a lot of people that have been able to find their way. I often tell my story because I want them to hear that, if I am where I am today, it is because I refuse to be what they told me I was. I refused to feel inferior.[31]

CHRISTI BELCOURT, MÉTIS VISUAL ARTIST AND AUTHOR

All Indigenous art traditions come from an understanding of, and connection with, the land and its spirits. So that knowledge is encoded in the work or art. When you look at Indigenous art around the world, there is always that direct connection to the land. That understanding of how we're supposed to live on the land is encoded into the design, the symbols and the things that we see.

This Painting is a Mirror by Christi Belcourt

It's no different with beadwork. So when I'm creating my art, it's not a simple transferring of the beadwork patterns onto the canvas; it has to have the meaning behind it. So there will be certain plants or symbols in the painting that have a specific reason or coding behind them. It's always a message about the respect for lands and waters: the respect we need to have for the earth and everything that is around us. As human beings, we are mistaken if we think we are superior to other species.[32]

MICHELLE GOOD, CREE AUTHOR

Hope is really all we have. . . . If we abandon hope then where will our energies be fired from? It has to be hope for the future, hope for the coming generations. . . . People say, "ah it hasn't changed," but I'm old enough, I can tell you it has.[33]

Indigenous athletes have also become more present and recognized, and have often reflected on the distinctive reality of being Indigenous and a sports star.

CAREY PRICE, ULKATCHO FIRST NATION, HOCKEY PLAYER FOR THE MONTREAL CANADIENS, 2016

I encourage First Nations youth to be leaders in their communities. Be proud of your heritage, and don't be discouraged by the improbable.[34]

BRYAN TROTTIER, CREE MÉTIS, WINNER OF SIX STANLEY CUPS WITH THE NEW YORK ISLANDERS

I don't know how big an inspiration I am for indigenous children, but I want to wear it with all my might. There's a certain pride I think we all have in where and how we grow up and our heritage. There's a lot of variety in First Nation; it's a very diverse group.

Some of them feel self-conscious about the blend they have, that maybe they're not 100 percent First Nation. But they have the bloodlines, and they're very creative and they're very athletic and talented. They all have the ability to make a difference, and I tell them it's OK to be homesick but to remember it takes courage to live your dreams.[35]

With the increasing role of Indigenous people in public life, and a growing public recognition and awareness of Indigenous Peoples, there has also come an awareness of the effects of colonization on issues of Indigenous identity. In addition to the many Indigenous people who are disconnected from their family, community, and culture because of a range of political, legal, and social forces, we have seen a number of instances of individuals claiming to be Indigenous when they are not; these individuals are often referred to as "pretendians." This has led to a particular focus on Indigenous identity fraud at universities and colleges.

DREW HAYDEN TAYLOR, OJIBWE PLAYWRIGHT, AUTHOR, AND JOURNALIST, ON WHY SOME PEOPLE PRETEND TO BE INDIGENOUS, 2022

It seems there are three major reasons for such a transfer of identity. First, these people want or need to join a culture or family, after having found little to embrace in their immediate background. They desire a sense of belonging. A launching point or direction from which to tackle the next segment of their lives. Not so different from joining the Boy Scouts or a street gang, though the world of Indigeneity has a greater spiritual and historical context to offer. Luckily, we also know how to tie knots and ride motorcycles. So, bonus bonus.

Second, there may be financial benefits for some to appropriate when holding high the eagle feather. Some potentially lucrative contracts and advantageous high-profile positions exist for those interested in riding that buffalo.

Third—and what I am finding to be the most common—is incorrect family lore. A tale told by a grandfather or uncle of having an Indigenous ancestor deep in the family history. The infamous Cherokee princess story, maybe, or something that came out of watching too many episodes of Jesse Jim on the Beachcombers. People take these tall tales to heart and believe them without bothering to validate them.[36]

JEAN TEILLET, MÉTIS LAWYER AND AUTHOR, IN *INDIGENOUS IDENTITY FRAUD: A REPORT FOR THE UNIVERSITY OF SASKATCHEWAN*, 2022

To put it bluntly, an individual who relies on deception to achieve a material advantage—who intentionally and falsely identifies as Indigenous to obtain a faculty or staff position, funding, or a student placement—is engaged in Indigenous identity fraud. There are two kinds of Indigenous identity fraud. The first kind—the fabricators—are individuals who fabricate an Indigenous identity out of thin air. The second kind—the embellishers—are individuals who embellish their connection to Indigeneity, either by exaggeration or misstatement, when they don an Indigenous identity based on illusive hearsay or rumors (family stories), or miniscule evidence (an ancestor from the 1600s, or a DNA test that reveals a small percentage of Native American ancestry). The advantage they gain is stolen, causes harm, and breaches our trust. These individuals are said to be "wannabees" or "pretendians." They are donning "redface" or "playing Indian" (Deloria, 1999). In this report these fabricators and embellishers are collectively called fraudsters.[37]

Indigenous people are also beginning to be more and more present and have an impact in the business, financial, and economic life of Canada.

This includes individuals being leaders in the business community, the expansion of Indigenous businesses, and Indigenous communities becoming major economic actors and building their economies as part of meeting the needs of their citizens and addressing socio-economic challenges. At the same time, many Canadian companies, like individuals across the country, are trying to understand their role and responsibility in the work of reconciliation, and coming to realize that they, too, must play a part in upholding the rights of Indigenous Peoples.

ERNIE DANIELS, PRESIDENT AND CEO, FIRST NATIONS FINANCE AUTHORITY, ON FIRST NATIONS ACCESS TO CAPITAL THROUGH THE BOND MARKETS

I get to see every day the successes of this. I see schools, I see roads, I see water treatment plants. I see First Nations really getting

Victoria, B.C.

involved in the transition from fossil fuels to green energy. . . . These loans help communities to build the necessary infrastructure that is really required in their communities. It also enables them to really build on their economic development. . . . I see a great partnership. I see First Nations taking a rightful place in this economy, and actually being a major contributor to the economy.[38]

The federal model for funding infrastructure has failed to deliver the housing, clean water and other critical infrastructure that will improve the living conditions in First Nations communities. . . . We believe there is a better way, a way that works with First Nations as partners rather than the colonial approach that's rooted in the almost 150-year-old Indian Act.[39]

CHIEF TERRANCE PAUL, MEMBERTOU FIRST NATION, 2015

Membertou's own revenues top $100 million. . . . We employ 700 people at peak seasons. Those are all people with jobs, who pay taxes, or buy consumer goods, pumping more money into the economy. . . .

People think we're getting something the rest aren't, that we don't want to work, that we don't pay taxes. . . . We do what needs to be done to educate the public. We are good to deal with, we improve the economy, improve the tax base of the city. The jobs here? The municipality benefits more than ourselves. We contribute.

Despite all the barriers, we're still here . . .[40]

KHELSILEM, SPOKESPERSON, SQUAMISH NATION SPEAKING ABOUT THE SEN̓ÁḴW DEVELOPMENT PROJECT, 2022

The nature of reconciliation is to start with the truth: it's about time First Nations can create value from the tiny parcels of reserve lands we were left with after past racist governments seized nearly everything. But it's also about Indigenous Peoples influencing Canada positively, as much as Canada has had a profound impact on Indigenous Peoples. We've had to change and sacrifice so much of who we are and give up so much of what belongs to us for Canada to exist. Our development of Sen'áḵw is as much of a benefit to the city as it is a tool to create wealth from our lands that will enhance the entire community.

Its legitimacy as an effort of reconciliation is evidenced by the broad collaboration between Indigenous and non-Indigenous governments, but also through the net positive impact, we will have on Indigenous and non-Indigenous communities.[41]

CHIEF CLARENCE LOUIE, OSOYOOS INDIAN BAND, 2023

Most of my people want to be self-supported. They want a good job. They want a regular paycheck. They want to be able to pay their own bills. They want to own nice things. They want to go on holidays.

Regarding our community, the entrepreneurial spirit goes back thousands of years. History books record that our people were entrepreneurial way back. People know about the fur trade—that was business and enterprise. Our people also traded with each other. . . . [T]he ancestral graves in our area prove that items that came from the far South and the far Northeast ended up in our area. There is archaeological evidence that our people had business relationships between tribes and nations long before the French and English showed up.

It's a challenge to keep the entrepreneurial spirit alive. A lot of damage has been done over the years due to colonialism. The colonial situation whether it was in Africa, New Zealand, or North America was intended to take over a race of people—the first thing you need to do is take away their economic ability to support themselves.[42]

Kamloopa Powwow

CHIEF JEN THOMAS, TSLEIL-WAUTUTH, ON THE JERICHO LANDS PROJECT, THE LARGEST DEVELOPMENT PROJECT IN VANCOUVER'S HISTORY, AND WHICH IS OWNED BY SQUAMISH, MUSQUEAM, AND TSLEIL-WAUTUTH NATIONS, 2024

In returning our culture to these lands, we honour our ancestors and Elders who taught us our traditions and stories. The efforts we make today, together with our relatives Squamish and Musqueam, are a once-in-a-lifetime opportunity to generate wealth that can be invested into our community to improve the quality of life for not only the current generations, but also for the next seven generations to come.[43]

TECK RESOURCES, INDIGENOUS PEOPLES POLICY, 2022

Teck respects the rights, cultures, interests, and aspirations of Indigenous Peoples and, in the spirit of reconciliation, is committed to building strong and lasting relationships that help us understand each other's perspectives and priorities. . . .

Teck engages with Indigenous Peoples potentially affected by our activities to:

- Build respectful relationships through early, inclusive dialogue and collaborative processes.

- Provide resources to build the capacity of both Indigenous Peoples and Teck to enable meaningful dialogue.

- Integrate Indigenous Peoples' knowledge and perspectives into decision making, throughout the mining life cycle, to enhance benefits and address impacts.

- Address adverse impacts to Indigenous rights, cultural heritage, livelihoods, health and wellbeing.

- Work to achieve and maintain the free, prior and informed consent of Indigenous Peoples when proposing new or substantially modified projects.

- Work with Indigenous Peoples to achieve self-determined community goals that provide lasting benefits.

We are dedicated to continually learning about the history, traditions, worldviews and rights of Indigenous Peoples where we operate. We are committed to working with Indigenous Peoples to provide intercultural awareness training and education for Teck team members.[44]

ROCCO ROSSI, PRESIDENT AND CEO, ONTARIO CHAMBER OF COMMERCE (OCC), UPON RELEASE OF *SHARING PROSPERITY*, AN INTRODUCTORY GUIDE TO ECONOMIC RECONCILIATION, 2023

The OCC recognizes that as a settler-led organization, we have the responsibility to take on this work and that reconciliation is an ongoing process of learning and action. Initial Steps we have taken to date include increasing the representation of Indigenous Peoples on our Board of Directors, applying Indigenous perspectives to our policy work, and committing to undertake continuous internal training. Nevertheless, there remains much work ahead. . . . This resource provides the business community with an introduction to the knowledge and know-how required to advance Truth and Reconciliation and build mutually beneficial relationships with Indigenous Peoples.[45]

DAVE MCKAY, PRESIDENT AND CEO, ROYAL BANK OF CANADA, IN *A CHOSEN JOURNEY: RBC INDIGENOUS PARTNERSHIP REPORT*, 2023

Our chosen journey is one rooted in partnership, humility and hope for our shared future. . . .

U'mista Culture Centre, Alert Bay

Much of my hope and optimism for the future comes from our chosen journey—one that's centred around reconciliation, inclusion and bringing generations together to build a future we can all be proud of.

In Canada, our country's reconciliation journey is interlinked with our ability to solve the many challenges of our time, which is why RBC's commitment to reconciliation is important. . . .

We also know Indigenous leadership and knowledge is a critical part of protecting our planet, and meaningful consultation with Indigenous Peoples is fundamental to our country's successful transition to a net-zero future. As a leading Canadian company, we take seriously the responsibility to support and partner with Indigenous communities as we cultivate a more inclusive path forward—one that protects the land, water and sky for generations to come.[46]

In the early 2000s, the Supreme Court of Canada continued to issue critical rulings in favour of the rights of Indigenous Peoples, and to urge Crown governments to take action that effects real change. These included the Haida decision in 2004, which affirmed the duty to consult and accommodate, and the Tsilhqot'in Nation decision in 2014, which for all intents and purposes settled the core legal issues related to the outstanding "Indian Land Question." In Tsilhqot'in, the court declared title existed on a territorial basis—in this instance more than 1,750 square kilometres—and confirmed that wherever title exists, Indigenous consent is the standard, and that the Crown has no beneficial or economic interest in the lands and resources subject to Indigenous title. In other words, the Crown has been infringing on Indigenous title throughout the history of Canada; it continues to do so today; and the risks and costs of continuing this pattern are high.

Ninstints totem poles (Anthony Island), Haida Gwaii

CHIEF JUSTICE BEVERLEY MCLACHLIN, IN *HAIDA NATION V. BRITISH COLUMBIA (MINISTER OF FORESTS)*, 2004

Where treaties remain to be concluded, the honour of the Crown requires negotiations leading to a just settlement of Aboriginal claims. . . . Treaties serve to reconcile pre-existing Aboriginal sovereignty with assumed Crown sovereignty, and to define Aboriginal rights guaranteed by s. 35 of the Constitution Act, 1982. Section 35 represents a promise of rights recognition, and "[i]t is always assumed that the Crown intends to fulfil its promises". . . . This promise is realized and sovereignty claims reconciled through the process of honourable negotiation. It is a corollary of s. 35 that the Crown act honourably in defining the rights it guarantees and in reconciling them with other rights and interests. This, in turn, implies a duty to consult and, if appropriate, accommodate.[47]

CHIEF JUSTICE BEVERLEY MCLACHLIN, IN *TSILHQOT'IN NATION V. BRITISH COLUMBIA*, 2014

With the declaration of title, the Tsilhqot'in have now established Aboriginal title to the portion of the lands designated by the trial judge. . . . This gives them the right to determine, subject to the inherent limits of group title held for future generations, the uses to which the land is put and to enjoy its economic fruits. As we have seen, this is not merely a right of first refusal with respect to Crown land management or usage plans. Rather, it is the right to proactively use and manage the land.

. . .

I add this. Governments and individuals proposing to use or exploit land, whether before or after a declaration of Aboriginal title, can avoid a charge of infringement or failure to adequately consult by obtaining the consent of the interested Aboriginal group.[48]

In 2015, Justin Trudeau became prime minister, promising transformative change based on recognition of Indigenous rights, respect, co-operation, and partnership. Three years later, he announced in the House of Commons that his government would enact a comprehensive Recognition

Teztan Biny, Tsilhqot'in Territory

and Implementation of Indigenous Rights Framework involving new laws, policies, and practices by the end of 2018.

PRIME MINISTER JUSTIN TRUDEAU'S DIRECTION TO ALL GOVERNMENT MINISTERS IN THEIR MANDATE LETTERS, 2015

I made a personal commitment to bring new leadership and a new tone to Ottawa. We made a commitment to Canadians to pursue our goals with a renewed sense of collaboration. Improved partnerships with provincial, territorial, and municipal governments are essential to deliver the real, positive change that we promised Canadians. No relationship is more important to me and to Canada than the one with Indigenous Peoples. It is time for a renewed, nation-to-nation relationship with Indigenous Peoples, based on recognition of rights, respect, co-operation, and partnership.[49]

PRIME MINISTER JUSTIN TRUDEAU, COMMITTING CANADA TO THE ESTABLISHMENT A NEW RECOGNITION AND IMPLEMENTATION OF INDIGENOUS RIGHTS FRAMEWORK, 2018

Last September, at the United Nations, I spoke to delegations from around the world and told some hard truths about Canada's long and complicated relationship with First Nations, Inuit, and Métis peoples.

I talked about the colonial approach that led to the discriminatory and paternalistic *Indian Act*.

A colonial approach that systematically ignored the history of the Métis Nation, and denied its peoples their rights.

And that, in the name of Canadian sovereignty, forced the relocation of entire Inuit communities—starving individuals, uprooting families, and causing generations of harm.

. . .

It's clear, Mr. Speaker, that Indigenous Peoples and all Canadians know it is past time for change.

At the same time, some view our government's commitments with some degree of scepticism—and if you look at how things have been handled in the past, it's hard to say that that scepticism is misplaced.

After all, it's not like we are the first government to recognize the need for change, and promise that we'd do things differently.

It's been more than 20 years since the Royal Commission on Aboriginal Peoples called for "the recognition of Aboriginal Peoples as self-governing nations with a unique place in Canada."

More than 30 years have passed since the Penner Report and the First Ministers' Conferences on the Rights of Aboriginal Peoples.

And last year marked 35 years since Aboriginal and treaty rights were recognized and affirmed through Section 35 of the *Constitution Act*.

You might recall . . . that the government of the day—led by my father—did not intend to include these rights at the outset.

It was the outspoken advocacy of First Nations, Inuit, and Métis peoples, supported by non-Indigenous Canadians, that forced the government to reconsider.

Imagine what that must have felt like, Mr. Speaker.

To have fought so hard, for so long, against colonialism. Rallying your communities, reaching out to Canadians, riding the "Constitution Express." And in the end, to finally be recognized and included. To see your rights enshrined and protected in the foundational document on which Canada's democracy rests.

Now imagine the mounting disappointment—the unsurprising and familiar heartache, and the rising tide of anger—when governments that had promised so much did so little to keep their word.

You see . . . the challenge—then and now—is that while Section 35 recognizes and affirms Aboriginal and treaty rights, those rights have not been implemented by our governments.

The work to give life to Section 35 was supposed to be done together with First Nations, Inuit, and Métis Peoples. And while there has been some success, progress has not been sustained, or carried out.

And so over time, it too often fell to the courts to pick up the pieces, and fill in the gaps.

More precisely, instead of outright recognizing and affirming Indigenous rights—as we promised we would—Indigenous Peoples were forced to prove, time and time again, through costly and drawn-out court challenges, that their rights existed, must be recognized and implemented.

Indigenous Peoples, like all Canadians, know this must change.

We know it, too.

. . .

And so today, I am pleased to announce that the government will develop—in full partnership with First Nations, Inuit, and Métis people—a new Recognition and Implementation of Indigenous Rights Framework that will include new ways to recognize and implement Indigenous Rights.

This will include new recognition and implementation of rights legislation.

Going forward, recognition of rights will guide all government relations with Indigenous Peoples.[50]

Not unlike the promises of governments in the past, the Trudeau government's promised transformative change did not materialize and remains outstanding. But some legislative progress was made. Between 1867 and 2019, there was no federal or provincial statute that recognized, respected, and upheld the rights of Indigenous Peoples. In 2019, the legislature of British Columbia unanimously passed the Declaration on the Rights of Indigenous Peoples Act *to implement the United Nations Declaration on the Rights of Indigenous Peoples. Canada passed a similar law—the* United Nations Declaration on the Rights of Indigenous Peoples Act*—in 2021. While these laws are largely only frameworks requiring further action and legal* *development, they are steps forward. A number of other recent statutes have express acknowledgements of the existence of Indigenous rights. While this is progress, significant work remains to change laws, policies, and practices of Crown governments. And the colonial Indian Act remains in place.*

DECLARATION ON THE RIGHTS OF INDIGENOUS PEOPLES ACT, B.C., 2019

2 The purposes of this Act are as follows:

(a) to affirm the application of the Declaration to the laws of British Columbia;

(b) to contribute to the implementation of the Declaration;

(c) to support the affirmation of, and develop relationships with, Indigenous governing bodies.

3 In consultation and cooperation with the Indigenous peoples in British Columbia, the government must take all measures necessary to ensure the laws of British Columbia are consistent with the Declaration.

4 (1) The government must prepare and implement an action plan to achieve the objectives of the Declaration.

(2) The action plan must be prepared and implemented in consultation and cooperation with the Indigenous peoples in British Columbia.

(3) The action plan must contain the date on or before which the government must initiate a review of the action plan.

(4) After the action plan is prepared, the minister must, as soon as practicable,

(a) lay the action plan before the Legislative Assembly if the Legislative Assembly is then sitting, or

(b) file the action plan with the Clerk of the Legislative Assembly if the Legislative Assembly is not sitting.

(5) The government may prepare a new action plan in accordance with this section.[51]

Declaration on the Rights of Indigenous Peoples Act, formally passed in the B.C. Legislative Assembly, 2019

WHEREAS CLAUSES FROM THE UNITED NATIONS DECLARATION ON THE RIGHTS OF INDIGENOUS PEOPLES ACT, CANADA, 2021

Whereas all doctrines, policies and practices based on or advocating the superiority of peoples or individuals on the basis of national origin or racial, religious, ethnic or cultural differences, including the doctrines of discovery and *terra nullius*, are racist, scientifically false, legally invalid, morally condemnable and socially unjust;

Whereas the Government of Canada rejects all forms of colonialism and is committed to advancing relations with Indigenous peoples that are based on good faith and on the principles of justice, democracy, equality, non-discrimination, good governance and respect for human rights;

Whereas the Declaration emphasizes the urgent need to respect and promote the inherent rights of Indigenous peoples of the world which derive from their political, economic and social structures and from their cultures, spiritual traditions, histories, philosophies and legal systems, especially their rights to their lands, territories and resources;

Whereas the Government of Canada recognizes that all relations with Indigenous peoples must be based on the recognition and implementation of the inherent right to self-determination, including the right of self-government;

Whereas the Government of Canada is committed to taking effective measures—including legislative, policy and administrative measures—at the national and international level, in consultation and cooperation with Indigenous peoples, to achieve the objectives of the Declaration;

Whereas the Government of Canada is committed to exploring, in consultation and cooperation with Indigenous peoples, measures related to monitoring, oversight, recourse or remedy or other accountability measures that will contribute to the achievement of those objectives;

Whereas the implementation of the Declaration can contribute to supporting sustainable development and responding to growing concerns relating to climate change and its impacts on Indigenous peoples;

Whereas the Government of Canada acknowledges that provincial, territorial and municipal governments each have the ability to establish their own approaches to contributing to the implementation of the Declaration by taking various measures that fall within their authority;

Whereas the Government of Canada welcomes opportunities to work cooperatively with those governments, Indigenous peoples and other sectors of society towards achieving the objectives of the Declaration;

Whereas the Declaration is affirmed as a source for the interpretation of Canadian law . . .[52]

Under the Justin Trudeau government, specific resolution was brought to some significant issues. One of the most notable was settling, in 2023, the long-standing discrimination in funding supports for Indigenous children after years of struggle and litigation through the Canadian Human Rights Tribunal. Another advance with respect to children and families was the passage of Bill C-92: An Act respecting First Nations, Inuit and Métis children, youth and families *in 2019, which establishes the mechanism for Indigenous jurisdiction over their children and families. Since its passage, several Indigenous governments across the country are in various stages of taking over control of their children. On February 9, 2024, the Supreme Court of Canada upheld Bill C-92 as constitutional and spoke to the importance of self-government and Indigenous Peoples caring for their children under their laws.*

STATEMENT OF PURPOSE OF BILL C-92: *AN ACT RESPECTING FIRST NATIONS, INUIT AND MÉTIS CHILDREN, YOUTH AND FAMILIES*, 2019

[To] affirm the inherent right of self-government, which includes jurisdiction in relation to child and family services.[53]

NATIONAL CHIEF PERRY BELLEGARDE, ASSEMBLY OF FIRST NATIONS ON BILL C-92, 2019

This legislation is first and foremost about First Nations children and their safety, their security and their future. The tragedy of thousands of First Nations children in care tells us we need a new approach. This legislation will recognize First Nations jurisdiction so they can build their own systems based on their own governance, laws and policies. Our focus has to be on prevention over apprehension, and keeping children close to their cultures and families. We need investments to support this work, and we need everyone to support this approach. The time is long overdue for First Nations to finally regain responsibility over our children.[54]

CINDY BLACKSTOCK, EXECUTIVE DIRECTOR OF FIRST NATIONS CHILD AND FAMILY CARING SOCIETY, ON WHAT IS NEEDED TO HELP ENSURE THAT DISCRIMINATION DOES NOT CONTINUE TO OCCUR, 2021

If we can raise a generation of non-Indigenous kids who don't normalize discrimination, and have the tools to peacefully and respectfully advocate for the end of this kind of apartheid system, then we'll be in a position where First Nations children never have to recover from their childhoods again. . . . And non-Indigenous children never have to say they're sorry.[55]

PATTY HAJDU, MINISTER OF INDIGENOUS SERVICES, ON THE SETTLEMENT OF CLAIMS REGARDING DISCRIMINATION AND FUNDING SUPPORTS, 2023

It's a historic day for so many First Nations families who have waited so long for this. Although nothing can make up for the harm and pain decades of underfunding caused, compensation is essential to moving forward. I sincerely thank the Assembly of First Nations, Moushoom and Trout class action plaintiffs and the First Nations Child and Family Caring Society—amongst others—for their work. Their leadership has pushed Canada to do the right thing and is moving us forward on the path to reconciliation. We will continue working with them on a historic reform of our programs so that this never happens again.[56]

ZACHEUS TROUT, CROSS LAKE FIRST NATION, MB, ONE OF THE LEAD PLAINTIFFS IN THE CANADIAN HUMAN RIGHTS TRIBUNAL LITIGATION, IN RESPONSE TO COURT APPROVAL OF THE SETTLEMENT, 2023

I hope this brings a change of how we look at Indigenous people and how we can move forward, reconciling all the differences between non-Indigenous and the Indigenous people right across Canada. . . . It's history that's been made here today.[57]

SUPREME COURT OF CANADA, "REFERENCE RE AN ACT RESPECTING FIRST NATIONS, INUIT AND MÉTIS CHILDREN, YOUTH AND FAMILIES" (BILL C-92), 2024

[7] The three elements of the purpose set out in s. 8 [of the Act] reflect Parliament's openness to using three different types of legal norms that will be interwoven in this framework for reconciliation to ensure the well-being of Indigenous children: the legislative authority of Indigenous peoples in relation to child and family services, the legislative provisions enacted by Parliament to establish national standards, and the international standards referred to in the Declaration. The metaphor of "braiding" together these three types of norms has been helpfully proposed to explain how the Declaration should be implemented in Canada, so as to "work out how state law and Indigenous law

Ghislain Picard (third from left, back row), Regional Chief of the Assembly of First Nations Quebec-Labrador (AFNQL), addresses a news conference where First Nations leaders responded to the Supreme Court of Canada decision on the federal Indigenous child welfare act, Ottawa, February 9, 2024

> could be interwoven, with guidance from international law, to form a single, strong rope." . . .
>
> [8] Announced in s. 8 and carried out by the Act as a whole, Parliament's effort to braid this "rope" with three strands constitutes the specific framework for reconciliation when it comes to Indigenous child and family services, in the spirit of the Declaration. Canada's commitment to implementing the Declaration and responding to the Truth and Reconciliation Commission's call to action is thus met immediately; this avoids the uncertainties of constitutional negotiations, the slowness of treaty settlements entered into on a piecemeal basis by the Crown and each of the various Indigenous communities concerned, and the inevitable conflicts associated with court settlements. . .[58]

<<<< >>>>

You are probably familiar with the expression "low man on the totem pole." This phrase is a mix of ignorance, appropriation, and racism. It infers that totem poles are depictions of social hierarchy, with the most important people at the top and the least important at the bottom, and that the pole itself should be seen as a reflection of the levels and distinctions between types of peoples. It reduces our artwork, our culture, to a casual bit of slang in a variety of contexts dissociated from First Nations.

Rather than depicting hierarchy and distinction, our totem poles are intended to convey connections between Clans, and the balance that exists between peoples. Each figure on a pole has distinct powers, roles, and responsibilities that must be fulfilled for the well-being of all. Rather than reflecting a hierarchy, which is more a European mode of social order, our poles reflect the communitarian worldviews that characterize Indigenous cultures and ways of life.

There is no "low man" on a totem pole. There are figures that together form a whole and, together, tell a story.

For me, the work of reconciliation today involves, at once, a process of deconstruction and a process of construction. We must deconstruct, take apart, dismantle what phrases like "low man on a totem pole" represent—the removing of Indigenous modes of social organization and governance, and the imposition of a foreign one, including the system imposed on First Nations by the Indian Act. At the same time, we must rebuild Indigenous nations and governments in ways that meet the challenges and realities of the contemporary world.

This constructive, rebuilding work is taking place across Canada. Indigenous people are pursuing this work in their own distinct ways, at different paces, and reflecting their own priorities. It is this work that is essential to our shared future as Canadians. Colonization, at

Gitanyow, B.C.

its core, is about disempowerment—the removal of the autonomy, self-determination, and sovereignty of a People. To say it another way, colonization is about removing the control any People should have over their own lives and well-being. Decolonization and reconciliation require re-establishing that control and exercising it in ways that best care for our children, families, and communities, as well as stewarding lands and resources.

At this moment in time, we are hearing a fundamental shift from what we have heard before. We are hearing voices that express how we are in the midst of a resurgence and revitalization of our ways. This work of construction is deepening every day, and it is these voices that will keep getting stronger and stronger.

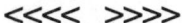

<<<< >>>>

Public attention regarding the need for reconciliation has continued to increase. The reports of unmarked burials at the sites of former residential schools—beginning in 2021 with the Tk'emlúps te Secwe'pemc announcing the detection of unmarked burials believed to hold the remains of 215 children who attended the Kamloops Indian Residential School—was a shock for many Canadians. Across the country, Indigenous communities continue to search and report on the discovery of unmarked burials at the sites of former residential schools, Indian hospitals, and other colonial institutions.

WILTON LITTLECHILD, CREE, FORMER MEMBER OF PARLIAMENT AND GRAND CHIEF OF THE CONFEDERACY OF TREATY SIX FIRST NATIONS, 2021

It was because the story was hidden that people didn't know about it. . . . It took sort of a real shock and awakening of the country. . . . My prayer and hope is that's the stage we're at now, that we will go on a path of reconciliation now that we know more of the truth. It took this shocking news to wake the country up in a sense, but

Vancouver Art Gallery, August 28, 2021

let's use that and say, "Now that we know the truth, what can we do about it?" I say let's work on a path to reconciliation.[59]

PRIME MINISTER JUSTIN TRUDEAU, 2021

As prime minister, I am appalled by the shameful policy that stole Indigenous children from their communities. . . . Sadly, this is not an exception or an isolated incident. . . . We're not going to hide from that. We have to acknowledge the truth. Residential schools were a reality—a tragedy that existed here, in our country, and we have to own up to it. Kids were taken from their families, returned damaged or not returned at all.[60]

CHIEF ROSANNE CASIMIR, TK'EMLÚPS TE SECWE'PEMC, 2021

[The death of children at the Kamloops Indian Residential School was] an unthinkable loss that was spoken about but never documented.[61]

Kamloops, B.C., June 4, 2021

KIMBERLY R. MURRAY, INDEPENDENT SPECIAL INTERLOCUTOR FOR MISSING CHILDREN AND UNMARKED GRAVES AND BURIAL SITES ASSOCIATED WITH INDIAN RESIDENTIAL SCHOOLS (CANADA), SUBMISSION TO THE UN EXPERT MECHANISM ON THE RIGHTS OF INDIGENOUS PEOPLES, 2023

[2] For over 100 years, more than 150,000 First Nation, Inuit and Métis children were taken from their parents and communities and placed in state-funded, church-run Indian Residential Schools. Based on significant documentary evidence and Survivor testimony, the TRC [Truth and Reconciliation Commission] concluded that many children who were forcibly taken to these institutions were subject to neglect, malnutrition, substandard health and living conditions, exposure to contagious diseases, mistreatment, medical experimentation, and extreme physical, sexual, spiritual and mental abuse by those entrusted with their care.

[3] Unfortunately, many First Nations, Inuit and Métis children were never returned home from Indian Residential Schools. Survivors have shared testimonies of children who were there one day then disappeared the next, of newborn babies being put into incinerators, of being forced to dig the graves of children who died, and of knowing where on former Indian Residential School grounds children are buried in unmarked graves.[62]

While public attention increases, and governments continue to struggle to advance the transformative shifts that have long been needed, Indigenous Peoples continue to work to revitalize their own governments and legal orders, rebuild their cultures and communities, and support a resurgence in their social and cultural life.

The Gwaii Haanas Legacy Pole, Lyell Island, Haida Gwaii, 2013

CHIEF DAN GEORGE OF THE TSLEIL-WAUTUTH NATION, 1974

My people's memory reaches into the beginning of all things.[63]

DR. JOHN BORROWS, CHIPPEWA OF NAWASH FIRST NATION, LEGAL SCHOLAR AND PROFESSOR, ON THE RELATIONSHIP BETWEEN THE REVITALIZATION OF INDIGENOUS LAWS AND RECONCILIATION

We have our own standards, principles, criteria, authority, measures, signposts, and guideposts. We have our own indicia for measuring how to regulate our affairs and how to resolve our disputes. . . . These things have been passed down to us and can be revitalized in ways that are contemporary, living, and relevant. . . . Our challenge is to see our languages, our songs, our stories, our relationship to the natural world and reason in relationship to them

“My people’s memory reaches into the beginning of all things.”

—Chief Dan George

and feel in relationship to them so that we can . . . make them live. We make them live by giving them application.[64]

I think [reconciliation] means anything that revitalizes Indigenous law. And by that, law is something that we do, it is an activity, it's something that is participatory, and allows for engagement.

And so, the idea of reconciliation being something about the revitalization of Indigenous law, is about seeing our participatory promises that can come alongside reconciliation. If Indigenous law becomes more prominent, I have often made this point that we cannot be reconciled with one another until we are also reconciled with the earth, and so if we reconcile Indigenous law that is going to help us reconcile our relationship with the earth . . . and if we are doing that as Indigenous peoples that is going to invite other Canadians into finding reconciliation with the earth.

The revitalization of Indigenous law puts other values forward as the standards for judgment in regard to law and reconciliation . . . so we have our grandmother and grandfather teachings, other nations have those similar things, love, respect, truth, humility, courage, honesty, wisdom . . . that is if we see law, not just as this external measure again, but something we can internalize around love, honest, humility etc. . . . these become things that help us make judgments . . . they become the touchstones, the criteria for the way we act together . . . and my hope then is that this reconciliation would then revitalize our material quality of life.[65]

LEANNE BETASAMOSAKE SIMPSON, MICHI SAAGIIG NISHNAABEG SCHOLAR, WRITER, AND ARTIST, ON THE LEGACY OF COLONIALISM, 2020

Over the past 200 years, and really the most intense degradation has occurred since the 1940s, which is in the lifespan of our old people—without our permission and without our consent, we have been systemically removed and dispossessed of most of our territory. We have fought back as most of our homeland has been stolen, clearcut, subdivided and sold to settlers from Europe and later, cottagers from Toronto. The last salmon navigated our waters about one hundred years ago; we no longer have eels or salmon in our territory, we no longer have old-growth white pine forests. Our rice beds were nearly destroyed, all but one tiny piece of prairie that exists in my reserve in Alderville has been destroyed. Ninety percent of our sugarbushes are under private ownership. Our most sacred spaces have been made into provincial parks for tourists, with concrete buildings on our teaching rocks. Our burial grounds, our mounds, have cottages built on top of them. The veins of our mother have lift-locks blocking them, and the shores of nearly every one of our lakes and rivers has a cottage or a home, making it nearly impossible for us to launch a canoe. Our rice has nearly been destroyed by raised water levels from the Trent-Severn Waterway, boat traffic, and sewage from the cottages. Our children have been taken away and sent to Residential schools, day schools, and now an education system that refuses to acknowledge our culture, our knowledge, our history and Indigenous experience.

Colonialism was and is a choice that Canadians make every day. It's a choice to maintain and uphold a system that is based on the hyper exploitation of the land and of Indigenous peoples. It's a choice to maintain a system that overwhelmingly promotes greed over creation.[66]

MI'KMAW ELDER ALBERT MARSHALL, ON ETUAPTMUMK (TWO-EYED SEEING)

Two-Eyed Seeing refers to a concept of learning to see from one eye with the strengths of Indigenous knowledges and ways of knowing—and seeing from the other eye with the strengths of Western knowledges and ways of knowing. . . .

It is believed that using *Two-Eyed Seeing* provides a pathway to co-existence, where long-standing Indigenous knowledge systems can be paired with Western scientific insights for an equitable and sustainable future.

In *Two-Eyed Seeing*, it is important to recognize that this concept does not assimilate either viewpoint. This guiding framework serves to build a co-existence and to complement both approaches. It creates an awareness and understanding that to move forward, both ways of knowing are beneficial, and recognizing and seeing both ways of knowing can only improve and strengthen our decision-making and future in all aspects.[67]

JEAN TEILLET, MÉTIS LAWYER AND AUTHOR, ON REBUILDING, 2024

So as much as we can push forward now . . . that means that the pull-back . . . they can only push you back so far . . . and there is one good thing about this. . . . I think that First Nations, Inuit, and Métis are much stronger than they were before . . . politically, financially, health-wise—I know there are lots of problems . . . but I think we are way better than we have ever been, and so that is really encouraging to my mind and we are standing firm on what we think needs to happen . . . and we are saying "no" now to them . . . and that is part of reconciliation . . . we are not always the ones that should be always compromising or always giving in because we need the money. We still need those things. . . . Reconciliation is having the effect of strengthening us and changing the mindset where Canadians are actually . . . accepting that there are other nations within this state . . . a state composed of many nations.

. . .

A confederation . . . an assembly of different nations working together as nations . . . that is my vision of where we will be . . . maybe it will take a hundred years, maybe it will never happen . . .

the Indigenous Nations will have control of their territories, lands, and resources and governments, and then the other governments will have to include them in the decision-making and the way this state is run . . . and we are a long way from that.[68]

ELDER FRANK NELSON, DZAWADA̲'ENUX̲W NATION, WITH ADVICE FOR THE NEXT GENERATION

"Maya'anł"; love, compassion, respect, honor, integrity. We don't exercise it. Most of the time we would like to think that we do. We can't just leave it hanging by the door in the Bighouse. That is what is missing in our lives. All of the things that have become a part of your administration, sometimes a lot of people aren't too happy with how things are administered in our village. I say this not to undermine our family, but sometimes we are too consumed by being governed by the book, by what Indian Affairs has laid down for us. There is no room for being compassionate to be able to address anything that we have to do to help our families. That part I would really recommend that we exercise to the best of our ability.[69]

ELDER CAROLE DAWSON, DZAWADA̲'ENUX̲W NATION, WITH ADVICE TO THE NEXT GENERATION

We need to remember our roots, we need to remember our origins. Not just remember them but to honour them. I personally feel that I have not done enough to honour my community, to honour my family, to pay homage to them. We have a very rich background and it is incumbent on us, not only to uphold that for ourselves, we need to share that with the universe. It has to echo back. The valleys are rich and wealthy in so many ways. Not just material things; we are rich in our memory. We are rich in our minds, our knowledge. We are rich in our traditions. All these things about Kingcome, they are powerful. They are medicine, our medicine. We need to share that medicine with other people.[70]

Kwakwaka'wakw button blanket

"We need to remember our roots, we need to remember our origins. Not just remember them but to honour them. . . . We have a very rich background . . . we are rich in our minds, our knowledge. We are rich in our traditions. . . they are powerful. They are medicine, our medicine. We need to share that medicine with other people."

—Elder Carole Dawson, Dzawada'enuxw Nation

THERESA HOLIZKI, SASKATCHEWAN HUMAN RIGHTS COMMISSION, 1993

The first thing is, we have to be able to share the power. Until we are going to make that leap, there is not going to be change.[71]

RICHARD WAGAMESE, AUTHOR, ON RECONCILIATION, 2012

Our neighbours in this country need to hear stories about our capacity for forgiveness, for self-examination, for compassion, and for our yearning for peace because they speak to our resiliency as a people. That is how reconciliation happens.

It is a big work, *reconciliation*. Quite simply, it means to create harmony. You create harmony with truth and you build truth out of humility. That is spiritual. That is truth. That is Indian. Within us, as nations of Aboriginal people and as individual members of those nations, we have an incredible capacity for survival, endurance, and forgiveness. In the reconciliation with ourselves first, we find the ability to create harmony with others, and that is where it has to start—in the fertile soil of our own hearts, minds, and spirits.

That, too, is Indian.[72]

One central aspect of the resurgence of Indigenous Peoples is the preservation and teaching of Indigenous languages. The Inuit languages of Inuvialuktun, Inuinnaqtun, and Inuktitut, the Métis language Michif, and the more than seventy First Nations languages spoken across Canada are all fundamental to Indigenous cultures, identities, and well-being, and a focus of efforts to ensure that Indigenous ways of knowing and being are passed on to future generations.

ELDER ELI TAYLOR, SIOUX VALLEY DAKOTA NATION, ON THE IMPORTANT OF LANGUAGE

The Aboriginal languages were given by the Creator as an integral part of life. Embodied in Aboriginal languages is our unique relationship to the Creator, our attitudes, beliefs, values and the fundamental notion of what is truth. Aboriginal language is an asset to one's own education, formal and informal. Aboriginal language contributes to greater pride in the history and culture of the community: greater involvement and interest of parents in the education of their children, and greater respect for Elders. Language is the principle means by which culture is accumulated, shared and

Ancestral Women Taking Back Their Dresses by Sherry Farrell Racette

transmitted from generation to generation. The key to identity and retention of culture is one's ancestral language.[73]

ELDER NORMAN FLEURY, MÉTIS NATION, ON MICHIF

Our Michif language is a gift from the Creator; it is a God-given language, gifted to the Métis Nation.[74]

EVA AARIAK, INUK, AS NUNAVUT LANGUAGES COMMISSIONER, ON LANGUAGE AND CULTURE

Who are you if you don't have culture? How do you feel? How do you see yourself? If you know who you are, if you know your language, your culture, if you know where you came from, then you are that much more confident in yourself, and you are ready to take on the challenges of life.[75]

At this moment in time, it is recognized that while progress is being made, fundamental changes are still needed if reconciliation is to truly advance. From continuing to learn the truth of our past; to fully recognizing and implementing Indigenous rights; to recognizing and respecting the roles and responsibilities of Indigenous governments; to addressing the continuing colonial Indian Act; to following through on the solutions to social, economic, and cultural challenges that have been identified time and again in studies and reports—it is understood that hard work remains ahead of us.

ELDER FRED KELLY, OJIBWAYS OF ONIGAMING, ON INTERDEPENDENCE

While international conflicts are fought between enemies on a very clear and simple proposition of win or lose, the choice here in Canada is one that must be made among friends and neighbours. We must face the underlying tensions. We must understand them and we must resolve them. Neither side believes that the other is going

Gitanyow, B.C.

anywhere. This is home. So, how do we live side-by-side and build a future of prosperity together? We share space in a common land. We constitute a society that is envied by other countries. We are economically interdependent. We have many social ties. Our children are married to one another through which we share generations of grandchildren. So inextricably tied are we that our options are also very clear and simple: we can all win or we can all lose.[76]

GOVERNOR GENERAL MICHAËLLE JEAN, AT THE RELAUNCH OF THE TRUTH AND RECONCILIATION COMMISSION OF CANADA, 2009

When the present does not recognize the wrongs of the past, the future takes its revenge. For that reason, we must never never turn away from the opportunity of confronting history together—the opportunity to right a historical wrong.[77]

STEPHEN LEWIS, HONORARY WITNESS STATEMENT, TRUTH AND RECONCILIATION COMMISSION OF CANADA, 2013

It seems to me that you can't restore the soul of a country through continued oppression on the First Peoples of this land. But you can restore the soul of a country in this elaborate design by bringing non-Aboriginal and Aboriginal forces together to understand, to conciliate, to share. The Commissioners and the Survivors and those who have come forward are so filled with love, generosity, courage, human decency in the face of everything, that it's almost supernatural, I can't get over it. I live with rage and I admit that. I have an emotional span that moves from rage to rage. But what I saw here in the last two days is truly memorable—it is the triumph of the human spirit over the worst that has been done to human beings. Thus, we look forward to the future rising from the ashes of the past.

I believe frankly, I've really learnt something. I've suffered a kind of happy conversion as I've witnessed what I have witnessed.

I actually believe that the commission will prevail. It will be seen as a remarkable exercise in reconciliation. I undertake and promise . . . to do whatever I can over the course of the remainder of my geriatric life to pursue the findings and recommendations and heart and soul of what the Commission is doing and will ultimately say.[78]

BEVERLEY MCLACHLIN, CHIEF JUSTICE OF THE SUPREME COURT OF CANADA, ON PLURALISM, 2015

The most glaring blemish on the Canadian historic record relates to our treatment of the First Nations that lived here at the time of colonization. An initial period of cooperative inter-reliance ground in norms of equality and mutual dependence was supplanted in the nineteenth century by the ethos of exclusion and cultural annihilation. . . . "Indianness" was not to be tolerated; rather it must be eliminated. In the buzz-word of the day, *assimilation*; in the language of the 21st century, *cultural genocide*.

We now understand that the policy of assimilation was wrong and that the only way forward is acknowledgement and acceptance of the distinct values, traditions and religions of the descendants of the original inhabitants of the land we call Canada. . . . Yet the legacy of intolerance lives on in the lives of First Nation people and their children—a legacy of too much poverty, too little education, and over-representation of aboriginal people in our courts.

Three lessons emerge from the Canadian experience with tolerance and intolerance. First, intolerance—the marginalization of difference—doesn't work. It may seem to provide a solution in the short term. But in the long run it is bound to fail. Second, intolerance imposes inhumane and unacceptable costs in terms of human suffering and lost human and economic potential. Third, the way forward is not to use intolerance to eliminate difference, but embrace tolerance in the spirit of reconciliation.[79]

Inukshuk at sunset, Nunavut

NATAN OBED, PRESIDENT OF INUIT TAPIRIIT KANATAMI, ON RECONCILIATION, 2016

Reconciliation is not just something that you do today that you didn't do yesterday. It's premised on action. So the Missing and Murdered Indigenous Women and Girls Inquiry, or the Truth and Reconciliation Commission's 94 Calls to Action, or the United Nations Declaration on the Rights of Indigenous Peoples—their acceptance and implementation are two different things. Accepting that they exist and saying that they're important allows for the Canadian government, and Canadians to think that we're actually doing something, when we aren't until we have implementation plans and actions associated with each one of those things, which are created from the ground up with Indigenous people. And that's where reconciliation breaks down.

Everyone wants in on reconciliation today, but often on non-Indigenous terms. You don't want true partnerships; you just want to be branded with that term, to feel good about the fact that you're doing something for us, with us. My central take on reconciliation is that it's not as easy as easy as it looks. And it should be hard.[80]

POPE FRANCIS, ON THE RESIDENTIAL SCHOOL SYSTEM, 2022

I condemned it, taking away children, changing culture, the mind, traditions, a so-called race. A whole culture. . . .

Yes, it's a technical word, genocide. I didn't use it because it didn't come to mind. But yes, I described it. Yes, it's a genocide.[81]

POPE FRANCIS, ON THE DOCTRINE OF DISCOVERY, 2022

It's true, it's bad. It's unjust. Even today it's used. That mentality, that we're superior and Indigenous people don't count, that's why we have to work on . . . what was done that was bad, but with the awareness that even today, that same colonialism exists.[82]

GORDON CAMPBELL, FORMER PREMIER OF BRITISH COLUMBIA, ON RECONCILIATION, 2024

One of the things that moves us away from success is political leadership saying "oh yes, I care about it" but then not doing anything about it. It is just a press release, it is not an action plan, it's not an execution plan, or review of what steps we have done after a year . . . and frankly one of the things I found in government was that there are no timelines . . . if it does not take place by this time it does not get done . . . you need people that say, "These are my goals and objectives, this is how I expect to get there, I am going to watch how I do and I am going to report back on how I do it."

. . .

I think there is a long way to go, and I think that long way requires people of good will to constantly work together to get there.[83]

Each day, more and more Canadians from all backgrounds are engaged in the work of reconciliation. From young to old, we all have a role to play, and Canada's future well-being demands that we continue to confront and address the legacy of the past.

CHIEF TED WILLIAMS, RAMA FIRST NATION, ON RECONCILIATION, 2024

I can't be waiting for someone else because I could be waiting forever.

. . .

That which you think about, talk about, dream about, write about over an extended period of time . . . has to . . . has to be brought into reality.[84]

KORYN JOHN, ONE OF THE ORGANIZERS OF THE SOARING EAGLES CAMP OCCUPATION BESIDE OLD CITY HALL IN TORONTO, ESTABLISHED IN RESPONSE TO CONCERNS WITH THE CRIMINAL JUSTICE SYSTEM, 2018

I think people need to be held accountable for their actions.

They're making it easy to kill Indigenous youth. We need to make it hard. We need to say you cannot get away with hurting us, killing us, abusing us. You can't get away with it anymore.

The more the youth stand up and stand strong and say we're not going to allow this to happen, then maybe the system will change.[85]

SAKOYA YEN, A GRADE NINE STUDENT WHO IS A MEMBER OF BEAR CLAN, WINDSOR-ESSEX, 2021

It's good to know that people do care and they do care about how things were stripped away. . . . It really sucked to see that people haven't changed much. . . . Maybe they can learn to be better as people if they realize how much of an impact the residential schools have had on the Indigenous children and community.[86]

Kamloopa Powwow

FRAN MORRISON, UPON HEARING OF THE HORRIFIC DISCOVERY OF THE REMAINS OF 215 CHILDREN NEAR KAMLOOPS INDIAN RESIDENTIAL SCHOOL AND DECIDING TO ATTEND A VIGIL ON THE SHUBENACADIE FIRST NATION, 2021

Somebody said to me before I went, "Aren't you nervous about going there?" and I said "why would I be nervous?" "Well, you're probably going to be the only white person there," and I looked at them and I said, "that's the kind of thinking that we have to stop."[87]

DR. MIKE KIRLEW, ON WORKING IN RURAL AND INDIGENOUS COMMUNITIES, 2017

The health-care system on reserves is far inferior to what other people get—period. . . . This is taking children's lives.

What makes you angry is that, unless you change the system, this is going to be an unfortunate narrative that's going to repeat itself.

You're triaging people based on race to an inferior system . . . That's what makes you angry.[88]

SAMANTA KRISHNAPILLAI, FOUNDER OF THE ON CANADA PROJECT, 2021

We, as non-Indigenous people who live on this land, do have a responsibility for reconciliation . . . . Learn the land, do the research, understand what truth and reconciliation is, and connect with your elected officials and demand better.[89]

ELSA KAKA, LAWYER AND CO-HOST OF "THE ORDINARY BLACK GIRL" PODCAST, ON RACISM AND WHITE FRAGILITY, 2020

I don't care about whether you have hate in your heart or how much you sympathize with my plight. I don't care if you like me.

What I do care about is if you turn a blind eye to the systems that hurt me.

I care about the actions you take against systemic racism.

Being a non-racist person may soothe the ego of some, but it does little to advance us toward an anti-racist society.

I care about dismantling a system that maims and murders Black and Indigenous people—a system that renders us powerless.

Creating meaningful change means centring the voices of Black and Indigenous people who have already been doing the work.

It means redirecting funds to services that address inequality, and it means voting for people who want to eradicate systemic racism, rather than uphold it.

None of this is possible if our government does not recognize that white feelings don't matter more than Black and Indigenous lives.[90]

Today, there is a recognition of our true history and our responsibility to build a better future. The solutions and steps that we know must be taken are increasingly understood. The need now is for more intense and focused action to implement these solutions in ways that transform the lives of children, families, and communities across Canada.

JUSTICE MURRAY SINCLAIR, DESCRIBING THE ONGOING WORK OF RECONCILIATION, 2012

The road we travel is equal in importance to the destination we seek. There are no shortcuts. When it comes to truth and reconciliation we are forced to go the distance.[91]

FORMER PRIME MINISTER PAUL MARTIN, CHANGING THE COURSE OF HISTORY, 2013

So how do we address this?

We do so by changing the course of history.

We do so by recognizing that natural resource development must be an opportunity to ensure that the status quo is abandoned in favor of change for the better.

"The road we travel is equal in importance to the destination we seek. There are no shortcuts. When it comes to truth and reconciliation we are forced to go the distance."

—Justice Murray Sinclair

We do so by ensuring that Aboriginal Canadians are at the table from the beginning of the development process on their lands.

We do so by ensuring that they are included as key participants, not just as laborers but also as skilled workers, managers, and owners.

We do so by confronting the consequences of our colonial past which continue unfortunately even unto today.

We do so by refusing to condone the repetitive breach of treaty rights, the damage arising from the Indian Act, and the political refusal to accept the inherent right of self-government.

We do so by refusing to accept the overt discrimination in the provision of the country's fundamental rights: in children's welfare, in universal healthcare, and in universal primary and secondary school education.

We do so by recognizing that whether our ancestors have been here since time immemorial or whether we arrived on these shores yesterday, that we must build this country together. That is how we will change the course of history![92]

GORD DOWNIE, LEAD SINGER OF THE TRAGICALLY HIP, IN AN INTERVIEW, AND IN AN HONOURING AT THE ASSEMBLY OF FIRST NATIONS, 2016

The last 150 years aren't as much worth celebrating as we think. . . . But the new 150 years can be years of building an actual nation. Imagine if they were part of us and we them, how incredibly cool it would make us? That's what's missing as we celebrate doughnuts and hockey.

. . .

It will take 150 years or seven generations to heal the wound of the residential school. . . . To become a country, and truly call ourselves Canada, it means we must become one. We must walk down a path of reconciliation from now on. Together, and forever. This is the first day of forever: the greatest day of my life, the greatest day of all of our lives.[93]

STEVEN POINT, FORMER LIEUTENANT GOVERNOR OF BRITISH COLUMBIA, ON RECONCILIATION, 2024

This kind of top-down social change does not work, you can't change people's hearts by changing a law in Ottawa, or changing a policy . . . even the UNDRIP [United Nations Declaration on the Rights of Indigenous Persons] that we see now . . . brought about a tremendous change in vision internationally which has touched us here in Canada . . . but how do you change the hearts and minds of Canadians generally—you can't go to them and say we got a new law here now—you have to like us now . . . that is not going to happen right.

. . .

The real change began happening when they found the 215 kids in Kamloops—because for the first time they had real and substantive evidence that something bad was going on—and somebody was covering it up . . . and people internationally . . . in this one moment started turning around—wondering what the hell is really going on

Steven Point, lieutenant governor of British Columbia, 2007

here—this a-ha moment in Canadian history . . . people had woken up . . . people started asking what can we do . . . that was the turning point at the people level.

. . .

We have to find ourself the strength and fortitude to break away from the bondage of the Indian Act and begin to create self-governing bodies that determine for our own self what we want to do with our children, what we want to do with health, with culture and language, and land development . . . all of that . . . in the territory that still has aboriginal title, that still has self-government, and that still has a strong relationship with the government under section 35 of the Constitution . . . and that we have to stop being afraid of stepping out on our own now. And we have to do that.[94]

GOVERNOR GENERAL MARY SIMON, REFLECTING ON THE ONE-YEAR ANNIVERSARY OF THE IDENTIFICATION OF UNMARKED BURIALS AT TK'EMLÚPS TE SECWE'PEMC, 2022

We, as Indigenous peoples, grow up with legends and myths, of creation and family. Eventually, we make our own stories, which we pass down to the next generation.

At this residential school and others like it across the country, churches and governments eradicated Indigenous languages and identity through corrupt policies. They took away our stories.

Over the years, too much of our culture, language and people have been lost because of residential schools, colonization and assimilation policies.

We still feel its impact today. We still experience trauma today.

For these children, their stories were cut short, but you won't let it end like this. By speaking up, you strip away the anonymity forced upon them by this school.

These were young boys and girls, with hopes and dreams, love in their hearts and their lives ahead of them. They had families and friends and were integral to their community and culture.

And it's up to all of us, across the country, to tell the stories of these kids, no different than any other child, no different than our children. To say in one voice: we failed them, and you.

We can never let that happen again.

The time for "we didn't know" is over. To all Canadians, I deliver this message. Indigenous families didn't know what happened to their children and many still don't. Most Canadians didn't know about residential schools. Now they do.

How, then, do we move forward from the shadows to the light and begin to heal?

Wherever I go in Canada or around the world, I vow to take your stories with me. I will share your stories and the stories of these children. I will do my part to bring their memories into the light.

I consider this a sacred responsibility, as governor general, as an honorary witness of the Truth and Reconciliation Commission, as a mother and a grandmother.

This is a responsibility all Canadians share. We all need to listen. We all need to understand.[95]

Design by Mulidzas (Kwakwaka'wakw Artist Curtis Wilson)[96]

K̓i'mola (many walking together)

For all that can be seen when one looks at the Kingcome pole, a foundational message is always conveyed—we are one with each other.

When the pole was raised this was a message that the Chiefs were conveying to the Crown, and, most important, to their own people, my people. A reminder that who we are can only be fully understood in relation to one another.

We started our telling of the history of Canada with origin stories. In my teachings, every origin story is open-ended. It has a beginning, but no end. Every generation of people has a responsibility to contribute another chapter to the story.

We are a story that has no end. A story that in every moment has something more to tell.

You, me, all of us are continuing to tell the story right now.

What is the chapter we are telling?

Well, I think some of this storytelling is exciting, new, and powerful.

Unlike times in the past, the voices of Indigenous people—regardless of gender, age, role, status, ability, or background—are being heard, and are part of telling the story. The breadth and scope of what these voices convey about how they are shaping their futures is unparalleled when compared to earlier chapters. Increasingly, Indigenous people are in every sphere of the life of Canada, visibly and proudly. And through their presence the story of Canada is changing.

And, as is already emerging, voices from all backgrounds are speaking to the issue of the place of Indigenous Peoples in Canada. We are at a moment where, for the first time, the future of Canada is truly being discussed by all of us, with Indigenous people at the table, and grappling with what that means. Today and onwards, we are finally beginning to do what should have been done in 1867. We are trying to collectively form a nation that includes the First Peoples of this land.

As we increasingly recognize that the next chapter of our story is a collective one, we also recognize that we each must play our part in its telling. Chief Ted Williams speaks of how we each have to rise to the challenge of playing our part. And taking the necessary steps forward starts with each and every one of us:

> A big part of the development of relationship, regardless of who they are with . . . starts with you. . . . I don't know you and you don't know me . . . but when I think of myself . . . I have to give of myself first.[1]

For many, this means challenging ourselves to understand and act in new ways. Businesswoman and author Arlene Dickinson has reflected on the path she is on, and has identified lessons that can help each of us reflect on our responsibilities:

> Awareness of the need for reconciliation is something that has come over time and is something that has evolved for me in terms of what it means. I think just truly understanding the impact of colonialism and then working actively to make change—that is what reconciliation is to me. It is not just knowing about colonialism, but it is actively working to change it.
>
> Reconciliation means to take up the challenges of helping to bridge relationships—to change the narrative and to move beyond performative statements on reconciliation. To be way more willing to do the hard work, because this is hard work, and you have to

actively be engaged in it. And so, I think that is an uncomfortable place for many people, where we kind of have to acknowledge that many of us have benefited from those colonial and racist structures. . . . It is hard for those of us who have been privileged, and benefited from it, to step back and say "wait a minute, this made my life better and other people's lives worse." I think some would have some defensive thoughts as a result of that—"Well it wasn't me, it was somebody else that. . . ," "This was before me, things are better now." But they are not better now for everyone. So, I think reconciliation is this active understanding of how the past actually benefitted us and being able to reconcile that personally without feeling like it wasn't me that did it, it was my ancestors that did it—which is not at all a reasonable way to think. And for me, with my profile, I think I have an opportunity to move the conversation and to effect change.[2]

The chapter we are telling requires following through with what we have long known needs to be done. As Dene leader Georges Erasmus says:

> I cannot see true Reconciliation happening in Canada unless the Royal Commission on Aboriginal Peoples is fully implemented. We need to get to a place or time in this country where the original Peoples of Turtle Island have ownership or control of enough Land and resources in our homelands to be fully Self Sufficient and Self Reliant. Along with Land and Resources there has to be political control so the inherent Right to Self-Government must be implemented across the country. The decolonization of Aboriginal Peoples must be central to the implementation of RCAP, or the rebirth of First Nations will not be complete.
>
> The most important thing I see happening to advance reconciliation is the coming forth of young Leaders assuming their rightful place in taking on the struggle to achieve our rightful place in this country.

The jury is still out on how the relationship between Indigenous and non-Indigenous People will evolve, but I tend to be optimistic, I think there will come a time when the non-Indigenous people in Canada will see a strong vibrant Aboriginal population as nothing to fear but rather something to support.[3]

Family by Jackson Robertson

Indigenous legal scholar John Borrows describes following through on what we know needs to be done, and how that involves the reimagination and transformation of social structures, systems, and spaces—and, in particular, law:

> Reconciliation is anything that revitalizes Indigenous law, and if we see law in that light, then it is not just about revitalizing law for Indigenous peoples, it is also about revitalizing law for Canadians more generally, because we would see law as something that is not just done by legislatures and the courts, as important as that is, not just done by chiefs and band councils, as important as they may be, but it is done by all Canadians and all Indigenous peoples . . . and it is something that sees us more fully engage with one another.[4]

What needs to be done also includes recognizing the necessity for unity in the face of injustice, as former governor general Michaëlle Jean says:

> The times call on all of us to unite across experiences—Blacks or people of African descent, First Nations, Inuit and Métis people, people of European, of Asian descent, humans of all stripes—around our future, the sacredness of life.
>
> Exclusion, exploitation, erasure are experiences Indigenous lives and Black lives have long shared in this country, and on this continent. That history has brought Black peoples and Indigenous peoples of the Americas to seal a tacit compact as allies in the process of reconciliation.[5]

We must also remember that the future we are building, the chapter we are adding to the story, also involves considerable healing and redress. The Kingcome pole continues to stand today, and it will into the future. But symbolic of how colonialism has caused intergenerational trauma and pain, the pole stands in a state of some decay. It needs care, repair, and attention. At one point in time, in the 1980s, the pole even had to be taken down and refurbished, and then put back up. As well, in our culture we understand poles are from the earth, and as such at some point in time they must return to the earth. When that occurs it raises questions and dialogue about whether the pole needs to be replaced—if something new should be erected or, at least for a period of time, we should let things settle as they are.

Chief Rosanne Casimir recounts how the change she sees happening includes learning and understanding that allows for healing and redress to occur:

> The unmarked graves brought truth to the world and the world stood with us in solidarity and unity. I express gratitude for the support of media who helped to share our truths in a respectful way and kept everyone engaged so that there could be a better understanding of our collective history and for helping us create space for our survivors to voice their history that they lived with the world and providing non-residential school survivors a better understanding of our true collective history. It is important to educate and do our part to do better and chart new and inclusive paths forward.
>
> People have a new awareness of the atrocities of residential school and its impacts on our people, although these truths were made public previously thru the residential school settlement.
>
> Everyone wants to learn more and how to do better for future generations and those not yet born.
>
> In the past we all have seen and know our territories have been exploited without equitable sharing, decisions were made without consent and an often-impoverished view of reciprocal obligations has dominated our government-to-government relationships. Today we see that as the past and are redefining history by changing our futures together. Today, we are all making real change with greater understanding as truth prevails.

> Reconciliation is more than resolve of wrongs, it is the hope that brings new beginnings, it allows traumas and truths to determine what justice is for each and every one towards the healing and the power to collectively make this world a better place for all our children.[6]

The necessity of truth-seeking and healing as part of reconciliation is reiterated by doctor and politician Jane Philpott:

> Reconciliation is like the healing of an old and festering wound. From the beginning of Canada there has been a serious rift between the First Peoples of this land and those of us who came (or whose ancestors came) from elsewhere. It is only recently that many Canadians are learning how much damage has been caused by that rift. It has caused sickness, pain, and death for the First Peoples of the land. The work of reconciliation is the intentional process of mending that broken relationship, making amends for the suffering, and resetting the agreements about how we are going to live together on this land.[7]

The reality is that today, many Indigenous nations are in a state of struggle, and many individuals continue to face struggles and obstacles in securing their health, safety, and well-being. There is tremendous healing work that still has to be done.

As we tell our chapter of the story, we also need to remember that the story is supposed to evolve and change, just as we each change as individuals.

When the totem pole was raised, it spoke, as totems always do, to enduring stories and messages that are beyond time—of Clans and Creation. But it also spoke *in* time: to the reality of colonization, to the Crown, and to the struggle for justice. Even more, when we look at the pole today, as we have in this book, we also see it in our own time and context, and see the ways it speaks to how we understand what is happening right now.

So it will be into the future. The story of Canada will continue to be shaped by our own struggles and efforts, and the chapters that unfold will be moulded by our choices and will. The Kingcome pole will keep standing, but we will continue to see in it new things, things we may not have seen before.

As we peer into the future and consider what we might see in the pole, we are helped by the visions of those who have, in various ways, been involved in the work of reconciliation over decades. Stó:lō leader, judge, and former lieutenant governor of British Columbia Steven Point recognizes that there are still divergent paths ahead of us—that we have choices to make:

> The future that I see has got two paths, one path is the path where we continue fighting over our philosophies, legal rights, and access to resources—and that is the fight that I see happened in other parts of the world . . . where they have never been able to do reconciliation . . . and you know we can continue battling if we want, and pass our conflicts on to the next generation and keep on fighting, OR we can accept the fact that we are all here today, we are all here, it has been a bit of an unhappy kind of relationship so far, there is some good things happening . . . and try to figure out within our Canadian legal structure how to reconcile our differences and how to live together, and help one another. My hope is that is where we can go. Unless people sort of figure out . . . that yes, we have differences . . . we have legal, political, historical and cultural differences but that we are all humans, that we all can live together . . . work together for mutual benefit . . . if we can't do that, you know we are binding ourselves to another 100 years of conflict.[8]

Métis lawyer Jean Teillet speaks of how, as mindsets keep changing, the waves of progress will keep building, and with that will come change:

> The attitudes are changing. I do not think it is anything other than a change in mindset. Not on our part, on the part of non-Indigenous Canadians. There is a shift in mindset. And it is having results, changes are happening. They are of course slow because I don't think you can turn that beast around that was all about assimilation or about just "ignoring" . . . that has been running for two-hundred-plus years, you can't turn that around in five years or ten years, it is going to take a long time to turn around, but it is changing. . . .
>
> About reconciliation . . . there will be a backlash . . . it happens every time there is a push forward . . . my uncle Roger used to call it the seventh wave . . . you go forward and there is this undertow or big wave that comes along that pulls you back . . . it doesn't pull you all the way back to where you were before, but it pulls you back. This is going to happen.[9]

And Gaagwiis Jason Alsop, president of the Council of the Haida Nation, spoke on the floor of the Legislative Assembly of British Columbia in April 2024 on the historic occasion of the introduction of legislation recognizing the Aboriginal title of the Haida to all of Haida Gwaii, sharing this vision of the future:

> There are over 150 years of colonization. It's going to take time to undo some of the harms, the things that aren't good, look at the things that are good.
>
> In our way, in trying to find answers for the future, we look back to the past. We look to our teachings, to our ancestors. One of the statements or teachings that guides us is a statement that was made by Chief [Lewis] Louis Collinson [1881–1970]. . . . He said:
>
> > "People are like trees, and groups of people are like forests. While the forests are composed of many different kinds of trees, these trees intertwine their roots so strongly that it is impossible for the

> strongest winds that blow on our islands to uproot the forest. For each tree strengthens its neighbour, and their roots are inextricably entwined. In the same way, the people of our islands, composed of members of Nations and races from all over the world, are beginning to intertwine their roots so strongly that no troubles will affect them. Just as one tree standing alone would soon be destroyed by the first strong wind which came along, so is it impossible for any person, any family or any community to stand alone against the troubles of the world."[10]

I must admit, I cannot fully say what will be new in the chapter we are telling right now. But I have a few guesses and hopes.

We will recognize that while every pole has a carver, a creator, we are all part of giving the pole meaning. In that way, as creators of meaning, we are also all carvers. We all have a part to play in shaping our story, and we must play our part. The past, and the present and future, are not things to look at from a distance, and imagine what they might have been, or might yet be. We need to take hold of that present and future, and help to shape them, mould them, and make them what they must be. The resurgence of Indigenous Peoples, cultures, and governments is part of this. But so too is non-Indigenous people working to break through the silos that colonialism has constructed between us, and getting involved in shaping where we are at and where we must go.

We will also see, if only metaphorically, totem poles extend to new heights. As I said earlier, in our traditions it is not the case that a taller totem pole is somehow a better totem pole. But it is always the case that a totem pole is reaching into the sky, drawing our eyes upward to the limitless possibilities of that sky. The totem pole always reminds us of what exists beyond our vision and sight, the invisible realities that are the most powerful forces in existence. The reality of love and connection between Clans and Peoples. The reality of the supernatural, the spiritual realm, that animates our existence. The reality of the unseen forces in the natural world that are the source of life, creation, and abundance.

The story of the future will not be the story of the past, and I believe it is one of limitless potential. For the first time, consciously, we are grappling with how to actualize the teaching of *ki'mola*—many walking together. In my tradition, we are created to move forward in unity, and believe that our potential—of each and every one of us, and all of us together—is reached only when we are all moving forward together, with no one left out or behind. We are now in that time of starting to walk together. As we do, we will start accomplishing things we had only dared to dream of before.

So, as we reach the end of our exploration of the Kingcome pole—of trying to examine our history from different angles and perspectives—we are all left with a challenge. To examine what we each can do to be on a path of walking together, and how we can stay on that path at a good pace. It is not, and will not, be easy. Much of the truly hard work remains before us. Just as my people now and in the future will have to make decisions about the future of the Kingcome pole—including how long it will stand or what will stand in its place—so too must we make decisions together that forge our shared future.

Nothing can be taken for granted.

The voices in this book tell us why. The reality and legacy of colonization does not stop when we say we do not want any of it anymore and call it out for how wrong it is. Colonization, and the racism and harms it carries with it, is embedded in how we got to this moment in time. We need to always be cognizant of that as we walk forward, and to not lose sight of the fact that, as we construct the future, we must also continually address the legacy we carry with us. As the African American author James Baldwin said, "the great force of history comes from the fact that we carry it within us, are unconsciously controlled by it . . . history is literally present in all that we do."[11]

I leave you with these similar words that I use whenever I speak on reconciliation across Canada: Have courage, be willing to be uncomfortable, and recognize that every contribution to shaping a more just future for Canada is a valuable and needed contribution. Building our future takes all of us. We need you. We need us. Together we walk.

We are one with each other. And I thank you for all you do to manifest that.

Acknowledgements

There are so many people to thank for making *Reconciling History* a reality, it is impossible to mention all of them. Below we have mentioned just a few.

We acknowledge and thank the generations of people who have worked to build a more just and equal Canada for Indigenous peoples. This includes contemporary leaders who generously agreed to be interviewed for this book: John Borrows, Gordon Campbell, Rosanne Casimir, Arlene Dickinson, Georges Erasmus, Michaëlle Jean, Jane Philpott, Steven Point, Jean Teillet, and Ted Williams.

Like any book, *Reconciling History* is the product of many people making distinct and important contributions. We are grateful to the McClelland & Stewart team at Penguin Random House Canada for their support on this project—specifically, our publisher Stephanie Sinclair, and our editor Doug Pepper. Linda Pruessen provided meticulous and amazing copy editing. Mary Rose MacLachlan helped immensely in identifying and arranging images, as did Katie Bray Kingissepp in providing research support. John Borrows, Clo Ostrove, Jane Philpott, and Pep Philpott reviewed the manuscript and provided invaluable insights that made it significantly better.

Our greatest gratitude goes to our families, who provide constant support.

For Roshan: Endless thanks to Cathy and Mary for their love and guidance; and to those who passed away in recent years: my beloved son, Darwyn, and my parents, Michele and Hossain, for the necessary lessons all three of them continue to provide.

For Jody: The lessons of my grandmother, Pugladee, I carry with me always; my father, Hereditary Chief Hemas Kla-Lee-Lee-Kla (Bill Wilson), and my mother, Sandy Wilson, for their love and guidance; my sister Kory; my nieces and nephew, Kaija, Kaylene, Kadence, Jamie, and Miles; and, to my husband, Tim Raybould, for your love and for always being by my side.

Finally, and importantly, to all the inbetweeners. *Gilakas'la* for courageously playing your role in your own spheres of influence, to create a more just, inclusive, and compassionate society. Reflecting the vision of the Musgamagw Dzawada̱'enux̱w Pole, you are agents of building a more united Canada, grounded in an understanding of the importance of strengthening and telling our shared story.

Notes

ODOODEM (TOTEM POLE)

1 An audio recording of Jim King’s translation of Chief Dick Webber’s speech that was made at the raising of the pole, and was passed along to me by Midori Nicholson.

2 Quoted in Gwi’molas Ryan Silas Douglas Nicolson, “‘Playing the Hand You’re Dealt’: An Analysis of Musgamakaw Dzawada̱’enux̱w Traditional Governance and Its Resurgence” (master’s thesis, University of Victoria, 2013), 6, https://dspace.library.uvic.ca/handle/1828/11535.

PART 1: FIRST ANCESTOR

1 Justo, “Ojibwe Creation Story: The Myth of Turtle Island,” Native Tribe Info, April 13, 2023, https://nativetribe.info/ojibwe-creation-story-the-myth-of-turtle-island/.

2 “Iroquois Creation Myth,” Commack School District, n.d., https://www.cs.williams.edu/~lindsey/myths/myths_12.html.

3 Stephen Augustine, “Mi’kmaq Creation Story,” History Museum, n.d., https://www.historymuseum.ca/wp-content/uploads/2020/06/Mikmaq-Creation-Story-EN.pdf.

4 Ron Russ, “Raven Butterfly and the First Haida,” Spirits of the West Coast Art Gallery, n.d., https://spiritsofthewestcoast.com/blogs/news/the-many-stories-of-raven.

5 Pauktuutit Inuit Women of Canada, *The Inuit Way: A Guide To Inuit Culture*, Chaire de Recherche Sentinelle Nord Sur Les Relations Avec Les Sociétés Inuit (Quebec City, QC: Université Laval, 2006), https://www.relations-inuit.chaire.ulaval.ca/sites/relations-inuit.chaire.ulaval.ca/files/InuitWay_e.pdf.

6 “Legend of Kiviuq,” quoted in *Amarok’s Song—The Journey to Nunavut*, directed by Martin Kreelak and Ole Gjerstad (National Film Board of Canada, Inuit Broadcasting Corporation, 1998), https://www.nfb.ca/film/amaroks_song_-_the_journey_to_nunavut/.

7 Canada, House of Commons, Standing Committee on Justice and Human Rights, Testimony, No. 135, 1st Session, 42 Parliament, February 27, 2019,

https://www.ourcommons.ca/DocumentViewer/en/42-1/just/meeting-135/evidence.

8 "Sleep Not Longer, O Choctaws and Chickasaws," History Is a Weapon, n.d., https://www.historyisaweapon.com/defcon1/tecumsehsleepnotlonger.html.

9 Quoted in Boyce Richardson, *People of Terra Nullius: Betrayal and Rebirth in Aboriginal Canada* (Vancouver: Douglas & McIntyre Ltd., 1993), 2, 5.

10 Richardson, *People of Terra Nullius*, 118–19.

11 "Letter to Prime Minister Wilfrid Laurier by the Chiefs of the Shuswap, Okanagan and Couteau Tribes," August 25, 1910, https://iitio.org/wp-content/uploads/2016/12/1910-Letter-to-PM-from-Secwepemec.pdf.

12 "Constitution of the Iroquois Nation," n.d., https://cscie12.dce.harvard.edu/ssi/iroquois/simple/1.shtml. The Great Law of Peace is dated 1451, though some sources say it goes back to c. 1190.

13 Franz Boas, "A Year Among the Eskimo," *Journal of the American Geographical Society of New York* 19 (1887): 383–402, https://www.jstor.org/stable/196741.

14 Quoted in Qikiqtani Inuit Association, *Qikiqtani Truth Commission: Community Histories 1950–1975* (Iqaluit, NU: Inhabit Media, 2014), 16, https://www.qtcommission.ca/sites/default/files/community/community_histories_iqaluit.pdf.

15 Quoted in Gwi'molas, "'Playing the Hand You're Dealt,'" 10–11, https://dspace.library.uvic.ca/handle/1828/11535.

16 Quoted in "The Story Box: Franz Boas, George Hunt, and the Making of Anthropology," Bard Graduate Center Gallery, February 14–July 7, 2019, https://www.bgc.bard.edu/files/Boas_PressBrochureFinal-2.pdf.

17 Diamond Jenness, *The People of the Twilight* (University of Chicago Press, 1928), 191.

18 René Dussault and Georges Erasmus, *Report of the Royal Commission on Aboriginal Peoples*, vol. 1: *Looking Forward, Looking Back* (Ottawa: Indian and Northern Affairs Canada, 1996), as summarized at "Highlights from the Report of the Royal Commission on Aboriginal Peoples," http://data2.archives.ca/e/e448/e011188230-01.pdf.

19 Pauktuutit, *The Inuit Way*, 4.

PART 2: RAVEN

1 "Letter to Prime Minister Wilfrid Laurier."

2 "Letter to Prime Minister Wilfrid Laurier."

3 "Letter to Prime Minister Wilfrid Laurier."

4 Quoted in "The Doctrine of Discovery and the Church's Complicity," Missio Alliance, October 12, 2020, https://www.missioalliance.org/the-doctrine-of-discovery-and-the-churchs-complicity/.

5 The Bull Romanus Pontifex (Nicholas V), January 8, 1455 (Granting the Portuguese a perpetual monopoly in trade with Africa), https://www.papalencyclicals.net/nicholo5/romanus-pontifex.htm.

6 Dussault and Erasmus, *Report of the Royal Commission on Aboriginal Peoples*, vol. 1, 43.

7 "Patent Granted by King Henry VII to John Cabot and His Sons, March 1496," Heritage Newfoundland & Labrador, https://www.heritage.nf.ca/articles/exploration/1496-cabot-patent.php#.

8 Richardson, *People of Terra Nullius*, 31–32.

9 Quoted in Robert MacBain, *Their Home and Native Land* (Toronto: Robert MacBain Books, 2016), 294.

10 Quoted in Arthur J. Ray and Donald B. Freeman, *"Give Us Good Measure": An Economic Analysis of Relations between the Indians and the Hudson's Bay Company before 1763* (Toronto: University of Toronto Press, 1978).

11 Ray and Freeman, *"Give Us Good Measure,"* 21.

12 "Letter to Prime Minister Wilfrid Laurier."

13 Quoted in Mark D. Walter, "Right and Remedies within Common Law and Indigenous Legal Traditions," in *The Right Relationship: Reimagining the Implementation of Historical Treaties*, eds. John Borrows and Michael Coyle (University of Toronto Press, 2017), 188.

14 "Text of the HBC's Royal Charter," Hudson's Bay Company, https://www.hbcheritage.ca/things/artifacts/the-charter-and-text.

15 Quoted in Donald Purich, *Our Land: Native Rights In Canada* (Toronto: James Lorimer, 1986), 80.

16 Government of Canada, "The Arrival of the Europeans: 17th Century Wars," 15, last modified April 19, 2018, https://www.canada.ca/en

/department-national-defence/services/military-history/history-heritage/popular-books/aboriginal-people-canadian-military/arrival-europeans-17th-century-wars.html.

17 Government of Canada, "The Arrival of the Europeans," 6–7.

18 David T. McNab, *Research Report on the Royal Proclamation of 1763 and British Indian Policy, 1750–1794* (Ottawa: Ministry of Natural Resources, 1979).

19 Cherokee v. Georgia, 1831, https://www.sfu.ca/~palys/USSC1831CherokeevGeorgia.pdf.

20 Quoted in Nathan Ince, "An Empire within an Empire: The Upper Canadian Indian Department, 1796–1845" (partial PhD diss., McGill University, 2021), 66.

21 "Royal Proclamation 1763," Indigenous Foundationsarts.ubc.ca, First Nations and Indigenous Studies, University of British Columbia, https://indigenousfoundations.arts.ubc.ca/royal_proclamation_1763/.

22 Dussault and Erasmus, *Report of the Royal Commission on Aboriginal Peoples*, vol. 1, 114.

23 Dussault and Erasmus, *Report of the Royal Commission on Aboriginal Peoples*, vol. 1, 117.

24 Quoted in "Haudenosaunee to the White Brothers Two Row Wampum 1613," Onondaga Nation, n.d., https://www.onondaganation.org/history/quotes/.

25 Grand Chief Michael Mitchell, "Akwesasne: An Unbroken Assertion of Sovereignty," in Boyce Richardson, ed., *Drumbeat: Anger and Renewal in Indian Country* (Toronto: Summerhill Press and Assembly of First Nations, 1989).

26 Ellen Gabriel, "Ka'swenh:tha—The Two Row Wampum: Reconciliation Through An Ancient Agreement," in *Reconciliation and The Way Forward,* eds. Shelagh Rogers, Mike Degagne, Glen Lowry, and Sara Fryer (Ottawa: Aboriginal Healing Foundation, 2014).

27 Quoted in John Borrows, *Wampum at Niagara: The Royal Proclamation, Canadian Legal History, and Self-Government* (1997), 230, https://www.sfu.ca/~palys/Borrows-WampumAtNiagara.pdf.

28 Borrows, *Wampum at Niagara*, 77. (Brackets in original.)

29 "Treaty Texts—1752 Peace and Friendship Treaty," Government of Canada, https://www.rcaanc-cirnac.gc.ca/eng/1100100029040/1581293867988.

30 Quoted in Stephen Patterson, "Eighteenth-Century Treaties: The Mi'kmaq, Maliseet, and Passamaquoddy Experience," *Native Studies Review* 18, no. 1 (2009): 45–46.

31 Quoted in Darren R. Préfontaine with Leah Dorion, "The Métis and the Spirit of Resistance," Métis Museum, n.d., 5, https://www.Métismuseum.ca/media/document.php/00740.Resistance.pdf.

32 Quoted in "Métis Culture Cards: The Métis Flag," Rupertsland Institute, May 29, 2019, http://www.rupertsland.org/wp-content/uploads/2019/06/Culture-Cards-29May2019.pdf?r=1.

33 Quoted in Gerhard J. Ens and Joe Sawchuk, *From New Peoples to New Nations: Aspects of Metis History and Identity from the Eighteenth to the Twenty-First Centuries* (Toronto: University of Toronto Press, 2015), 102.

34 "Métis Laws," Legal Aid Saskatchewan, accessed June 17, 2023, https://gladue.usask.ca/Métis_democratic_laws.

35 "Louis Riel," Manitoba Métis Federation, n.d., https://www.mmf.mb.ca/louis-riel.

36 Julia Skelly, "Thelma Chalifoux," Canadian Encyclopedia, October 25, 2018, https://www.thecanadianencyclopedia.ca/en/article/thelma-chalifoux.

37 Quoted in Council of the Haida Nation, *Haida Laas: Journal of the Haida Nation* (March 2009), 15, https://www.haidanation.ca/wp-content/uploads/2017/03/jl_mar.09.pdf.

38 Quoted in Robert Boyd, "Smallpox in the Pacific Northwest: The First Epidemics," *BC Studies* 101, no.1 (1994): 22, https://ojs.library.ubc.ca/index.php/bcstudies/article/download/864/905/3662.

39 Boyd, "Smallpox in the Pacific Northwest," 13.

40 Quoted in Sheldon Krasowski, *No Surrender: The Land Remains Indigenous* (Regina: University of Regina Press, 2019), 6. (Recorded by Beryl M. Cryer, retelling the history of the Nanaimo Treaty.)

41 Archibald Barclay to James Douglas, December 1849, as quoted in Derek Pethick, *James Douglas: Servant of Two Empires* (Vancouver: Mitchell Press 1969), 77–78.

42 J. Trutch, "Memorandum on a Letter treating of condition of the Indians in Vancouver Island addressed to Secretary to the Aborigines Protection

Society by Mr. Wm. Sebright Green," January 13, 1870, https://bcgenesis.uvic.ca/B70008.html.

43 "Indians in British Columbia" (from an Occasional Correspondent, Kamloops, B.C., October 15, 1877), *The Times* (UK), December 7, 1877, 3.

44 Quoted in "Louis Riel," Barrie Métis Council, https://barriemetiscouncil.com/metis-history/service.php?id=1.

45 "Louis Riel Quotes," Manitoba Métis Foundation, https://www.mmf.mb.ca/.

46 "Louis Riel Quotes."

47 Duncan Campbell Scott, "Indian Affairs, 1763–1841," in *Canada and Its Provinces*, vol. 4, eds. Adam Shortt and A.G. Doughty (Toronto: T. and A. Constable, 1913), 329–62.

48 Dispatch from the Earl of Gosford, Quebec City, to Lord Glenelg, Downing Street, London, quoted in Andrew Armitage, "Canada: The General Structure of Canadian Indian Policy," in *Comparing the Policy of Aboriginal Assimilation: Australia, Canada, and New Zealand* (Vancouver: University of British Columbia Press, 1995), 75, https://files.eric.ed.gov/fulltext/ED403094.pdf.

49 Duncan Campbell Scott, "Indian, 1840–1867," in *Canada and Its Provinces*, vol. 5, eds. Shortt and Doughty, 695–725.

50 British Parliamentary Papers, "Report of the House of Commons Select Committee on Aborigines, 1837," in *Correspondence Returns and Other Papers Relating to Canada and the Indian Problem Therein, 1839* (Dublin: Irish University Press, 1969), 44, in Armitage, *Comparing the Policy of Aboriginal Assimilation.*

51 Richardson, *People of Terra Nullius*, 57.

52 Quoted in Boyce Richardson, *People of Terra Nullius: Betrayal and Rebirth in Aboriginal Canada* (Vancouver: Douglas & McIntyre Ltd., 1993), 56-57.

53 Quoted in "Inuit History and Heritage," Inuit Tapiriit Kanatami, 2016, 12, https://www.itk.ca/wp-content/uploads/2016/07/5000YearHeritage_0.pdf.

54 Quoted in "Inuit History and Heritage," 12.

55 British North American Act, 1867, SS 1867, c 3, https://www.canlii.org/en/sk/laws/stat/ss-1867-c-3/latest/ss-1867-c-3.html.

56 R. v. Secretary of State for Foreign and Commonwealth Affairs, ex parte Indian Association of Alberta, [1982], quoted in René Dussault and

Georges Erasmus, *Report of the Royal Commission on Aboriginal Peoples*, vol. 2: *Restructuring the Relationship, Part One* (Ottawa: Indian and Northern Affairs Canada, 1996), 210.

57 Quoted in Robin Fisher, "Joseph Trutch and the Indian Land Policy," *BC Studies* 12 (Winter 1971–72): 11, https://ojs.library.ubc.ca/index.php/bcstudies/article/download/719/761/3084.

58 Quoted in Gerry St. Germain and Lillian E. Dyck, "First Nations Elections: The Choice Is Inherently Theirs," Report of the Standing Senate Committee on Aboriginal Peoples (Ottawa: 2010), 4, https://publications.gc.ca/collections/collection_2011/sen/yc28-0/YC28-0-403-3-eng.pdf.

59 Evidence given by Deputy Superintendent-General Duncan Campbell Scott in his remarks to the 1920 Special Committee of the House of Commons, National Archives of Canada, Record Group 10, vol. 6810, file 470-2-3, vol. 7, 55 (L-3) and 63 (N-3).

60 Richardson, *People of Terra Nullius*, 5.

61 Quoted in Matthew McRae, "The Chaotic Story of the Right to Vote in Canada," Canadian Museum of Human Rights, September 12, 2019, https://humanrights.ca/story/the-chaotic-story-of-the-right-to-vote-in-canada.

62 APTN National News, "'A Lament for Confederation': A Speech by Chief Dan George in 1967," APTN News, July 1, 2017, https://www.aptnnews.ca/national-news/a-lament-for-confederation-a-speech-by-chief-dan-george-in-1967/.

63 Quoted in "The Role of the Churches," Facing History and Ourselves, 2012, https://www.facinghistory.org/stolen-lives-indigenous-peoples-canada-and-indian-residential-schools/chapter-3/role-churches.

64 "The Role of the Churches."

65 "The Role of the Churches."

66 Quoted in Ronald Wright, *Stolen Continents: The "New World" Through Indian Eyes* (Toronto, Penguin, 1993), 313.

67 "Quotes from Sir John A. Macdonald, Author of Canada's Genocide of Indigenous Peoples," Two Row Times, n.d., https://tworowtimes.com/opinion/quotes-from-sir-john-a-macdonald-author-of-canadas-genocide-of-indigenous-people-2/#.

68 Canada, Debates of the House of Commons, April 27, 1882, 4th Session, 4th Parliament, 1186.

69 Indian Act, 1876. S.C. 1876, c.18 (39 Vict.).

70 Session of the 6th Parliament of the Dominion of Canada, 1887, quoted in *Stolen Lives: The Indigenous Peoples of Canada and the Indian Residential Schools* (Facing History and Ourselves, 2018), 37, https://www.facinghistory.org/stolen-lives-indigenous-peoples-canada-and-indian-residential-schools/chapter-3/introduction.

71 Department of the Interior, *Annual Report for the year ended 30th June, 1876*, quoted in Dussault and Erasmus, *Report of the Royal Commission on Aboriginal Peoples*, vol. 1: 277–78.

72 Quoted in Mark Kennedy, "'Simply a Savage': How the Residential Schools Came to Be," *Ottawa Citizen*, May 22, 2015, https://ottawacitizen.com/news/politics/simply-a-savage-how-the-residential-schools-came-to-be.

73 Canada, *Debates of the House of Commons*, May 22, 1883, 1st Session, 5th Parliament, 1376.

74 Department of the Interior, *Annual Report for the year ended 30th June, 1876*, xiv.

75 Canada, *Debates of the House of Commons*, May 9, 1883, 1st Session, 5th Parliament, 1107–8.

76 Sessional report by A.E. Forget, Indian Commissioner, 1897, quoted in *Where Are The Children? Healing the Legacy of The Residential Schools* (Aboriginal Healing Foundation, National Archives of Canada and National Library of Canada—Legacy of Hope Foundation, 2003), 17.

PART 3: WOLF

1 Richardson, *People of Terra Nullius*, 45.

2 Richardson, *People of Terra Nullius*, 46–47.

3 Quoted in Megan Harvey, "Story People: Sto:lo-State Relations and Indigenous Literacies in British Columbia, 1864–1874," *Journal of the Canadian Historical Association* 24, no. 1 (May 12, 2014): 51–88, https://www.erudit.org/en/journals/jcha/1900-v1-n1-jcha01400/1024997ar/.

4 Quoted in Calder et al. v. Attorney General of British Columbia, [1973] S.C.R. 313 (Can.), https://www.canlii.org/en/ca/scc/doc/1973/1973canlii4/1973canlii4.html, and preceded by this statement: "The Nisga'a answer to government assertions of absolute ownership of the land within their boundaries was made as early as 1888 before the first Royal Commission to visit the Nass Valley."

5 Riel's complete speech can be found in Michael Bliss, ed., *The Queen vs. Louis Riel* (Toronto: University of Toronto Press, 1974), 311–25.

6 Adam Gaudry, "Gabriel Dumont," Canadian Encyclopedia, last edited, September 9, 2019, https://www.thecanadianencyclopedia.ca/en/article/dumont-gabriel.

7 Claude Adams, "Metis Sacred Ground," Metis Museum, n.d., https://www.metismuseum.ca/media/document.php/148697.Boucher%20221.pdf.

8 "Louis Riel," Manitoba Métis Federation, n.d., https://www.mmf.mb.ca/louis-riel.

9 "Louis Riel," Barrie Métis Council, n.d., https://barriemetiscouncil.com/metis-history/service.php?id=1.

10 Quoted in Robert N. Wilkins, "Opinion: Sir John A's Popularity in Montreal Did Not Last," *Gazette* (Montreal), last updated July 12, 2020, https://montrealgazette.com/news/local-news/opinion-sir-john-a-s-popularity-in-montreal-did-not-last.

11 Quoted in Louis Riel, *Justice Must Be Done* (Winnipeg: Manitoba Métis Federation Press, 1979), iv, https://www.metismuseum.ca/media/document.php/12596.Louis%20Riel%20Part%2001.pdf.

12 Royal Commission on Aboriginal Peoples, "Public Hearings, Discussion Paper 2, Focusing the Dialogue" (Ottawa: Canada Communication Group Publishing, 1993), 42.

13 Crown-Indigenous Relations and Northern Affairs Canada, "The Numbered Treaties (1871–1921)," last modified March 15, 2023, https://www.rcaanc-cirnac.gc.ca/eng/1360948213124/1544620003549.

14 Quoted in Truth and Reconciliation Commission, *Final Report,* vol.1: *Canada's Residential Schools: The History, Part 1* (Montreal: McGill-Queen's University Press, 2015), 119.

15 "Treaties 1 and 2 Between Her Majesty The Queen and The Chippewa and Cree Indians of Manitoba and Country Adjacent with Adhesions," Treaty Texts—Treaties No. 1 and No. 2, Government of Canada, https://www.rcaanc-cirnac.gc.ca/eng/1100100028664/1581294165927.

16 Quoted in George F.G. Stanley, *The Birth of Western Canada: The History of the Riel Rebellions* (Toronto: University of Toronto Press, 1961), 216.

17 Quoted in "Treaty Negotiations, July 1871 to October 1873, Between Canada and First Nations of Manitoba and the Northwest Territories," Confederation Debates, 1865–1994, 2–3 and 10, https://hcmc.uvic.ca/confederation/en/Morris_Chapter_05.html.

18 Quoted in Alexander Morris, *The Treaties of Canada with the Indians of Manitoba and the NorthWest Territories Including the Negotiations on Which They Were Based and Other Information Related Thereto* (Saskatoon, SK: Fifth House, 1991), 211, 233, and 239.

19 Quoted in Sheldon Kirk Krasowski, "Mediating the Numbered Treaties: Eyewitness Accounts of Treaties Between the Crown and Indigenous Peoples, 1871–1876" (PhD diss., University of Regina, 2011), 270, https://ourspace.uregina.ca/server/api/core/bitstreams/656fb86d-b5c5-4fe7-83f1-a05b49aeafc0/content.

20 Quoted in Michael Asch, *On Being Here To Stay: Treaties and Aboriginal Rights in Canada* (Toronto: University of Toronto Press, 2014), 114.

21 Quoted in Harold Cardinal and Walter Hildebrand, *Treaty Elders of Saskatchewan: Our Dream Is That Our Peoples Will One Day Be Clearly Recognized as Nations* (Calgary: University of Calgary Press, 2000), 32.

22 Cardinal and Hildebrand, *Treaty Elders of Saskatchewan*, 20.

23 Claudette Commanda, executive director, First Nations Confederacy of Cultural Education Centres, testimony to the Standing Committee on Indigenous Peoples, Issue No. 26, 1st Session, 42 Parliament, September 27, 2017, https://publications.gc.ca/collections/collection_2017/sen/yc28/YC28-421-26.pdf.

24 Purich, *Our Land*, 151.

25 Purich, *Our Land*, 117.

26 Quoted in "Creator—Land–People: Negotiations Continue (1876)," Treaty 6 Education, n.d., https://treaty6education.lskysd.ca/negotiations.html.

27 Quoted in Gina Starblanket and Dallas Hunt, "COVID-19, The Numbered Treaties and The Politics of Life: A Special Report," Yellowhead Institute, June 2020, https://yellowheadinstitute.org/wp-content/uploads/2020/06/yi-special-report-covid19-and-treaties.pdf.

28 Quoted in Treaty 7 Elders and Tribal Council with Walter Hildebrandt, Dorothy First Rider, and Sarah Carter, *The True Spirit and Original Intent of Treaty 7* (Montreal: McGill-Queen's University Press, 1996), 129.

29 Quoted in "Hearing Indigenous Voices 4," Yukon Schools, Feb. 2018, http://lss.yukonschools.ca/uploads/4/5/5/0/45508033/yukon_blanket_activity_scrolls_feb_2018.pdf.

30 "Treaty Implementation: Fulfilling the Covenant," Office of the Treaty Commission, Saskatoon, SK, 2007, 46–47, http://www.otc.ca/public/uploads/resource_photo/55757_TreatyWeb.pdf.

31 This occurred in 1953 and 1955. The RCMP, acting as representatives of the Department of Resources and Development, moved Inuit from Inukjuak (formerly called Port Harrison) in Northern Quebec, and Mittimatalik (Pond Inlet), in what is now Nunavut, to settle two locations on the High Arctic islands. (See "Historical Events in RCMP-Indigenous Relations," Royal Canadian Mounted Police, last modified May 31, 2022, https://www.rcmp-grc.gc.ca/en/historical-events-rcmp-indigenous-relations.)

32 "Inuit History and Heritage."

33 William M. Halliday, *Potlatch and Totem, and the Recollections of an Indian Agent* (London: J.M. Dent & Sons, 1935), 4.

34 Quoted in Joy Inglis and Harry Assu, *Assu of Cape Mudge: Recollections of a Coastal Indian Chief* (Vancouver: University of British Columbia Press, 2006), 103–4.

35 Jane Spoangle, "'We Call It Prison Island': Inuk Man Remembers Forced Relocation to Grise Fiord," CBC News, June 30, 2017, https://www.cbc.ca/news/canada/north/forced-relocation-high-arctic-inuit-1.4182600.

36 Qikiqtani Inuit Association, *Qikiqtani Truth Commission*, 27.

37 Darcy Anne Mitchell, "The Allied Indian Tribes of British Columbia: A Study in Pressure Group Behaviour" (master's thesis, University of British Columbia, 1977), 1, https://open.library.ubc.ca/media/stream/pdf/831/1.0094337/1.

38 Mitchell, "The Allied Indian Tribes of British Columbia," 130.
39 Mitchell, "The Allied Indian Tribes of British Columbia," 21–22.
40 St. Catharines Milling and Lumber Co. v. R. [1887], 13 S.C.R. 577, 596–97.
41 "To the League of Nations: The Red Man's Appeal for Justice," August 6, 1923, http://cendoc.docip.org/collect/deskaheh/index/assoc/HASH0102/5e23c4be.dir/R612-11-28075-30626-8.pdf.
42 Special Joint Committee on the Senate and House of Commons Appointed to Inquire into the Allied Tribes of British Columbia, Session 1926–27 (Ottawa: King's Printer, 1927), https://parl.canadiana.ca/view/oop.com_SOCHOC_1601_1_1/5 .
43 Indian Act, R.S.C., ch. 1–5.
44 Dussault and Erasmus, *Report of the Royal Commission on Aboriginal Peoples*, vol. 1, 556.
45 McKenzie Porter, "Warrior," *Maclean's*, September 1, 1952, 49.
46 "Aboriginal Veterans Quotes," Comox Valley Schools, June 25, 2001, https://www.comoxvalleyschools.ca/indigenous-education/wp-content/uploads/sites/25/2021/06/Aboriginal-Veterans-Quotes-Forgotten-Warriors.pdf.
47 "Dr. Gilbert C. Monture," *Tekawennake*, May 12, 1971, 1.
48 "Aboriginal Veterans Quotes," Comox Valley Schools.
49 Quoted in Harold McGill, "Two Decades Later: The Second World War," Annual Report of the Indian Affairs Branch of the Department of Mines and Resources, 1939–1940, 183 (Indian Affairs became a branch in this department in 1936).
50 Dussault and Erasmus, *Report of the Royal Commission on Aboriginal Peoples*, vol. 1, 556.
51 Canada, Department of Northern Affairs and National Resources, Annual Report, 1955, quoted in Truth and Reconciliation Commission of Canada, *The Final Report of the Truth and Reconciliation Commission of Canada*, vol. 2: *Canada's Residential Schools: The Inuit and Northern Experience* (Montreal: McGill-Queen's University Press, 2015), 76.
52 Qikiqtani Inuit Association, *Qikiqtani Truth Commission: Community Histories 1950–1975* (Iqaluit, NU: Inhabit Media, 2014), 33, https://www.qtcommission.ca/sites/default/files/community/community_histories_iqaluit.pdf.

53 Qikiqtani Inuit Association, *Qikiqtani Truth Commission*, 26.

54 Qikiqtani Inuit Association, *Qikiqtani Truth Commission*, 27.

55 Quoted in Truth and Reconciliation Commission *The Final Report of the Truth and Reconciliation Commission of Canada*, vol. 2: *Canada's Residential Schools*, 79.

56 Zach Parrot, "The Indian Act," Canadian Encyclopedia, last edited September 23, 2022, https://www.thecanadianencyclopedia.ca/en/article/indian-act#:~:text=A%20new%20and%20revised%20Indian,and%20sun%20dance%20were%20removed.

57 John Leslie and Ron Maguire, eds., *The Historical Development of the Indian Act* (Ottawa: Indian Affairs and Northern Affairs Canada, 1978), 132. https://publications.gc.ca/collections/collection_2017/aanc-inac/R32-342-1984-eng.pdf.

58 John Giokas, "The Indian Act: Evolution, Overview, and Options for Amendment and Transition," March 22, 1995, 54–55, https://publications.gc.ca/collections/collection_2016/bcp-pco/Z1-1991-1-41-130-eng.pdf.

59 Giokas, "The Indian Act," 56.

60 Leslie and Maguire, eds., *The Historical Development of the Indian Act*, 133.

61 Leslie and Maguire, eds., *The Historical Development of the Indian Act*, 146.

62 Prime Minister Diefenbaker, speech to the House of Commons on January 19, 1960, as reported in Hansard, 3rd Session, 24th Parliament, 8 Elizabeth II, 1960, House of Commons Canada Bill C-2 1952-53, C. 41, An Act to amend the Indian Act, quoted at Diefenbaker Canada Centre, https://diefenbaker.usask.ca/exhibits/online-exhibits-content/the-enfranchisement-of-aboriginal-peoples-in-canada-en.php.

63 "Memo form Ellen Fairclough, Superintendent-General of Indian Affairs and Minister of Citizenship and Immigration to PM Diefenbaker," quoted at Diefenbaker Canada Centre, https://diefenbaker.usask.ca/exhibits/online-exhibits-content/the-enfranchisement-of-aboriginal-peoples-in-canada-en.php.

64 Quoted in Eric Jamieson, *The Native Voice: The Story of How Maisie Hurley and Canada's First Aboriginal Newspaper Changed a Nation* (Qualicum Beach, B.C.: Caitlin Press Inc., 2016).

65 Quoted in "First Nations Right to Vote Granted 50 Years Ago," CBC News, July 1, 2010, https://www.cbc.ca/news/canada/north/first-nations-right-to-vote-granted-50-years-ago-1.899354.

66 Indian Act, 1876, S.C. 1876, c. 18.

67 Indian Act, 1951, S.C. 1951, c. 29.

68 Quoted at "Elsie Knott," Women and Gender Equality Canada, Government of Canada, n.d., https://women-gender-equality.canada.ca/en/commemorations-celebrations/women-impact/trailblazers/elsie-knott.html.

69 Quoted at CraigBaird, "Mary Two-Axe Early," Canadian History Ehx, September 11, 2021, https://canadaehx.com/2021/09/11/mary-two-axe-earley/.

70 Quoted at CraigBaird, "Mary Two-Axe Early."

71 Quoted at Wayne Brown, "Electoral Insight—Aboriginal Participation in Elections," Elections Canada, November 2003, https://www.elections.ca/content.aspx?section=res&dir=eim/issue9&document=p10&lang=e#ftn4.

72 Quoted at CraigBaird, "Mary Two-Axe Early."

73 McIvor v. Canada [2009] B.C.J. No. 669, http://www.kahnawake.com/org/docs/McIvorDecision.pdf.

74 Marion Buller, Michèle Audette, Brian Eyolfson, and Qajaq Robinson, *Reclaiming Power and Place: Executive Summary of the Final Report*, vol. 1a (Canada: National Inquiry into Missing and Murdered Indigenous Women and Girls, 2019), 1–2, https://www.mmiwg-ffada.ca/wp-content/uploads/2019/06/Executive_Summary.pdf.

75 Marion Buller, Michèle Audette, Brian Eyolfson, and Qajaq Robinson, *Reclaiming Power and Place: Executive Summary of the Final* Report, vol. 1b (Canada: National Inquiry into Missing and Murdered Indigenous Women and Girls, 2019), 167, https://www.mmiwg-ffada.ca/wp-content/uploads/2019/06/Final_Report_Vol_1b-1.pdf.

76 Quoted in Larry Loyie, Wayne K. Spear, and Constance Brissenden, *Residential Schools: With the Words and Images of Survivors*. (Brantford, ON: Indigenous Education Press and Shingwauk Residential Schools Centre, 2014) 11.

77 Quoted in Nicholas Pescod, "Author Shares Experiences from Residential Schools," *Nanaimo News Bulletin*, February 18, 2014,

https://www.nanaimobulletin.com/entertainment/author-shares-experiences-from-residential-schools-1013051.

78 Quoted in Meghan Thompson, "Chief Bev Sellars Shares Her Story of Residential School," *Martlet*, September 12, 2013, https://martlet.ca/chief-bev-sellars-shares-her-story-of-residential-school/.

79 Loyie, Spear, and Brissenden, *Residential Schools*, 35.

80 Loyie, Spear, and Brissenden, *Residential Schools*, 34.

81 Karina Roman, "St. Anne's Residential School: One Survivor's Story," CBC News, December 18, 2013, https://www.cbc.ca/news/politics/st-anne-s-residential-school-one-survivor-s-story-1.2467924.

82 Loyie, Spear, and Brissenden, *Residential Schools*, 37.

83 Jonathan Chang et al., "Stories from Canada's Indigenous Residential School Survivors," WBUR, July 28, 2021, https://www.wbur.org/onpoint/2021/07/28/stories-from-survivors-of-canadas-indigenous-residential-schools.

84 Loyie, Spear, and Brissenden, *Residential Schools*, 39.

85 Loyie, Spear, and Brissenden, *Residential Schools*, 41.

86 Loyie, Spear, and Brissenden, *Residential Schools*, 42.

87 Karla, Renic, "'Stripped of Love': Mi'kmaw Woman Shares Story of Years in Residential School," Global News, September 30, 2022, https://globalnews.ca/news/9167731/mikmaw-woman-residential-school-story-ns/.

88 Loyie, Spear, and Brissenden, *Residential Schools*, 56.

89 Loyie, Spear, and Brissenden, *Residential Schools*, 58.

90 Loyie, Spear, and Brissenden, *Residential Schools*, 79.

91 KC-NIWESG, "Three Residential School Survivors and the Brutality That Shaped Their Lives," Issuu, August, 2021, https://issuu.com/kci-niwesq/docs/kci-niwesq-issue_5-august_2021/s/13146168.

92 KC-NIWESG, "Three Residential School Survivors."

93 Loyie, Spear, and Brissenden, *Residential Schools*, 80.

94 Loyie, Spear, and Brissenden, *Residential Schools*, 81.

95 P.H. Bryce, "Report on the Indian Schools of Manitoba and the NorthWest Territories" (Ottawa: Government Printing Bureau, 1907), https://publications.gc.ca/collections/collection_2018/aanc-inac/R5-681-1907-eng.pdf.

96 Quoted in "The Healing Has Begun: An Operation Update from the Aboriginal Healing Foundation," May 2022, https://www.ahf.ca/files/the-healing-has-begun.pdf.

97 "Sixties Scoop Survivors Recall Painful Memories in Ontario," CBC News, August 23, 2016, https://www.cbc.ca/news/canada/toronto/sixties-scoop-supporters-1.3732037.

98 Edwin C. Kimelman, *No Quiet Place: Final Report to the Honourable Muriel Smith, Minister of Community Services / Review Committee on Indian and Métis Adoptions and Placements* (Manitoba: Review Committee on Indian and Métis Adoptions and Placements, 1985), 274, https://indigenousfoundations.arts.ubc.ca/sixties_scoop/.

99 Blair Crawford, "'The Sadness That Never Goes Away': Sixties School Survivor Battles to Be Recognized as Indigenous," *Ottawa Citizen*, January 8, 2019, https://ottawacitizen.com/news/local-news/the-past-that-will-never-heal-sixties-scoop-survivor-battles-to-be-recognized-as-indigenous/.

100 Ashifa Kassam, "Ratio of Indigenous Children in Canada Welfare System Is 'Humanitarian Crisis,'" *The Guardian*, November 4, 2017, https://www.theguardian.com/world/2017/nov/04/indigenous-children-canada-welfare-system-humanitarian-crisis.

101 "Cindy Blackstock Quotes," AZ Quotes, n.d., https://www.azquotes.com/author/96321-Cindy_Blackstock#google_vignette.

102 Elizabeth McSheffrey, "'Breathe Life into Our Own Laws': Visions for the Future of Indigenous Child Welfare in B.C.," Global News, June 16, 2022, https://globalnews.ca/news/8912080/visions-future-indigenous-child-welfare-bc/#:~:text=.

103 First Nations Child and Family Caring Society of Canada et al. v. Attorney General of Canada, 2019 CHRT 39, September 6, 2019, https://fncaringsociety.com/sites/default/files/2019_chrt_39.pdf/.

104 "Two Indians Challenge Powers of White Man," *Daily Free Press*, July 8, 1963.

105 Regina v. White and Bob, CANLII, 643 (SCC), September 12, 1963, para. 22–23.

106 Quoted in David Wiwchar, "Berger Helped Launch Land Claims Industry," Ammsa.com, 2003, https://ammsa.com/publications/windspeaker/berger-helped-launch-land-claims-industry

107 Quoted in Hamar Foster, Jeremy H.A. Webber, and Heather Raven, eds., *Let Right Be Done: Aboriginal Title, the Calder Case, and the Future of Indigenous Rights* (Vancouver: UBC Press, 2007), 202, https://scholars.wlu.ca/cgi/viewcontent.cgi?article=3119&context=etd.

108 Quoted in "Honouring Our Past—Dr. Frank Calder," Nisga'a Lisims Government, n.d., https://www.nisgaanation.ca/news/honouring-our-past-dr-frank-calder.

109 Quoted in Terry Fenge and Jim Aldridge, *Keeping Promises: The Royal Proclamation of 1763, Aboriginal Rights, and Treaties in Canada* (Montreal: McGill-Queen's University Press, 2015), 109.

110 "Billy Diamond: In His Own Words," Cree Nation of Waskaganish, n.d. https://waskaganish.ca/billy-diamond/.

111 Quoted in "Presentation by the Cree Nation Before the Royal Commission on Aboriginal Affairs," May 28, 1993, 13–14, https://data2.archives.ca/rcap/pdf/rcap-545.pdf.

112 "Presentation by Cree Nation," 14.

113 "Billy Diamond: In His Own Words."

114 Quoted in Mark Hume, "No. 6: Frank Calder," *Globe and Mail*, April 3, 2005, https://www.theglobeandmail.com/news/national/no-6-frank-calder/article1116728/.

115 Quoted in H.A.C. Cairns, S.M. Jamieson, and K. Lysyk, *A Survey of the Contemporary Indians of Canada*, vol. 1 (Canada: Indian Affairs Branch, 1966), https://caid.ca/HawRep1a1966.pdf.

116 Cairns, et. al., *A Survey of the Contemporary Indians of Canada*, 13.

117 From the Foreword, "Statement of the Government of Canada on Indian Policy, 1969," https://epe.lac-bac.gc.ca/100/200/301/inac-ainc/indian_policy-e/cp1969_e.pdf.

118 "Prime Minister Pierre Elliot Trudeau: Remarks on Indian Aboriginal Treaty Rights: Part of a Speech Given August 8th, 1969 in Vancouver British Columbia," Internet Archive, https://archive.org/details/primeministertruoounse.

119 "Statement of the Government of Canada on Indian Policy, 1969."

120 Quoted in Martin Lawrence, *Chrétien: The Will to Win* (Toronto: Lester, 1995), 195.

121 Harold Cardinal, *The Unjust Society: The Tragedy of Canada's Indians* (Edmonton: H.G. Hurtig, 1969), 139.

122 Cardinal, *The Unjust Society*, 140.

123 Quoted in Naithan Lagace, "The White Paper, 1969," Canadian Encyclopedia, last edited June 2020, https://www.thecanadianencyclopedia.ca/en/article/the-white-paper-1969.

124 Dussault and Erasmus, *Report of the Royal Commission on Aboriginal Peoples*, vol. 1, 205.

125 Assembly of First Nations, "Charter of the Assembly of First Nations" (1985), https://www.afn.ca/wp-content/uploads/2021/09/AFN-Charter-Ammended-06JUL2021.pdf.

126 "National Representational Organization for Inuit in Canada," Inuit Tapiriit Kanatami, n.d., https://www.itk.ca.

127 "Home," Métis National Council, n.d., https://www2.Métisnation.ca.

128 Quoted in the MacKenzie Valley Pipeline Inquiry, *The Report of the MacKenzie Valley Pipeline Inquiry*, "Epilogue: Themes for the National Interest," Prince of Wales Northern Heritage Centre, 1977, https://www.pwnhc.ca/extras/berger/report/BergerV1_ch12_e.pdf.

129 Quoted in "Natives Speak Out," Canada: A People's History (CBC), n.d., https://www.cbc.ca/history/EPISCONTENTSE1EP17CH2PA1LE.html.

130 "Natives Speak Out."

131 Quoted in "Berger Commission," Canadian Encyclopedia, last edited November 12, 2020, https://www.thecanadianencyclopedia.ca/en/article/berger-commission.

132 Quoted in Karilyn Toovey, "Decolonizing or Recolonizing: Indigenous Peoples and the Law in Canada" (master's thesis, University of Lethbridge, 2005), 13, https://dspace.library.uvic.ca/bitstream/handle/1828/744/toovey_2005.pdf.

133 Union of British Columbia Indian Chiefs, Special General Assembly, May 14 and 15, 1981, Vancouver, BC, https://constitution.ubcic.bc.ca/sites/constitution.ubcic.bc.ca/files/OCRSGA1981-05-14&15(NoClippings).pdf.

134 Quoted in Union of British Columbia Indian Chiefs, "The Indian Nations and the Federal Government's View on the Constitution," 13,

https://constitution.ubcic.bc.ca/sites/constitution.ubcic.bc.ca/files/OCRIndianNations&FederalGovView.pdf.

135 Constitution Act, 1982, being Schedule B to the Canada Act 1982 (UK), 1982, c 11.

136 Maurice Bulbulian, *Dancing Around the Table*, Parts 1 (National Film Board of Canada, 1987), https://www.nfb.ca/film/dancing_around_the_table_1/.

137 Secretariat of the Conference, "Federal-Provincial Conference of First Ministers on Aboriginal Constitutional Matters," Document 800-17/004, Primary Documents.ca, March 15–16, 1983, https://primarydocuments.ca/wp-content/uploads/2018/07/1stMinConfAboVerb1983Mar15.pdf.

138 "Federal-Provincial Conference of First Ministers on Aboriginal Constitutional Matters," 128.

139 "First Ministers' Conference on Aboriginal Constitutional Matters," March 26–27, 1987, Document 800-23/004, https://primarydocuments.ca/wp-content/uploads/2018/07/FirstMinsAboriginalVerb1987Mar26.pdf.

140 "First Ministers' Conference on Aboriginal Constitutional Matters," March 26–27, 1987.

141 Jamie Bradburn, "The Penner Report," Canadian Encyclopedia, March 16, 2023, https://www.thecanadianencyclopedia.ca/en/article/the-penner-report.

142 Quoted in Peter A. Cumming and Diana Ginn, "First Nations Self-Government in Canada," *Nordic Journal of International Law* 55, no. 1–2 (1986): 86–116, https://digitalcommons.osgoode.yorku.ca/cgi/viewcontent.cgi?referer=&httpsredir=1&article=1884&context=scholarly_works.

143 "First Ministers' Conference on Aboriginal Constitutional Matters," April 2, 1985, 9–11, https://primarydocuments.ca/wp-content/uploads/1985/04/FirstMinsConfVerb1985Apr2.pdf.

144 Quoted in Carol Etkin, "The Sechelt Indian Band: An Analysis of a New Form of Native Self-Government," n.d., http://courses.learninglibrary.com/tllflash/AFOA/AFM%206/PDFs/SecheltIndianBand_Etkin.pdf.

145 René Dussault and Georges Erasmus, *Report of the Royal Commission on Aboriginal Peoples*, vol. 5: *Renewal* (Ottawa: Indian and Northern Affairs Canada, 1996), 1.

146 Quoted in Allan Levine, "Native Leader Elijah Harper Helped Scuttle Meech Lake," *Globe and Mail*, May 20, 2013, https://www.theglobeandmail.com/news/politics/native-leader-elijah-harper-helped-scuttle-meech-lake/article12033338/.

147 Levine, "Native Leader Elijah Harper."

148 Dussault and Erasmus, *Report of the Royal Commission on Aboriginal Peoples*, vol. 1, 209.

149 "25 Years since Elijah Harper Said 'No' to Meech Lake Accord," CBC News, June 11, 2015, https://www.cbc.ca/news/canada/manitoba/25-years-since-elijah-harper-said-no-to-the-meech-lake-accord-1.3110439.

150 "Charlottetown Accord," Canadian Encyclopedia, last edited October 14, 2014, https://www.thecanadianencyclopedia.ca/en/article/charlottetown-accord-document.

151 Wright, *Stolen Continents*, 332.

152 "Georges Erasmus on Self-Government, 1990" (speech, Empire Club of Canada, November 29, 1990), http://greatcanadianspeeches.ca/2018/03/27/george-erasmus-on-self-government-1990/.

153 Brian Mulroney to Tony Penikett (Government Leader, Yukon Territory) and Dennis Patterson (Government Leader, Northwest Territories), 15 November 1990, PCO 2150-1, Identification Number 34788, TRC Document Number TRC3379, https://www.aptntv.ca/news/wp-content/uploads/sites/4/2015/04/MulroneylettersstoNWTandYukon.pdf.

154 Dussault and Erasmus, *Report of the Royal Commission on Aboriginal Peoples*, vol.1.

155 "Federal Government Makes Untimely Response to RCAP," *Saskatchewan Indian*, Spring 1998, https://epe.lac-bac.gc.ca/100/205/301/ic/cdc/saskindian/a98spr10.htm.

156 "Federal Government Makes Untimely Response to RCAP."

157 The Royal Commission of Aboriginal Peoples logo, by Joseph Sagaj, represents the four divisions of humanity — in essence, all sectors of Canadian society—coming together to join hands, to establish a basic relationship. The circle they form represents their mutual willingness to join one another in finding ways to make their relationship more balanced and mutually

beneficial. At the centre of the circle is a bear's claw. This represents the healing that must take place during this process. After so much misunderstanding, anger, alienation, and division, the time has come to repair the fractures in relations between Aboriginal peoples and Canadian society. This healing will occur when the various components that make up Canadian society come together to embrace and affirm the fundamental principles that promote balanced and mutually beneficial co-existence.

158 Quoted in *Delgamuukw: The People, The Strength, and the Unity Behind the Historic Decision* (British Columbia: Gitxsan Chief's Office, 2010), 3.

159 *Delgamuukw*, 5.

160 *Delgamuukw*, 7.

161 Delgamuukw v. British Columbia, [1997] 3 S.C.R. 1010 (Can.), para 186, https://scc-csc.lexum.com/scc-csc/scc-csc/en/item/1569/index.do?q=%5B1997%D+3+SCR+1010.

162 Haida Nation v. British Columbia (Minister of Forests), [2004] S.C.R. 73 (Can.), https://scc-csc.lexum.com/scc-csc/scc-csc/en/item/2189/index.do.

163 Mikisew Cree First Nation v. Canada (Minister of Canadian Heritage), [2005] 3 S.C.R. 388 (Can.), para 1, https://scc-csc.lexum.com/scc-csc/scc-csc/en/item/17288/index.do.

164 R. v. Powley, [2003] 2 SCR 207, para 13, https://scc-csc.lexum.com/scc-csc/scc-csc/en/item/2076/index.do.

165 Manitoba Métis Federation Inc. v. Canada (Attorney General), 2013 SCC 14.

166 Daniels v. Canada (Indian Affairs and Northern Development), 2016 SCC 12.

167 Quoted in "The Creation of Nunavut," Listening To Our Past, n.d., http://www.traditional-knowledge.ca/english/the-creation-nunavut-s153.html.

168 Currently, there are seven First Nations implementing modern treaties under three Final Agreements signed under the B.C. Treaty Process: Maa-Nulth First Nations (comprising Huu-ay-aht First Nations, Ka:'yu:'k't'h'/Che:k'tles7et'h' First Nations, Toquaht Nation, Uchucklesaht Tribe, and Yuułuʔiłʔatḥ [Ucluelet] First Nation); Tla'amin Nation; and Tsawwassen First Nation (See *2021 Annual Report*, BC Treaty Commission, 12, https://bctreaty.ca/reports/2021-annual-report/.)

169 Quoted in "Principals and Parties: Treaties and Agreements," BC Treaty Commission, n.d., http://www.bctreaty.ca/principals-and-parties.

170 Douglas R. Eyford, *A New Direction: Advancing Aboriginal and Treaty Rights* (Ottawa: Crown-Indigenous Relationship and Northern Affairs Canada, 2015), https://www.rcaanc-cirnac.gc.ca/DAM/DAM-CIRNAC-RCAANC/DAM-TAG/STAGING/texte-text/eyford_newDirection-report_april2015_1427810490332_eng.pdf.

171 Public Legal Education Association of Saskatchewan, "From Dream to Reality: The Story of Treaty Land Entitlement" (Grasswood, SK: Office of the Treaty Commission, 2011), https://teachers.plea.org/uploads/content/FromDreamToReality.pdf.

172 R. v. Gladue [1999] 1 SCR 688, https://scc-csc.lexum.com/scc-csc/scc-csc/en/item/1695/index.do.

173 The British Columbia First Nations Justice Council logo, by Jamin Zuroski, of three salmon represents the past, present, and future. We draw upon the tools, protocols, and teachings of our ancestors; recognize and contend with the challenges of today; and work toward our common goal of returning home to self-determined approaches to justice.

174 "B.C. First Nations Justice Strategy," February 2020, https://bcfnjc.com/wp-content/uploads/2022/04/BCFNJC_Justice-Strategy_February-2020.pdf.

175 Priscilla Wolf, "'I Miss My Son So Much': Colten Boushies' Mother Demands Change in Justice System," APTN, August 10, 2021, https://www.aptnnews.ca/national-news/i-miss-my-son-so-much-colten-boushies-mother-demands-change-in-justice-system/.

176 Buller, Audette, Eyolfson, and Robinson, *Reclaiming Power and Place*, vol. 1a, 5.

177 The National Inquiry into Missing and Murdered Indigenous Women and Girls logo, by Meky Ottawa (lead artist), revisits the traditional roots of female Indigenous expression and empowerment. The design combines the traditional symbols of First Nations, Métis, and Inuit women.

Indigenous women have always been story tellers through the shell work, beadwork, and weaving patterns they have passed down from generation to generation. While design differs across the nation, floral prints are often used.

The "dot art" within the flower and leaves of the logo emphasizes symmetry, balance, and harmony and the use of the connected lines also represents our interconnectedness to each other. The black lines and dots that tie it all together represent the traditional tattoos of Inuit women.

178 Buller, Audette, Eyolfson, and Robinson, *Reclaiming Power and Place*, vol. 1a., 57.

179 Buller, Audette, Eyolfson, and Robinson, *Reclaiming Power and Place*, vol. 1a, 53.

180 Buller, Audette, Eyolfson, and Robinson, *Reclaiming Power and Place*, vol. 1a., 66.

181 Quoted in Katie Hyslop, "The Kelowna Accord, Racism and the Child Welfare Crisis," *The Tyee*, May 22, 2018, https://thetyee.ca/News/2018/05/22/Kelowna-Accord-Racism-Child-Welfare/.

182 "The Métis Nation Welcomes the Passing of Bill C-292: An Act to Implement the Kelowna Accord," NationTalk, March 22, 2007, https://nationtalk.ca/story/the-metis-nation-welcomes-the-passing-of-bill-c-292-an-act-to-implement-the-kelowna-accord.

PART FOUR: THUNDERBIRD

1 Dussault and Erasmus, *Report of the Royal Commission on Aboriginal Peoples*, vol. 2: *Restructuring the Relationship*, xi.

2 "Schedule N: Mandate for the Truth and Reconciliation Commission," Government of Canada, https://www.residentialschoolsettlement.ca/SCHEDULE_N.pdf.

3 "Indian Residential Schools Statement of Apology—Prime Minister Stephen Harper," Government of Canada, June 11, 2008, https://www.ourcommons.ca/DocumentViewer/en/39-2/house/sitting-110/hansard.

4 "The Day of the Apology," Government of Canada, June 11, 2008, https://www.rcaanc-cirnac.gc.ca/eng/1100100015697/1571589725919.

5 Quoted in Joanna Smith, "School 'Atrocity' Affected Generations, Survivor Says," *Toronto Star*, June 11, 2008, https://www.thestar.com/news/canada/2008/06/11/schools_atrocity_affected_generations_survivor_says.html.

6 Quoted in "Harper Apologizes for Residential School Abuse," CTV News, June 11, 2008, https://www.ctvnews.ca/harper-apologizes-for-residential-school-abuse-1.301603.

7 "Indian Residential Schools Statement of Apology—Mary Simon, President, Inuit Tapiriit Kanatami," Government of Canada, June 11, 2008, https://www.rcaanc-cirnac.gc.ca/eng/1100100015707/1571590053915.
8 "Indian Residential Schools Statement of Apology—Beverley Jacobs, President, Native Women's Association," Government of Canada, June 11, 2008, https://www.rcaanc-cirnac.gc.ca/eng/1100100015717/1571590149046.
9 Truth and Reconciliation Commission of Canada, *Honouring the Truth, Reconciling for the Future,* 315–16.
10 Truth and Reconciliation Commission of Canada, *Honouring the Truth, Reconciling for the Future: Summary of the Final Report of the Truth and Reconciliation Commission*, 1, https://ehprnh2mwo3.exactdn.com/wp-content/uploads/2021/01/Executive_Summary_English_Web.pdf.
11 Truth and Reconciliation Commission of Canada, *Honouring the Truth, Reconciling for the Future,* 316–17.
12 Buller, Audette, Eyolfson, and Robinson, *Reclaiming Power and* Place, vol. 1a, 6.
13 UN General Assembly, United Nations Declaration on the Rights of Indigenous Peoples, October 2, 2007, 8–9, 19, 20, https://www.un.org/development/desa/indigenouspeoples/wp-content/uploads/sites/19/2018/11/UNDRIP_E_web.pdf.
14 "General Assembly Adopts Declaration on Rights of Indigenous Peoples; 'Major Step Forward' Towards Human Rights for All, says President," United Nations, September 13, 2007, https://www.un.org/press/en/2007/ga10612.doc.htm.
15 Quoted in "Canada Votes 'No' as UN Native Rights Declaration Passes," CBC News, September 13, 2007, https://www.cbc.ca/news/canada/canada-votes-no-as-un-native-rights-declaration-passes-1.632160.
16 "Canada Votes 'No'."
17 "Speech Delivered at the United Nations Permanent Forum on Indigenous Issues, New York, May 10," Indigenous and Northern Affairs Canada (Hon. Carolyn Bennett), May 10, 2016, https://www.canada.ca/en/indigenous-northern-affairs/news/2016/05/speech-delivered-at-the-united-nations-permanent-forum-on-indigenous-issues-new-york-may-10-.html.

18 Quoted in Heather Scoffield, "Assembly of First Nations Asks UN to See if Ottawa's Meeting Legal Obligations," Global News, December 6, 2011, https://globalnews.ca/news/186079/assembly-of-first-nations-asks-un-to-see-if-ottawas-meeting-legal-obligations/.

19 Idle No More, "Vision," n.d., https://idlenomore.ca/about-the-movement/.

20 Wab Kinew, "From a Grassroots Hashtag to a Real Opportunity for Change," *Free Press*, December 6, 2012, https://www.winnipegfreepress.com/arts-and-life/life/2012/12/06/from-a-grassroots-hashtag-to-a-real-opportunity-for-change-kinewview.

21 Quoted in Sarah Van Gelder, "Why Canada's Indigenous Uprising Is About All of Us," *YES!*, February 8, 2013, https://www.yesmagazine.org/issue/issues-how-cooperatives-are-driving-the-new-economy/2013/02/08/why-canada2019s-indigenous-uprising-is-about-all-of-us.

22 "First Nations Meeting with PM Thrown into Disarray," CBC News, January 10, 2013 [video], https://www.cbc.ca/news/politics/first-nations-meeting-with-om-thrown-into-disarray-1.1381808.

23 Canada, House of Commons, Standing Committee on Justice and Human Rights, Testimony, No. 135, 1st Session, 42 Parliament, February 27, 2019, https://www.ourcommons.ca/DocumentViewer/en/42-1/just/meeting-135/evidence.

24 Quoted in Shannon Proudfoot, "Mumilaaq Qaqqaq: 'It's Time to Face the Scale of Justice,'" *Maclean's*, June 16, 2021, https://macleans.ca/politics/ottawa/mumilaaq-qaqqaq-its-time-to-face-the-scale-of-justice/.

25 An explanation of this expression's origins can be found on Linternaute, https://www.linternaute.fr/expression/langue-francaise/928/avoir-un-nom-a-coucher-dehors/.

26 Government of Canada, "The Honourable Michelle O'Bonsawin's questionnaire," Office of the Commissioner for Federal Judicial Affairs Canada, 2022, https://www.fja.gc.ca/scc-csc/2022/nominee-candidat-eng.html.

27 Quoted in Alex Karpa, "How Wab Kinew's Victory Can Inspire the Next Generation," CityNews, October 6, 2023, https://winnipeg.citynews.ca/2023/10/06/how-wab-kinews-victory-can-inspire-the-next-generation/.

28 Karpa, "How Wab Kinew's Victory Can Inspire the Next Generation."

29 Quoted in Carolyne Weldon, "Remembering Acclaimed Inuit Artist Kenojuak Ashevak," NFB Blog, January 9, 2013, https://blog.nfb.ca/blog/2013/01/09/inuit-artist-kenojuak-ashevak/.

30 Quoted in Murray Whyte, "Ken Monkman Fills in the Blanks in Canadian History," *Toronto Star*, January 22, 2017, https://www.thestar.com/entertainment/visual-arts/kent-monkman-fills-in-the-blanks-in-canadian-history/article_fe928e36-316e-5537-be0f-d9f0e2515319.html.

31 "Abenaki Filmmaker Alanis Obomsawin on Her Legendary Career and the Power of Storytelling," CBC Radio, December 30, 2020, https://www.cbc.ca/radio/writersandcompany/abenaki-filmmaker-alanis-obomsawin-on-her-legendary-career-and-the-power-of-storytelling-1.5850622.

32 Quoted in Becky Rynor, "From the Heart: An Interview with Christi Belcourt," National Gallery of Canada, October 2, 2015, https://www.gallery.ca/magazine/artists/from-the-heart-an-interview-with-christi-belcourt.

33 Quoted in Jane Willsie, "In Conversation with Michelle Good," University of British Columbia, n.d., https://greencollege.ubc.ca/blog/conversation-michelle-good-author-lawyer-and-voice-wisdom.

34 "Carey Price," Indspire, n.d., https://indspire.ca/laureate/carey-price/.

35 Matthew Gourlie, "In Their Own Words: The Stories of Great Saskatchewan Indigenous Athletes," Saskatchewan Sports Hall of Fame, February 25, 2022, https://sasksportshalloffame.com/in-their-own-words-the-stories-of-great-saskatchewan-indigenous-athletes/.

36 Drew Hayden Taylor, "Why Do Some People Pretend to Be Indigenous," TVO Today, July 12, 2022, https://www.tvo.org/article/why-do-some-people-pretend-to-be-indigenous.

37 Jean Teillet, "Indigenous Identity Fraud: A Report for the University of Saskatchewan," October 17, 2022, https://indigenous.usask.ca/documents/deybwewin--taapwaywin--tapwewin-verification/jean-teillet-report.pdf.

38 First Nations Finance Authority, "Stronger Together," YouTube Video, 5:31, May 26, 2021. https://www.youtube.com/watch?v=C34izANefBE&t=88s.

39 First Nations Finance Authority, "First Nations Urge Canada to Choose Partnership over Paternalism in Federal Budget by Enacting Collaborative Funding Model to Close the Infrastructure Gap," Cision, March 22, 2023,

https://www.newswire.ca/news-releases/first-nations-urge-canada-to-choose-partnership-over-paternalism-in-federal-budget-by-enacting-collaborative-funding-model-to-close-the-infrastructure-gap-883807513.html.

40 Quoted in Trina Roache, "Boosting First Nation Economies a Part of Reconciliation," APTN, June 26, 2015, https://www.aptnnews.ca/national-news/boosting-first-nation-economies-part-reconciliation/.

41 "Khelsilam and Mindy Wright: Reconciliation is Building Something Better for Indigenous and Non-Indigenous Communities," Khelsilam, September 23, 2022, https://khelsilem.substack.com/p/khelsilem-and-mindy-wight-reconciliation.

42 Quoted in Richard J. Goossen, "Clarence Louie, Chief, Osooyos Indian Band: Life and Entrepreneurial Lessons (Part 1), ELO Network, June 27, 2023, https://www.entrepreneurialleaders.com/blog/434/Clarence-Louie-Chief-Osoyoos-Indian-Band-Life--Entrepreneurial-Lessons-Part-I.

43 "ʔəy̓alməxʷ/Iy̓álmexw /Jericho Lands to Become Future Complete Community," City of Vancouver, January 24, 2024, https://vancouver.ca/news-calendar/jericho-lands-to-become-future-complete-community-jan-2024.aspx.

44 Teck Resources, "Indigenous Peoples Policy," April 25, 2022, https://www.teck.com/media/Indigenous-Peoples-Policy.pdf.

45 Quoted in "The Robust Indigenous Economy Makes Economic Reconciliation An Urgent Business Imperative," Canadian Council for Aboriginal Business, November 23, 2023, https://www.ccab.com/the-robust-indigenous-economy-makes-economic-reconciliation-an-urgent-business-imperative/.

46 "A Chosen Journey: RBC Indigenous Partnership Report 2023" https://www.rbc.com/indigenous/_assets-custom/pdfs/A-Chosen-Journey-2023_ENG.pdf.

47 Haida Nation v. British Columbia (Minister of Forests), [2004] S.C.R. 73 (Can.), para 20, https://scc-csc.lexum.com/scc-csc/scc-csc/en/item/2189/index.do.

48 Tsilhqot'in Nation v. British Columbia [2014], 2 S.C.R. 257 (Can.), paras 97 and 94, https://scc-csc.lexum.com/scc-csc/scc-csc/en/item/14246/index.do.

49 "Archived—Minister of National Defence Mandate Letter," Prime Minister of Canada, November 12, 2015, https://www.pm.gc.ca/en/mandate-letters/2015/11/12/archived-minister-national-defence-mandate-letter.

50 "Remarks by the Prime Minister in the House of Commons on the Recognition and Implementation of Rights Framework," Prime Minister of Canada, February 14, 2018, https://pm.gc.ca/en/news/speeches/2018/02/14/remarks-prime-minister-house-commons-recognition-and-implementation-rights.

51 Declaration on the Rights of Indigenous Peoples Act [SBC 2019], Chapter 44, assented to November 28, 2019, Victoria, B.C., https://www.bclaws.gov.bc.ca/civix/document/id/complete/statreg/19044.

52 Canada. *United Nations Declaration on the Rights of Indigenous Peoples Act*. Ottawa, ON, 2021, https://laws-lois.justice.gc.ca/eng/acts/U-2.2/page-1.html.

53 Bill C-92: An Act respecting First Nations, Inuit and Métis children, youth and families [S.C. 2019, c. 24], assented to June 21, 2019, https://laws.justice.gc.ca/eng/acts/f-11.73/FullText.html.

54 Indigenous Services Canada, "Government of Canada, Assembly of First Nations, Inuit Tapiriit Kanatami, Métis National Council Celebrate the Introduction of Bill C-92," Cision, February 28, 2019, https://www.newswire.ca/news-releases/government-of-canada-assembly-of-first-nations-inuit-tapiriit-kanatami-Métis-national-council-celebrate-the-introduction-of-bill-c-92-884314752.html.

55 Marie-Danielle Smith, "Cindy Blackstock: A Relentless Champion for Indigenous Children's Rights," *Maclean's*, January 18, 2021, https://macleans.ca/society/cindy-blackstock-a-relentless-champion-for-indigenous-childrens-rights/.

56 Indigenous Services Canada, "Federal Court Approves Settlement Agreement to Compensate First Nations Children and Families," Government of Canada, October 24, 2023, https://www.canada.ca/en/indigenous-services-canada/news/2023/10/federal-court-approves-settlement-agreement-to-compensate-first-nations-children-and-families.html.

57 Darren Major and Olivia Stefanovich, "Judge Approves Historic $23B First Nations Child Welfare Compensation Agreement," CBC News, October 24,

2023, https://www.cbc.ca/news/politics/judge-approves-23-billion-first-nations-child-welfare-agreement-1.7006351.

58 Reference re An Act respecting First Nations, Inuit and Métis children, youth and families [2024 SCC 5].

59 Quoted in Phil Heidenreich, "'The Story Was Hidden': How Residential School Graves Shocked and Shaped Canada in 2021," Global News, December 31, 2021, https://globalnews.ca/news/8458351/canada-residential-schools-unmarked-graves-indigenous-impact/.

60 Quoted in "Calls to Find All Unmarked Graves after Grim Residential School Discovery," *The Guardian*, June 1, 2021, https://www.theguardian.com/world/2021/jun/01/calls-to-find-all-canadas-indigenous-mass-graves-after-grim-residential-school-discovery.

61 "Calls to Find All Unmarked Graves."

62 Kimberly R. Murray, *Submission to the UN Expert Mechanism on the Rights of Indigenous Peoples*, Office of the Independent Special Interlocutor for Missing Children and Unmarked Burial Sites associated with Indian Residential Schools, March 3, 2023, https://osi-bis.ca/wp-content/uploads/2023/03/Submission-the-UN-Expert-Mechanism-on-the-Rights-of-Indigenous-Peoples_Monitoring-UNDRIP-Implementation_March-2023_FINAL.pdf.

63 Dan George, *My Heart Soars* (Surrey, B.C.: Hancock House, 1974).

64 Quoted in *National Gathering on Unmarked Burials: Upholding Indigenous Laws in the Search and Recovery of Missing Children*, Office of the Independent Special Interlocutor for Missing Children and Unmarked Burial Sites associated with Indian Residential Schools, 2023,15, https://osi-bis.ca/wp-content/uploads/2023/11/OSI-SummaryReport_Toronto_2023_web.pdf.

65 John Borrows, interview with author, January 29, 2024.

66 Quoted in Teddy Zegeye-Gebrehiwot, Elizabeth Carlson-Manathara and Gladys Rowe, *Stories of Decolonization: Land Dispossession and Settlement*" (video), March 3, 2020, https://www.storiesofdecolonization.org/film-one.html.

67 "The Concepts of Netukulimk and Two-Eyed Seeing," L'Nuey, accessed June 26, 2023, https://lnuey.ca/wp-content/uploads/2021/03/CONCEPTS-FactSheet_2021.pdf.

68 Jean Teillet, interview with author, January 26, 2024.

69 Quoted in Maya'xala xan's K'walsk'wal'yakw, *"Honouring our Elders" of the Musgamagw Dzawada̱'enux̱w, Musgamagw* (Dzawada̱'enux̱w Tribal Council, First Choice Books, 2015), 16.

70 Quoted in K'walsk'wal'yakw, *"Honouring our Elders,"* 85.

71 Quoted in Royal Commission on Aboriginal Peoples, "Public Hearing, Discussion Paper 2, Focusing the Dialogue" (Ottawa: Canada Communication Group Publishing, 1993), 13.

72 Quoted in Glen Rogers et al. eds., *Speaking My Truth: Reflections on Reconciliation & Residential School* (Aboriginal Healing Foundation, 2012), 161.

73 Quoted in Brian Slattery, "The Generative Structure of Aboriginal Rights" in *From Recognition to Reconciliation: Essays on the Constitutional Entrenchment of Aboriginal & Treaty Rights*, ed. Patrick Macklem and Douglas Sanderson (Toronto: University of Toronto Press, 2016,) 113.

74 Quoted in "The Spirit of the Michef Language," Métis Gathering, n.d., https://metisgathering.ca/michif-language/about-michif/.

75 Quoted in Nadine Fabbi, "Inuktitut: the Inuit Language," April 22, 2016, https://leapintothevoidwithme.wordpress.com/2016/04/22/inuktitut-the-inuit-language/.

76 Fred Kelly, "Confessions of a Born Again Pagan," in Marlene Brant Castellano, Linda Archibald, and Mike Degagne, eds., *From Truth to Reconciliation: Transforming the Legacy of Residential Schools* (Ottawa: Aboriginal Healing Foundation, 2011), 15, 29.

77 Quoted in Bob Joseph, *21 Things You May Not Have Known About the Indian Act: Helping Canadians Make Reconciliation with Indigenous Peoples a Reality* (Vancouver, Indigenous Relations Press, 2018), 7–8.

78 Stephen Lewis, "Remarks at Vancouver Truth and Reconciliation Event, September 2013," in Shelagh Rogers, Mike DeGagné, Glen Lowry, and Sara Fryer, eds., *Reconciliation and the Way Forward* (Ottawa: Aboriginal Healing Foundation, 2014), 146–47.

79 Beverley McLachlin, "Reconciling Unity and Diversity in the Modern Era: Tolerance and Intolerance," Annual Pluralism Lecture, Global Centre for Pluralism, 2015, https://www.pluralism.ca/wp-content/uploads/2017/10/APL2015_BeverleyMcLachlin_Lecture.pdf.

80 Quoted in Kiera L. Ladner and Myra J. Tai, eds., *Surviving Canada: Indigenous Peoples Celebrate 150 Years of Betrayal* (Winnipeg, MB: ARP Books, 2017), 63.

81 Ka'nhehsí:io Deer, "Pope Says Genocide Took Place at Canada's Residential Schools," CBC News, July 30, 2022, https://www.cbc.ca/news/indigenous/pope-francis-residential-schools-genocide-1.6537203.

82 Quoted in Deer, "Pope Says Genocide Took Place at Canada's Residential Schools."

83 Gordon Campbell, interview with author, January 30, 2024.

84 Chief Ted Williams, interview with author, January 26, 2024.

85 Quoted in Rhiannon Johnson, "Indigenous Youth Set Up Protest Camp outside Toronto's Old City Hall," CBC News, March 6, 2018, https://www.cbc.ca/news/indigenous/youth-soaring-eagles-camp-old-city-hall-toronto-1.4563297.

86 Quoted in Jacob Barker,"Generations Reflect on What Truth and Reconciliation Is in Windsor-Essex," CBC News, September 30, 2021, https://www.cbc.ca/news/canada/windsor/national-day-truth-reconciliation-youth-elder-1.6194486.

87 Quoted in Ryan MacDonald, "Want to Be an Ally for Indigenous People? Here's How You Can Help," CTV News, June 2, 2021, https://atlantic.ctvnews.ca/want-to-be-an-ally-for-indigenous-people-here-s-how-you-can-help-1.5454156.

88 Quoted in Alex Ballingal, "Mike Kirlew, the Doctor-Advocate Fighting for Better Indigenous Health Care," *Toronto Star*, March 5, 2017, https://www.thestar.com/news/canada/mike-kirlew-the-doctor-advocate-fighting-for-better-indigenous-health-care/article_37e4e89c-bd3c-53ce-b184-4e559f8b24b5.html.

89 Ryan MacDonald, "Want to Be an Ally for Indigenous People?"

90 Elsa Kaka, "Why Is Being Called 'Racist' More Offensive Than Racism Itself? White Fragility Silences Voices, Says Advocate," CBC News, June 20, 2020, https://www.cbc.ca/news/canada/manitoba/pov-racism-white-fragility-1.5619647.

91 Quoted in Jocelyn Thorpe, "Truth and Reconciliation," NiCHE, October 24, 2012, https://niche-canada.org/2012/10/24/truth-and-reconciliation/.

92 Paul Martin, *Aboriginal Canada Today: Changing the Course of History*, The Symons Medal Series (Ottawa: University of Ottawa Press, 2013), 237–38.

93 Quoted in Jesse Kinos-Goodin, "By Questioning Canada's Past, Gord Downie Fought for a Better Future," CBC, October 18, 2017, https://www.cbc.ca/music/read/by-questioning-canada-s-past-gord-downie-fought-for-a-better-future-1.5000274.

94 Steven Point, interview with the author, February 1, 2024.

95 Mary Simon, "Through the Eyes of the North: Our Collective Responsibility" (Courchene Lecture, Queen's University, Kingston, ON, April 12, 2022), https://www.gg.ca/en/media/news/2022/queens-university-courchene-lecture-through-eyes-north-our-collective-responsibility.

96 "This design was created while I thought about who I was as a person and where I came from. I like to describe myself as coming from the four corners of the Kwakwaka'wakw territory.

"My Parental grandparents come from Axwamees (Wakeman Sound), We Wai Kai (Cape Mudge); my Maternal grandparents come from Ba'as (Blunden Harbour), and Wei Wai Kum (Campbell River). With this being said, though, we all still live within one larger Country, that being Canada. I wanted to create a design that represents where I came from but also representing the Country we live in."

—Mulidzas (Kwakwaka'wakw Artist Curtis Wilson)

K̲̓I'MOLA

1 Chief Ted Williams, interview with author.

2 Arlene Dickinson, interview with author, February 9, 2024.

3 Georges Erasmus, email to author, February 12, 2024.

4 John Borrows, interview with author.

5 Michaëlle Jean, email to author, April 13, 2024.

6 Chief Rosanne Casimir, email to author, February 13, 2024.

7 Jane Philpott, email to author, February 16, 2024.

8 Steven Point, interview with author.

9 Jean Teillet, interview with author.

10 Legislative Assembly of British Columbia, Debates (Hansard), 42nd Parliament, 5th Session, April 22, 2024, https://www.leg.bc.ca/documents-data/debate-transcripts/42nd-parliament/5th-session.

11 James Baldwin, *Collected Essays* (New York: Library of America, 1998), 723.

Illustration Credits

ODOODEM

p. 5 © Ryan Dawson

p. 7 "Chiefs in Regalia", Photographer: Amy Wakefield (1934-1937) / Collection of the Anglican Archives

p. 8 © Adelaide de Menil, George and Joanne MacDonald Northwest Coast Image Archive, Simon Fraser University

PART 1: FIRST ANCESTOR

p. 21 *Sky Woman Geezhigo-Quae*, by Donald Chrétien. Copyright © Donald Chrétien

p. 23 Photo courtesy of Spirits of the West Coast Art Gallery

p. 25 © House of Commons Collection, Ottawa / © Collection de la Chambre des communes, Ottawa

p. 26 Edward S. Curtis Collection (Library of Congress)

p. 38 René Dussault and Georges Erasmus, *Report of the Royal Commission on Aboriginal Peoples*, vol. 1: *Looking Forward, Looking Back* (Ottawa: Indian and Northern Affairs Canada, 1996), 21.

PART 2: RAVEN

p. 45 Permission of Kamloops Museum, KMA 6337

p. 61 Courtesy of The University of Waterloo

p. 67 Info633933 / Dreamstime.com

p. 70 © House of Commons Collection, Ottawa / © Collection de la Chambre des communes, Ottawa

p. 77 "Louis Riel, Manitoba", 1869, (CU1297348) by Unknown. Courtesy of Louis Riel Collection, Libraries and Cultural Resources Digital Collections, University of Calgary

p. 85 "Poundmaker, Cree chief", 1885, (CU184413) by Steele and Company. Courtesy of Glenbow Library and Archives Collection, Libraries and Cultural Resources Digital Collections, University of Calgary

p. 92 Archives Deschâtelets-NDC

p. 94–95 Library and Archives Canada / Annual report of the Department of Indian Affairs 1896 / OCLC 1771148

PART 3: WOLF

p. 108 "Louis Riel and his associates.", [ca. 1869], (CU175250) by Larsen, Ryder. Courtesy of Louis Riel Collection, Libraries and Cultural Resources Digital Collections, University of Calgary.

p. 109 Courtesy of Métis Nation of Alberta

p. 114 Image: © Manitoba Museum, Winnipeg, MB.

p. 118 "Sweetgrass, head chief of the Cree in St. Boniface Manitoba," 1872-06, (CU184333) by Unknown. Courtesy of Glenbow Library and Archives Collection, Libraries and Cultural Resources Digital Collections, University of Calgary.

p. 125 Museum of Archaeology and Anthropology, Cambridge, T 142655 PAT

p. 127 Copyright © GABRIEL ZARÁTE. Photo courtesy of Nunatsiaq News.

p. 130 From Leslie A. Robertson, *Standing Up*, published by UBC Press.

p. 133 Dept. of National Defence / Library and Archives Canada / PA-129070.

p. 134 Christopher J. Woods / Canada. Dept. of National Defence / Library and Archives Canada / PA-142289

p. 143 Photo courtesy of the National Film Board of Canada.

p. 146 Dept. Indian and Northern Affairs / Library and Archives Canada / e011080274

p. 148 Bud Glunz / National Film Board of Canada. Photothèque / PA-134110

p. 151 Courtesy of Tim Raybould

p. 153 Deschâtelets-NDC Archives

p. 155 Courtesy of First Nations Child & Family Caring Society

p. 160 Nisga'a Lisims Government Communications Department

p. 163 The Canadian Press / Fred Chartrand

p. 167 The Canadian Press / R. Mac

p. 172 From the NFB documentary *Fort Good Hope*, 1977 (dir. Ron Orieux)

p. 174 CP photo / Carl Bigras

p. 176 © Government of Canada. Reproduced with the permission of the Minister of Public Works and Government Services Canada (2012)

p. 180 (top) CBC Licensing

p. 180 (bottom) Centre for Mennonite Brethren Studies, Winnipeg, NP149-01-5486. Reprinted by permission.

p. 183 CP / Chuck Mitchell

p. 188 The Canadian Press / Tom Hanson

p. 192 The Canadian Press

p. 194 The Canadian Press / Shaney Komulainen

p. 197 Crown-Indigenous Relations and Northern Affairs Canada

p. 199 SuperStock / Chris Jaksa / All Canada Photos

p. 201 CP photo / Tom Hanson

p. 205 Photo courtesy of Nunatsiaq News

p. 207 CP photo / Tom Hanson

p. 211 BC First Nations Justice Council

p. 212 National Inquiry into Missing and Murdered Indigenous Women and Girls

PART 4: THUNDERBIRD

p. 225 The Canadian Press / Tom Hanson

p. 230 The Canadian Press / Adrian Wyld

p. 232 Courtesy of Tim Raybould

p. 238 Idle No More

p. 239 Paul Mckinnon / Dreamstime.com

p. 242 The Canadian Press / Adrian Wyld

p. 244 The Canadian Press / John Woods

p. 245 Image: *Northern Flash, 2022* by Kyle Natkusiak Aleekuk, photo courtesy of Onsite Gallery, Toronto ON

p. 246 *This Painting is a Mirror* (2012) by Christi Belcourt, acrylic on canvas. Indigenous Art Collection, Crown-Indigenous Relations and Northern Affairs Canada. Photographer: Lawrence Cook.

p. 250 Minnystock / Dreamstime.com

p. 253 Courtesy of Tim Raybould

p. 256 SuperStock / Witold Skrypczak / Alamy

p. 258 SuperStock / Chris Cheadle / All Canada Photos

p. 259 Tsilhqot’in National Government
p. 264 Ministry of Indigenous Relations and Reconciliation / B.C. Government
p. 268 The Canadian Press / Sean Kilpatrick
p. 270 Courtesy of Tim Raybould
p. 272 EB Adventure Photography / Shutterstock
p. 273 The Canadian Press / Darryl Dyck
p. 275 J. SHAFTO / Parks Canada
p. 281 Courtesy of Jody Wilson-Raybould
p. 284 SK Arts Permanent Collection, 1992-003
p. 286 Courtesy of Tim Raybould
p. 289 shaunl / iStockphoto
p. 292 (top and bottom) Courtesy of Tim Raybould
p. 297 Courtesy of Tim Raybould
p. 300–301 Designed by Kwakwaka’wakw artist, Curtis Wilson. Image courtesy of The Flag Shop.

Ḵ̓I’MOLA

p. 308 Courtesy of Jody Wilson-Raybould
p. 317 SuperStock / Chris Cheadle / All Canada Photos